The Traumatic Screen

The Traumatic Screen

The Films of Christopher Nolan

Stuart Joy

 **intellect**

Bristol, UK / Chicago, USA

First published in the UK in 2020 by
Intellect, The Mill, Parnall Road, Fishponds, Bristol, BS16 3JG, UK

First published in the USA in 2020 by
Intellect, The University of Chicago Press, 1427 E. 60th Street,
Chicago, IL 60637, USA

A catalogue record for this book is available from
the British Library.

Cover designer: Aleksandra Szumlas
Copy editor: MPS Technologies
Production manager: Emma Berrill
Typesetting: Contentra Technologies

Print ISBN 978-1-78938-202-0 (hardback)
Print ISBN 978-1-78938-219-8 (paperback)
ePDF ISBN 978-1-78938-204-4
ePub ISBN 978-1-78938-203-7

Printed and bound by Print on Demand, United Kingdom

To find out about all our publications, please visit
www.intellectbooks.com.
There, you can subscribe to our e-newsletter,
browse or download our current catalogue,
and buy any titles that are in print.

This is a peer-reviewed publication.

Dedicated with love to my parents

Contents

Acknowledgements   viii
List of Illustrations   ix

Introduction   1
1. The Traumatic Screen: Trauma, Psychoanalysis and Cinema   16
2. Revisiting the Scene of the Crime: Repressing the Past in *Insomnia*   37
3. *Batman Begins*, Again: The Temporality of Trauma in *The Dark Knight* Trilogy   53
4. Looking for the Secret: Trauma and Desire in *The Prestige*   71
5. The Dream Has Become Their Reality: Acting-Out and Working-Through Trauma in *Inception*   95
6. Beyond the Void: *Interstellar* and the Possibility of Post-Traumatic Growth   113
7. Keep Calm and Carry On: Combating Cultural Trauma in *Dunkirk*   133
8. Conclusion: Ending at the Beginning with *Doodlebug*, *Following* and *Memento*   146

References   160
Index   179

Acknowledgements

Take a moment to consider your achievement

– Cutter, *The Prestige*

First, I would like to thank Dr Jacqueline Furby and Dr Claire Hines for their unwavering support and encouragement. You have both been a constant source of thoughtful advice, calm reassurance and intellectually stimulating conversation over the years. Without both of you, I simply would not be where I am today. Likewise, I would like to express my gratitude to Professor Edward Chaney, Professor Maurice Owen and Professor Karen Randell for their helpful guidance. Sincere thanks are extended to Darren Kerr, Paul Marchbank and Professor Rod Pilling for their financial and institutional support while writing this book. I would also like to thank several scholars including Dr Donna Peberdy, Dr Devon Campbell-Hall, Professor Will Brooker, Dr Sorcha Ní Fhlainn, Dr Francesca Brencio, Dr Erin-Hill Parks, Dr Frances Pheasant-Kelley, Dr Tony M. Vinci and Dr Paul Sutton who have all contributed, in various ways, to the development of my ideas. I would particularly like to thank Dr Terence McSweeney whose feedback and guidance have been invaluable. Special thanks to my friend Kierren Darke for his willingness to act as a sounding board for my ideas and lastly, very special thanks are due to my family and my wife Sophie Joy Cross for their kindness, understanding and patience.

List of Illustrations

1. Dormer looking screen left, *Insomnia*, p. 43.
2. Subsequent shot (implied POV) of the Alaskan landscape, *Insomnia*, p. 43.
3. A plane comes into view from screen right as part of the same continuous shot, *Insomnia*, p. 43.
4. A momentary glimpse of the swarming bats, *Batman Begins*, p. 57.
5. Young Wayne at the opera, *Batman Begins*, p. 57.
6. Thomas Wayne is shot attempting to protect his wife, *Batman Begins*, p. 57.
7. Wayne falling down the well, *Batman Begins*, p. 63.
8. The well in the process of being sealed, *Batman Begins*, p. 63.
9. Wayne attempts to escape 'the pit' without the use of a safety rope, *The Dark Knight Rises*, p. 63.
10. Julia's lifeless body floats in the tank, *The Prestige*, p. 78.
11. An unknown person stands hunched over a sink with their head submerged underwater, *The Prestige*, p. 78.
12. Julia struggling underwater, *The Prestige*, p. 78.
13. *a* Borden sat facing off-screen right, *The Prestige*, p. 85.
14. *a* Borden in a medium-shot framing him in profile facing right, *The Prestige*, p. 86.
15. Angier sat in another row at the same performance, *The Prestige*, p. 86.
16. The framing and movement of the previous shots are duplicated but the two men have now switched places, *The Prestige*, p. 86.
17. An unknown figure inserts an object into the barrel of the gun, *The Prestige*, p. 87.
18. The camera tilts upward to reveal a disguised Angier, *The Prestige*, p. 87.
19. The disfigured hand of *a* Borden rests on top of the cage, *The Prestige*, p. 87.
20. The camera tilts upward to reveal *a* disguised Borden, *The Prestige*, p. 87.
21. Angier looking off-screen right, *The Prestige*, p. 88.
22. Angier once again looks off-screen right while recounting the trick from memory, *The Prestige*, p. 88.
23. Cutter looks off-screen left, *The Prestige*, p. 88.

Introduction

I've done really well so far in my career by trusting the audience to be as dissatisfied with convention as I am.

— Christopher Nolan (2010: 18)

Trauma haunts the cinema of Christopher Nolan. Beginning with his short film *Doodlebug* (1997) and ending with *Dunkirk* (2017), his films strive to articulate and understand the complexities of trauma. His recurring interest in aligning us with characters who have been traumatized and his repeated return to stories that involve loss thematically anchors each of his films in the experience of trauma. But beyond this, trauma is also explored through our own relationship to his films which frequently feature complex timelines that demand and even reward multiple viewings. These intricate narrative puzzles encourage us to return to them in such a way that emulates the cognitive shifts of traumatic memory – just as those who have undergone a traumatic experience must remember the past in the hope of moving forward, we too must recall our experience if we are to understand what we have seen. Take, for example, Nolan's debut feature *Following* (1998). In this film, our own experience of trying to make sense of the discontinuous episodic timeline is paralleled by the protagonist's inability to comprehend how he is framed for murder by the mysterious stranger Cobb (Alex Haw). In *Memento* (2000), the non-linear narrative functions to place the audience in the shoes of Leonard Shelby (Guy Pearce), a man with no short-term memory who seeks vengeance for the rape and murder of his wife. Likewise, in *Insomnia* (2002), Detective Dormer's (Al Pacino) own actions are the result of a traumatic event that subtly disrupts the linear chronological order of the film from the outset. Elsewhere, Nolan's turn to the superhero film with *Batman Begins* (2005) and its sequels, *The Dark Knight* (2008) and *The Dark Knight Rises* (2012), places an emphasis on Bruce Wayne's (Christian Bale) childhood and in doing so proves to be fertile ground for the exploration of the character's traumatic past via flashbacks and other temporal slippages. As with a number of other films directed by Nolan including *Memento* and *Insomnia*, in *The Prestige* (2006) and later *Inception* (2010), it is principally

1

a woman, or more precisely the death of a woman, that fractures the narrative structure and provides an insight into how trauma is manifested in these films. This trend continues in *Interstellar* (2014) although, in this instance, allusions to the death of Cooper's (Matthew McConaughey) wife serve as the necessary backdrop for exploring his strained relationship with his children whom he is forced to abandon in a story that involves actual time-travel. Finally, in *Dunkirk*, it is the trauma of battle that underpins the fragmented narrative of a group of soldiers desperately trying to flee the beaches of Northern France amid the Second World War.

The way that trauma is handled in these films corresponds to widely agreed-upon definitions of trauma as an overwhelming response to an unexpected event that can be neither fully understood nor fully assimilated but rather acquires significance after the fact in its repetition (Caruth 1996: 4). This emphasis places these films at the intersection between cinema and psychoanalysis and so my principle focus in this book is how Nolan attempts to represent trauma and how the spectator encounters it primarily in relation to a psychoanalytical framework. Indeed, it seems to me that it is important to move beyond an understanding of these films as being a simple way of attempting to *represent* trauma and consider instead how trauma is vicariously experienced – that is, how Nolan's films *speak* to the spectator. Before proceeding any further, then, it is worthwhile at this stage to qualify my own engagement with trauma. While much of what I go on to discuss involves identifying a signifier for the experience of trauma – whether that be Cobb's (Leonardo DiCaprio) involvement in his wife's death in *Inception* or Cooper's attempts to alleviate the guilt attached to his choice to abandon his children in *Interstellar* – I am less interested in the individual event than I am in suggesting that the pathology of the traumatic experience should not be defined by the event itself or the distortion of that event, but rather by the structure of the experience. In the context of Nolan's films, this experience is evident not only in terms of form and content through a series of visual and narrative repetitions but also through the spectator's engagement with each of his films. I am arguing that Nolan's films not only contain attempts to represent traumatic events, but also that our experience of these films means that they can be understood as a distinct form of trauma cinema.

Who Is Christopher Nolan?

Born in London in 1970, Nolan began making films from an early age with his father's super 8mm camera and an assortment of action figures. The son of American and British parents, Nolan spent much of his childhood moving back and forth between the United Kingdom and the United States. However, upon returning to England, he pursued an interest in filmmaking while he studied for his degree in English Literature at University College London, producing several short 16mm films with the college film society. These films included *Larceny* (1996) and *Doodlebug* (1997). From his breakthrough feature film *Following* to *Dunkirk*, the inventiveness of his work combined with his increasing ability to successfully court a mass audience has rendered the traditional divisions between mainstream and independent cinema somewhat arbitrary as the boundaries between the two have increasingly blurred. Indeed, such dualistic thinking is problematic when it comes to a discussion of Nolan's cinema because the use of binary oppositions such as popular and personal or art and commerce can only offer a partial insight into his films. Rather than operating within a popular conception of American cinema as either Hollywood or not-Hollywood, Nolan's films seemingly transcend the inherent limitations of these categories, offering instead a unifying approach that has enabled him to earn a reputation as a director able to work within the apparent confines of Hollywood, while at the same time, exercising sufficient creative control to retain a measure of independence and convey his own personal artistic vision.

This approach to film, that certain directors – commonly referred to as auteurs – could be considered artists within the commercial constraints of popular cinema, was principally introduced into the United States of America by the writer and critic Andrew Sarris. His influential article, 'Notes on the auteur theory in 1962', followed by *The American Cinema: Directors and Directions 1929–1968* (1968) distilled much of the French filmmaker François Truffaut's (see 1954) initial ideas by establishing three main premises of the auteur theory: technical competence; personal style; and, most importantly, interior meaning (Sarris 1962: 7). Sarris argued that the financial imperatives of Hollywood film production resulted in a tension between the auteur and their material, a tension that produced the interior meaning of the film. According to Sarris, the auteur's vision was often forged precisely because of these restrictions rather than despite them. As such, Sarris suggested that a measure of technical competence and a distinguishable personality could emerge through a critical examination of the thematic preoccupations, repeated structures and similarities in formal style within a director's body of work. Of course, the notion that the principal meaning of a film comes solely from the director is heavily contested and the anxiety over authorial intention is an ongoing point of discussion. Nevertheless, the continued significance of the auteur theory can be measured not least by the more general trend of film publications that are frequently based on the works of individual directors. These critical studies often tend to emphasize a director's personal vision and formal choices as the basis for an understanding of a film's creator, wider sociopolitical issues as well as stylistic and thematic consistencies within a body of work.

The auteur theory, then, might reveal some connections between the content of Nolan's films and the reality of his life experiences. For instance, in many respects, Nolan's engagement with trauma is unsurprising if one considers some of the antecedents of his films. *Following*, for example, was based on Nolan's own experience of being burgled (see Mottram 2002: 96). Equally, his personal admiration for film noir – evident in films as varied as *Memento*, *Insomnia*, *The Dark Knight* trilogy and *Inception* – stems from what he perceives to be the genre's ability to translate everyday anxieties into a heightened realm of expression (Nolan 2010: 11). Along similar lines, it is tempting to read *Inception* as perhaps Nolan's most personal film because it may relate to his own experience of coming to terms with the death of his father who passed away in 2009, a year prior its release (Shone 2014). The film's subplot, involving a son's desperate attempt to gain his dying father's approval, may resonate with Nolan's own personal experiences of grief. *Inception* also emphasizes the themes of parental failure and redemption which emerge in several of his films including *The Prestige* and *The Dark Knight* trilogy, both of which are linked by an obsession with failing or absent fathers leading up to a catharsis of sorts in *Inception* and *Interstellar*. Speaking about the demands of filming on location while being away from his family Nolan has remarked:

> There is a lot of guilt for that. A lot of guilt. The very sadness of saying goodbye to people is a massive expression of the love you feel for them. For me, the film is really about being a father. The sense of your life passing you by and your kids growing up before your eyes.
>
> (Shone 2014)

While Nolan's personal life is not necessarily or with any certainty related to his creative output, it is interesting to note how integral his nationality and literary background are to the construction of his filmmaking persona. Beyond the combination of critical praise and high box-office returns, Nolan's position within American cinema as a British émigré working within the Hollywood system might distinguish him from his contemporaries, positioning him as a natural successor to the likes of British director Ridley Scott. Aside from Scott, Nolan has regularly been compared to Stanley Kubrick who also studied literature at university. Like Kubrick, Nolan possesses a marked interest in the complex interaction of narrative and characterization. For example, when questioned about his unusual approach to narrative following the release of *Insomnia* in 2002, Nolan's thoughts immediately returned to his time at university: 'I wasn't a very good student, but one thing I did get from it […] was that I started thinking about the narrative freedoms that authors had enjoyed for centuries' (Andrew 2002). This awareness of the apparent restrictions of classical film narration in contrast to the relative freedoms afforded to writers and novelists emerges in Nolan's feature-length directorial debut *Following*. Shot over the course of a year on a budget of $6000 (Box Office Mojo 2016), the film was nominated for a British Independent Film Award and led to the financing for his follow-up, the critically acclaimed *Memento*. *Following*'s fractured timeline and characters introduce Nolan's interest in exploring narrative structure, a dominant theme throughout most of his films. *Memento* and later, *The Prestige*, *Inception* and *Dunkirk*, all seek to explore and extend the limits of film structure and technique.

Among his other connections to Kubrick, Nolan has also chosen a life away from the public eye and yet, as with Kubrick, his seeming inaccessibility has only furthered his mythic status. Throughout his career Nolan has often opted to give the minimum contractual number of promotional interviews and very little is known about his personal life, which he guards with great secrecy (Naughton 2014). He rarely talks about the complexities of his films, preferring instead to maintain a level of mystery that emphasizes the central ambiguities of each narrative. In an interview for *The Hollywood Reporter*, for instance, he discussed his desire to disentangle his films from what he perceives to be the limiting effects of his biography:

> I don't want people to know anything about me. I mean, I'm not being facetious. The more you know about somebody who makes the films, the less you can just watch the movies – that's my feeling. I mean, you have to do a certain amount of promotion for the film, you have to put yourself out there, but I actually don't want people to have me in mind at all when they're watching the films.
>
> (Feinberg 2015)

Clearly, Nolan feels that too much information about him as a filmmaker detracts from the viewing experience and that any such biographical information is therefore unnecessary. However, his reluctance to embrace his own personal narrative is a choice that in an unexpected way emphasizes control or rather a desire for control, as another one of the central themes of his films.

Mastery and obsession with control, two central aspects that can be understood within the broader context of trauma, run as a continuous theme through Nolan's films. For example, while the director's DVD commentary on *Memento* provides a conventional insight into the film's production history, Nolan offers multiple different recorded conclusions to the final scene but insists that he has a full, definitive interpretation of the film that he keeps to himself (see Hill-Parks 2010: 106–07). Similarly, the question implicit in the final moments of *Inception* (i.e. does Cobb's totem keep spinning?) has confounded critics and audiences alike resulting in numerous blog posts, articles and the publication of two edited volumes (both called *Inception and Philosophy* [2011]), all of which provide multiple theories concerning whether Cobb remains in a dream or in reality. Once again, in this instance Nolan has refused to provide audiences with a definitive conclusion to the film, preferring instead to allow the ambiguity of the ending to encourage them to create their own meaning. However, at the same time, he positions himself as the singular authoritative voice behind the film by retaining a complete understanding of how each film ends. In an interview for the *New York Times* he emphasizes his belief that to render the ambiguity of his films satisfying from an audience perspective he must maintain an objective position of power and authority:

> The only way to be productively ambiguous, is that you have to know the answer for you — but also know why, objectively speaking. If you do some-thing unknowable, there's no answer for the audience, because you didn't have an answer. It becomes about ambiguity for ambiguity's sake. There has to be a sense of reality in the film. If you don't have rules, then what I'm doing would be formless. I feel better with consistent rules.
>
> (Lewis-Kraus 2014)

All of Nolan's films are to an extent organized according to a set of thematic or formal rules. In *Following*, the unemployed writer (Jeremy Theobald) who shad-ows strangers to gather material for a new book abandons his own strict rules that dictate who he must follow, ultimately leading to his downfall. In *Memento*, Leonard Shelby manipulates the system of notes and tattoos that he uses to perpet-uate the seemingly never-ending search for those involved in his wife's apparent rape and murder. In *Insomnia*, Nolan's debut studio film, a corrupt detective defaults to bending the rules to obtain a conviction and later conceal his own mistakes. Following the critical and commercial success of *Insomnia*, Nolan was presented with an opportunity to reimagine one of DC Comics' most treasured icons, Batman. The resulting film, *Batman Begins*, successfully grounded the story of the Caped Crusader in a convincing reality and in doing so defied traditional genre conventions. The sequels, *The Dark Knight* and *The Dark Knight Rises*, continued to mine Nolan's fascination with rules and systems through an examination of a host of post-9/11 anxieties such as terrorism, mass surveillance, torture, the global recession and class warfare. In between making *The Dark Knight* trilogy, Nolan wrote and directed *The Prestige* and later *Inception*. Whereas the former replicates in its structure the three stages of a magic trick, in the latter, a heist film set in the mind of a business heir, he exposes the rules, techniques and modes of representation from both narrative cinema and video games.

Interstellar continues Nolan's fascination with rules and control on the grandest scale by focusing on the laws of physics. In the film, a team of astronauts must travel across space and time to discover a new planet that will replace a dying Earth. The film has attracted comparisons to Kubrick's genre-defining *2001: A Space Odyssey* (1968), a connection that Nolan doesn't shy away from:

> I put it like this: you can't make a science-fiction film pretending that *2001* doesn't exist but I think *2001*'s relationship with humanity is more philosophical, more abstract. I wanted to embrace the metaphysics, but relate it to something more obviously human, like love.
>
> (Collin 2014)

To hear Nolan emphasize the emotional dimension of the film is arguably at odds with one of the more common criticisms directed at him – that he is primarily a technical filmmaker whose understanding of form frequently overshadows the performances of his actors (see Lawrence 2010; Bevan 2012; Jones 2012). But another way of approaching Nolan's filmmaking is to suggest that while the scale of his films has increased exponentially since *Doodlebug* and *Following*, very few other directors have continued to pursue such a complex combination of form and characterization. At the same time, Nolan has maintained an engagement with a set of repeated themes achieving both critical and commercial success. Reflecting on *Interstellar*, film critic Mark Kermode encapsulates this view, noting that:

> While the end result may not represent the pinnacle of Nolan's extraordinary career, it nevertheless reaffirms him as cinema's leading blockbuster auteur, a director who can stamp his singular vision on to every frame of a gargantuan team effort in the manner of Spielberg, Cameron and Kubrick. 'Whose subconscious are we in?' asked Ellen Page in *Inception*. The answer here, *as always*, is unmistakably Nolan's.
>
> (Kermode 2014, emphasis added)

In many ways, *Interstellar* reflects on the passing of an ambitious space age. But, perhaps more than this, the film also contains an underlying concern with the passing of an age in cinema marked by the increasing move towards digital technologies at the expense of film. Many of Nolan's contemporaries have already shifted to digital forms of film production, and yet he is one of the few remaining vocal advocates for the continued use of 35mm film stock while also choosing to shoot parts of *The Dark Knight* and *The Dark Knight Rises* in IMAX 70mm – a practice that he continued with *Interstellar* and *Dunkirk*. Shot using a combination of 35mm anamorphic film and 70mm IMAX film, both *Interstellar* and *Dunkirk* reinforce Nolan's enduring commitment to celluloid, and increasingly to IMAX, demonstrating his desire to provide the audience with an enhanced experience of film-as-film to offer, as he says, 'something special, something extraordinary' (Feinberg 2015). He strives to advance the traditional art and craft of filmmaking by emphasizing the aesthetic virtues of celluloid while spearheading a discourse surrounding film formats that posit film-as-film as a form of authentic cinema. It is for these reasons that Nolan is not only the writer, producer and director of his films but as a filmmaker who oversees all aspects of production while also controlling cultural and industrial factors outside of the film.

Nolan's reluctance to employ a second unit, preferring instead to shoot the entire film himself, is further testament to his desire for full control of his artistic vision. Referring to his approach to *The Dark Knight* trilogy he remarks:

> Let me put it this way: If I don't need to be directing the shots that go in the movie, why do I need to be there at all? The screen is the same size for every shot. The little shot of, say, a watch on someone's wrist, will occupy the same screen size as the shot of a thousand people running down the street. Everything is equally weighted and needs to be considered with equal care, I really do believe that. I don't understand the criteria for parceling [sic] things off [...]. Having said that, there are fantastic filmmakers who use second and third units successfully. So it all comes back to the question of defining what a director does. Each of us works in different ways. It's really helped me keep more of *my personality* in these big films. There's a danger with big-action fare that the presence of the filmmaker is watered down, it can become very neutral, so I've tried to keep *my point of view* in every aspect of these films.
>
> (Ressner 2012, emphasis added)

The clarity of vision and level of personal accountability demonstrated in Nolan's response emphasizes his position as the primary creator – the auteur. However, elsewhere he also portrays himself as someone appreciative of the collaborative nature of commercial filmmaking. As part of an interview for *The Hollywood Report*'s annual roundtable, he remarked:

> The thing is, you go on a set and I don't shoot the film, I don't record the sound. You sit there in the middle of it all trying to be a conductor or something, I don't know, trying to be helpful, trying to be a lens for everybody else's input.
>
> (Galloway 2014)

As such, if one considers Nolan to be an auteur in line with the romantic conception of the theory, it is not necessarily just Nolan who contributes to that construct but also his collaborators both in front of and behind the camera. For example, Nolan has chosen to repeatedly work with a number of actors such as Michael Caine and Christian Bale as well as Cillian Murphy, Tom Hardy, Ken Watanabe, Marion Cotillard and Anne Hathaway, among others. Since *Memento*, he has often shared a writing credit with his brother Jonathan, while cinematographer Wally Pfister, editor Lee Smith, production designer Nathan Crowley, visual effects supervisor Paul Franklin, composers Hans Zimmer and David Julyan and perhaps, most importantly, his longest-standing collaborator – his wife and producer Emma Thomas – have all been involved in many of his films.

Beyond the cast and crew of Nolan's films, his affiliation with Warner Bros. has proven to be both hugely productive and mutually beneficial. Where Warner Bros. have profited greatly from the financial successes of his films, Nolan has been the primary beneficiary of the studio's willingness to support his development as a filmmaker. By entrusting him with increasingly larger budgets and one of their most lucrative franchises, Warner Bros. demonstrated a firm commitment to the cultivation of Nolan's directorial persona. However, it could be argued that for every 'personal' or original film that Nolan directed during those formative years, he subsequently returned to direct another instalment of what would become *The Dark Knight* trilogy, a series more overtly aimed at a mass audience. This pattern of alternating between mainstream and more personal productions is not one that Nolan consciously acknowledges, preferring instead to maintain his creative freedom *within* the studio system:

> There are filmmakers who pride themselves on 'one for the studio, one for me', and I just don't see it that way. I have an opportunity that very few filmmakers get, to do something on a huge scale that *I can control completely and make as personal as I want.*
>
> (Collin 2014, emphasis added)

Even in his commercial blockbusters for Warner Bros., it is not difficult to locate Nolan's personal themes. His interest in psychological dramas, his repeated experiments with narrative form and his ongoing exploration of time, memory and identity have now become widely accepted (Brooker 2012: 22).

Despite the apparent links between Nolan's personal life and his creative output, the assumption that the two are inherently connected needs to be viewed with some scepticism, since when one speaks of Nolan as a director one tends to be referring to set of stylistic and thematic traits that have been identified by fans and scholars alike, and not the man himself. Such a standpoint recalls Michel Foucault's 'author-function' which positions the author not as an individual who exists independently of the text but rather as a label that exists only in relation to the work associated with them (1977: 123). Along these lines, it is more useful to trace the development of Nolan's engagement with trauma independently from his personal biography. This method is largely in keeping with the development of the auteur theory as a critical tool, which now considers a range of other methodological perspectives designed to enhance the flexibility and durability of the discourse. Will Brooker reinforces this view with his comments on authorship noting that:

> While more conservative and traditional auteur theory saw the film as the deliberate expression of an individual artist – a real person with a biography and background that could help to explain their intentions – semiological and structuralist studies of authorship identified patterns of repetition and opposition within a body of work, whether consciously expressed or not. Within this model, a director tells the same story repeatedly but with variations; distinct themes and preoccupations emerge from the *oeuvre* as if through recurring dreams.
>
> (2012: 5)

The analysis undertaken in this book, therefore, subscribes to the belief that the mark of the auteur becomes evident in the consistency of themes and style of the artist when measured across a filmography meaning that the mark of an auteur lies in the work itself.

Current Scholarship on Christopher Nolan

The critical discourse related to Nolan can be broken down into the following themes, which include, but are not limited to time, memory, identity and narrative. Despite the possible intersection of these research topics with the field of trauma theory, discussions of Nolan's work in this context are fragmented and in need of collating. Therefore, I will attempt to synthesize some of the existing approaches to his work and elevate the discussion by uniting some of the disparate threads. Significantly, there has yet to be a comprehensive engagement with the representation of trauma in Nolan's films from a psychoanalytic perspective. Instead, scholars have frequently opted to emphasize the textual features and reception of his individual films. Todd McGowan's monograph titled *The Fictional Christopher Nolan* (2012a), my own co-edited collection *The Cinema of Christopher Nolan: Imagining the Impossible* (2015a), Jason T. Eberl and George A. Dunn's edited collection *The Philosophy of Christopher Nolan* (2017) and Darren Mooney's *Christopher Nolan* (2018) are the only current books that exist entirely devoted to a number of his films. Yet, none of these texts adopt a sustained psychoanalytical approach to Nolan's work.

It should be noted that several books have emerged over the past decade focusing exclusively on individual films, including Andrew Kania's edited collection focusing on *Memento* (2009), Claire Molloy's *Memento* (2010), two edited volumes – both called *Inception and Philosophy* – and David Carter's *Inception* (2019). Understandably, these texts do not extensively locate these films within the broader context of Nolan's filmmaking and none of them embrace a psychoanalytic approach. In addition to these books, there has been an increase in journal articles about Nolan's films. For example, those authors focusing on *The Dark Knight* trilogy frequently draw attention to allegories of post-9/11 anxiety including the 'War on Terror' and more recently the post-2008 economic recession (see Fisher 2006; Lewis 2009; Toh 2010; Muller 2011; Pheasant-Kelly 2011). Elsewhere, a number of authors have written about *The Prestige* and *Insomnia* although, comparatively speaking, there is a limited amount of academic engagement with these films when viewed within the wider discourse around Nolan's cinema (see Garcia 2006; McGowan 2007a; Michaels 2007; Bhatnagar 2009; Heilmann 2009; Joseph 2011; Gassert 2012; McGowan 2012; Tembo 2015; Blouin 2016). It is also worthwhile recognizing that there has been only a fleeting acknowledgement of Nolan's short film *Doodlebug* as well as his first feature film *Following* (see de Valk and Arnold 2013; Kealey 2015). While *Doodlebug* has been referred to as an example of a good short film, discussions of *Following* are frequently limited to direct comparisons with *Memento*. This is perhaps unsurprising given the critical success of the latter, but Nolan's earliest films should not be overlooked as they demonstrate some of the defining features that have since become hallmarks of his work – notably his interest in experimental narrative structures.

In many ways, it is the centrality of time within Nolan's films that permits a wider discussion of trauma – something that is mirrored by the significance of time to trauma studies (see Caruth 1996). It should come as no surprise, then, that a number of authors have identified issues relating to time as being central to understanding Nolan's filmmaking (see Gargett 2002; Clark 2002; Trifonova 2002; Parker 2004; Lyons 2006; Wilson 2008; Kiss 2012; Brown 2014; Panek 2014; Russo 2014; King 2014; Burnetts 2015; Furby 2015; Gutiérrez-Jones 2015; Kania 2015). The vast majority of academics who draw attention to the various aspects of time in Nolan's films often focus on *Memento*. A central question posed by many authors concerns if, and how, Leonard can maintain some semblance of identity given that his apparent 'condition' renders him unable to form new memories (see Thomas 2003; Kornbluh 2004; Little 2005; Heckman 2008; Kang 2006; Smith 2007; Hanley 2009; McKenna 2009; Morrissey 2011; Botez 2015; Perdigao 2015). Scholars have understandably concentrated on *Memento*'s representation of time given the film's narrative conceit of aligning the audience with Leonard via its formal structure. Belinda Morrissey and Peter Thomas, for example, offer commentaries on how the spectator vicariously engages in the cognitive processes associated with trauma. In separate pieces, they propose that *Memento*'s non-linear timeline can be understood as the cinematic equivalent of the way traumatic memory is often fragmented and repressed.

Nolan's focus on time not only provides a way of identifying with some of his most psychologically damaged central characters, but it also potentially offers a unique insight into both the creation of the film text and the relationship between the spectator and the screen. Take, for example, his attempts to heighten tension via parallel editing, which reach a climax in *Inception*. Several authors have highlighted how the thematic device of a dream functions as an exploration of narrative discourse (see Kiss 2012; Brown 2014; Panek 2014; Russo 2014; King 2014; Burnetts 2015; Furby 2015; Kania 2015; Olson 2015). In the film, a group of criminals attempt to infiltrate the mind of a business heir using a futuristic tech-nology that allows them to enter another person's dreams. From one perspective, alternating between the different layers of the dream world provides a sense of structural cohesion within the film yielding a seamless flow of linear *horizontal* time across the different *vertically* organized planes of action. From another view-point, the cuts between multiple different times and locations overtly expose the editing process revealing the artifice of the film and by extension, the contradic-tory position of the spectator in relation to the text. Focusing on *The Prestige* and *Inception*, Jonathan R. Olson suggests that Nolan's films simultaneously support the audience's immersion in the narrative while frequently contesting conven-tional aspects of mainstream cinema by disrupting their suspension of disbelief. Olson foregrounds Nolan's use of stage magic and shared dreams which, while acting as allegories of cinema and of Nolan's personal practice of filmmaking, circumvent the danger of dismantling the audience's immersion in the illusion of film. The point is that these films solicit the spectator's participation in the form of their wilful ignorance while highlighting the conditions of reception. It is the spectator's willing investment in the reality of the fiction presented that subsumes their knowledge of the truth or, to paraphrase *Inception*'s own expression, it is the truth they once knew but chose to forget.

Elsewhere, Jacqueline Furby provides perhaps the most comprehensive analy-sis of Nolan's cinema in relation to time arguing that whilst *Interstellar* is the first of his films to overtly engage with time-travel in the story, all his films play with temporality and narrative organization. By exploring the different kinds of time(s) and modes of time (travel) that operate in Nolan's films, she considers why it was inevitable that Nolan would eventually tell a science-fiction-based story about time-travel. Even though Furby's work shares an affinity with my own, the main difference between our approaches becomes evident in relation to desire. Where Furby suggests that the spectator's enjoyment of Nolan's films emerges from 'seeking the solution' (2015: 264) to his most complex narratives puzzles, I argue that this search is misleading for the fundamental reason that such a desire implies that a solution can be found. Instead, my argument is based, at least in part, on the notion that the spectator's enjoyment of Nolan's films is rooted in *not* obtaining the solution, or as Cutter (Michael Caine) puts it in the closing moments of *The Prestige*, 'You're looking for the secret. But you won't find it, because, of course, you're not really looking. You don't really want to work it out. You want to be fooled'. It is this cyclical process that most clearly emulates the temporal logic of trauma.

Structure of the Book

While much academic research has been concerned with Nolan's preoccupation with the overlapping strands of identity, time, memory and narrative, these aspects will form a foundation for my in-depth analysis which goes on to foreground the ways through which trauma and memory are presented at the level of theme, structure and *mise-en-scène* as well as the spectator's compulsion to repeat and replay his films. In what follows, Chapter 1 presents a detailed explanation of my approach to Nolan's films by focusing on the central psychoanalytic frameworks employed alongside a summary of how they overlap with cinema.

Chapter 2, 'Revisiting the Scene of the Crime: Repressing the Past in *Insomnia*', begins by analysing a scene taken from the film's DVD release. Even though this scene was not included in the film's theatrical run, it nevertheless contains several of the key issues that will feature prominently throughout this book. This chapter goes on to argue that Nolan's representation of trauma can be principally understood through the Freudian concept of *Nachträglichkeit* and its subsequent reformulation by Lacan as *après-coup* and Laplanche as *afterwardsness*. I argue that the key to understanding *Insomnia*'s narrative relationship to the experience of trauma resides in comprehending a cinematic deception that is induced in the spectator from the outset of the film. I propose that *Insomnia*'s narrative logic is predicated on the structural principles underlying the psychological mechanisms of trauma as the film draws attention to the process of reconstructing the past out of the present.

In Chapter 3, I begin by considering Nolan's treatment of trauma in the context of *The Dark Knight* trilogy by predominantly analysing the first entry into the series, *Batman Begins*. This chapter focuses on the film's narrative structure and thematic content alongside a broader consideration of the spectator's extra-diegetic relationship to the trilogy. Specifically, I argue that these films represent trauma from within them, that is, from the position of the protagonist but also from outside the text from the perspective of the spectator. Furthermore, I suggest that Nolan's trilogy engages in a complicated dialogue with the previous films in the franchise that effectively encourages the spectator to experience the temporal logic of trauma whereby their knowledge of the past is re-written in light of a renewed understanding of the present.

Although the spectator may be confused by the organization of time and space in many of Nolan's films, multiple viewings reveal that the complex logic of narrative composition cues the spectator to emulate the character's subjective experience of trauma, thereby vicariously experiencing the structure of trauma themselves. I explore these ideas in Chapter 4, 'Looking for the Secret: Trauma and Desire in *The Prestige*', by principally drawing on the pattern of repetition that figures among the after-effects of a traumatic experience. I argue that the presence of repeated motifs, visual metaphors and signifiers alongside the over-arching structure of the film, one that imitates the deceptive qualities of a magic trick, represents a multifaceted conception of the cognitive processes associated with a traumatic experience. The purpose of this chapter is to foreground the relationship between loss and desire by considering *The Prestige* in line with the Lacanian concept of 'lack' (1977c: xi), a state of existence inscribed in the human subject and on society. I put forward that through the repetition of loss or rather lack, one reveals the presence of trauma.

In Chapter 5 I argue that *Inception* represents an tonal shift in Nolan's treatment of trauma as, unlike his other protagonists who frequently remain caught in the wake of a loss that they are unable to overcome, Cobb is seemingly redeemed at the level of the narrative through his ability to work-through his relationship to the unconscious trauma that forms the basis of his identity. By accepting responsibility for his role in his wife's death, he can achieve a catharsis of sorts by the end of the film, albeit one that is constructed from the fiction he uses to achieve it. Furthermore, what Nolan reveals in *Inception* is the broader interaction between the spectator and the film, which extends beyond the internal structural logic and thematic emphasis on working-through the past to understand the present. In this chapter, therefore, I provide an analysis of *Inception* in relation to the Freudian concepts of acting-out and working-through.

Chapter 6 continues to emphasize Nolan's movement away from the indeterminate resolution of the traumatic experience evident in his earlier films towards an overly melodramatic vision of love and paternal redemption. In 'Beyond the Void: *Interstellar* and the Possibilities of Post-Traumatic Growth', I argue that *Interstellar* can be understood as representing a fundamental departure from his other films in several significant ways. Chief amongst them is that it dispenses with the innovative narrative structure and experimental form that defined so much of his earlier career. Instead, *Interstellar* bears little resemblance to his other films but shares a number of characteristics with the classical Hollywood narrative. This chapter draws attention to *Interstellar*'s contradictory relationship with Nolan's films to date by suggesting that, while it rejects the atemporal formal structure that is so central to his engagement with trauma evident in most of his previous films, *Interstellar* remains in keeping with his interest in trauma through thematic enactments of nostalgia, repetition and return.

In 'Keep Calm and Carry On: Combating Cultural Trauma in *Dunkirk*' I argue that, while Nolan continues to examine the themes of trauma and loss in his films, *Dunkirk*'s focus on the cultural trauma of the Second World War engages in a discourse about the past that contains an implicit political dimension. My own approach to studying *Dunkirk*, then, begins by acknowledging a necessary shift in my own critical analysis of his work. While the film represents a continuation of the themes of trauma and loss, *Dunkirk*'s focus on the cultural trauma of the Second World War requires a broader understanding of the distinction between individual and collective memories, and the formation of identity. For this reason, I begin by briefly discussing the psychoanalytic origins of cultural trauma before going on to address the various ways that nostalgia interacts with the cultural trauma of the Second World War to serve as a potent source of national identity in times of social, economic and political uncertainty.

Lastly, the final chapter of this book seeks to address a number of the themes that run throughout it by uniting the previous discussions of Nolan's other films into a reflection on the development of his work. In order to do so, I return to Nolan's short film *Doodlebug*, his debut feature film *Following* and the critically acclaimed follow-up *Memento*. Here, I put forward that, even though there have been substantial changes in Nolan's attitude towards trauma, one can find evidence of stylistic and thematic consistencies that emerge through his treatment of film endings.

The Traumatic Screen: Trauma, Psychoanalysis and Cinema

How can I heal? How am I supposed to heal if I can't feel time?

– Leonard Shelby, *Memento*

Towards the end of *Memento*, Natalie (Carrie-Anne Moss) invites Leonard (Guy Pearce) back to her apartment where she tells him to make himself feel at home while she goes to work. He sits down on her sofa and begins to watch television but finds himself mindlessly flicking through the various channels. On one occasion, he glances at the remote control and notices the tattoo that reads 'Remember Sammy Jankis' etched on his left hand. The film then cuts to a fleeting close-up of someone preparing a syringe before returning to Leonard who subsequently switches off the television and proceeds to review the case file relating to the attack on his wife. In this short sequence, it is the intervening shot of the syringe or 'micro shot' as Berys Gaut calls it (2011: 34), which is revealing for a number of reasons. Chief among these is that this single shot functions as a signifier of the underlying unconscious trauma that defines Leonard's identity, namely his apparent role in the death of his wife. This fleeting shot is also significant because it momentarily reveals that what is arguably repressed by the character is similarly repressed by the narrative, despite the film's complex structure. To be clear, *Memento* has two distinct plot threads: the first is presented in colour running chronologically backwards charting Leonard's quest to find the man he believes killed his wife. The second, made distinct using black and white film stock, runs chronologically forwards and recounts Leonard's relationship to a man called Sammy Jankis (Stephen Tobolowsky).

According to Leonard, Sammy Jankis also suffered from the same condition of anterograde amnesia having been involved in a car accident. Leonard's description of Sammy's disorder is a means to position both himself and others, not to mention the spectator, relative to his own subjective experience: 'I guess I tell people about Sammy to help them understand. Sammy's story helps me understand my own situation', he says. Unlike Leonard, we are told that Sammy was unable to develop a system for coping with his condition. Sammy should have been able to learn through repetition, but failed to do so in a series of scientific tests. Therefore, his diabetic wife (Harriet Sansom Harris) began to suspect that he might have been feigning his injury to claim an insurance pay-out. To discover the truth, she decided to administer her own test by getting him to repeatedly inject her daily dose of insulin over a short period of time. Unfortunately, Sammy failed this final test leading to his wife's eventual death and his confinement in a mental institution. The tattoo, 'Remember Sammy Jankis', that is prominently visible between Leonard's left thumb and forefinger is, therefore, a poignant reminder of Sammy's failure, an example that functions as an indication of what Leonard could become.

During the film's climax, Teddy (Joe Pantoliano) casts doubt on Leonard's version of events, thereby retroactively undermining the credibility of his telling of the story of Sammy Jankis. Not only does Teddy intimate that Leonard's own wife survived her assault, but he also suggests that – like Sammy's wife – she grew suspicious of the injury inflicted upon him during the altercation. It is Teddy's claim that it was Leonard's wife, not Sammy's, who had diabetes that casts the largest shadow of uncertainty over the entire narrative while simultaneously providing at least one plausible explanation for Leonard's actions throughout the film. Even though the narrative frames Teddy as an untrustworthy character throughout, his argument is strengthened for the spectator by a series of micro shots that appear momentarily on-screen as he offers his alternative account of Leonard's life following the attack that led to his condition. Among them is a duplicate of the earlier micro shot of someone preparing a syringe. In this instance, the micro shot is followed by another that reveals the identity of the person readying it to be Leonard. Even though these two instances of the same micro shot are separated by over twenty minutes, its reappearance during Teddy's accusations calls into question Leonard's own awareness of his likely role in the death of his wife. Gaut, for instance, acknowledges that when Leonard glances at the tattoo on his left hand in Natalie's apartment, the glimpse of the syringe 'is not prompted by any accusations of Teddy's about Leonard having killed his wife: it is a spontaneous image, and we have no reason to deny that it is a memory' (2011: 34). At this moment, then, Leonard's investment in the narrative of Sammy Jankis is momentarily ruptured by the reality of his involvement in her death, which appears as a fleeting flashback. His subsequent decision to open the doctored case file related to the attack upon his wife seems to confirm his reluctance to confront the truth, preferring instead to reaffirm the foundation of the lie upon which his identity is built.

The way that the spectator is provided with narrative information parallels, at least to some degree, Leonard's own inability to prevent the repressed past from irrupting into the present. The shot of the syringe serves as a trace of that repression in a way that points towards the potential of film to *represent* the structure of the traumatic experience on and through the screen, and it is precisely when these types of shots occur that the film *speaks* to the spectator. Trauma manifests in other ways throughout Nolan's corpus of films. There is a moment in *Inception*, for example, when Cobb (Leonardo DiCaprio) – an expert at infiltrating the human mind via a form of dream-sharing technology – tells Ariadne (Ellen Page) that the reason he obsessively returns to a collection of his own memories stored in the form of a traversable elevator is because they are moments he regrets, 'memories that I have to change'. As film scholar Frances Pheasant-Kelly points out, the elevator is a rather crude visualization of Freud's topographical model of the mind (2015: 110–11).[1] Nonetheless, this simple metaphor serves as an interesting indication of the ways in which psychoanalysis has permeated popular culture in relation to our understanding of the mind. Nolan's engagement with memory, repression and trauma is frequently more complex than this example indicates, but it demonstrates that there exists a potential to use Nolan's films to understand the structure of the traumatic experience.

Trauma Cinema

Many have argued that music, dance, theatre, poetry, films (and other visual media) are able to bear witness to, record and even shape trauma. Some notable contributions in the field of screen studies include the works of Siegfried Kracauer (2004) and Anton Kaes (2011) on Weimar era German cinema, Fabio Vighi (2006) on Italian film, Nurith Gertz and George Khleifi (2008) on Palestinian cinema and Raz Yosef (2011) on contemporary Israeli cinema. An engagement with trauma within screen studies is not, as this brief list would appear to indicate, restricted to a discussion of national film industries but also includes a variety of different genres such as the war film, horror, superheroes and, among others, melodrama. Similarly, I am not the first person to suggest that an individual filmmaker has evidenced a sustained engagement with trauma across several of their films. A number of academics, for example, have written about Roman Polanski, Andrei Tarkovsky, David Lynch and Michael Haneke, to name a few (see Wexman 1987; Ishii-Gonzales 2004; Mactaggart 2010; Stewart 2010; Skakov 2012; Elm 2014; Weber 2014). Yet Nolan, whose films have together so far generated more than $4.75 billion (Box Office Mojo 2018) in revenue worldwide, is undoubtedly the most commercially successful director to have so consistently attempted to depict traumatized individuals and traumatic events.

The increase in attention related to the study of trauma cinema roughly correlates to the emergence of trauma theory as a bourgeoning discourse in the humanities during the early 1990s. Taken together, Shoshana Felman and Dori Laub's *Testimony: Crises of Witnessing in Literature, Psychoanalysis and History* (1992) alongside Cathy Caruth's edited collection *Trauma: Explorations in Memory* (1995) and her monograph *Unclaimed Experience: Trauma, Narrative and History* (1996) mark a significant point of departure for the study of trauma. For Caruth, the privileged position that literature occupies in relation to trauma studies is located in the original contributions of Sigmund Freud to the field of psychoanalysis (1996: 3). According to Caruth, like the traumatic experience, literature forgoes an objective truth in favour of the gaps associated with a subjective reality and the role of the literary critic is to identify where these gaps emerge from within the text. However, her own discussion of the film *Hiroshima Mon Amor* (1959) indicates that literature is not the exclusive domain of trauma studies and that the screen theorist can also determine how trauma might be communicated. For Claire Sisco King the principle advantage that cinema maintains over all other arts in terms of trauma is the combination of sight and sound images that can transcend the boundaries of time and space. She writes that:

> As a visual medium composed of moving images, the cinema embodies the visuality of traumatic symptoms – as in hallucinations, flashbacks, and nightmares experienced by survivors. Films have a specific capacity to embody traumatic sensibilities and destabilize the purported cohesiveness of the 'I' through assaults on the eye.
>
> (2011: 33)

In many respects, cinema has always been uniquely positioned to confront traumatic experiences. Glen O. Gabbard, for example, argues that '[a] great many films depend on the recreation of infantile trauma and anxieties in the audience to compel re-viewings of the film over time' (2007: xv). To demonstrate his point he adds, 'how many love stories capitalize on the fact that the audience relives their own lost loves each time they sit through the breakup of a relationship on the screen?' (2007: xv). Elsewhere in the same edited collection, Andrea Sabbadini goes even further when she suggests that 'all films represent some sort of loss and, indeed, are themselves (among many other things, of course) forms of mourning and of recovering lost objects' (2007: 4). Here Sabbadini is primarily referring to the intrinsic loss attached to the medium itself, which presents the absent past (the filmed event) in the present via the optical illusion of motion that is achieved by the projection of still images at 24 frames per second. But her statement might also allude to the position that film occupies within our own lives as a cultural artefact that exists outside of time. Films share with literature, music and other forms of artistic expression a timeless quality that ensures they can be returned to again and again in the hope of recapturing our first encounter with them. We are perhaps aware on some level that, while we may have changed, the film itself remains fundamentally the same. It is only our perception of it that has been altered by the passage of time.

If, as Gabbard and Sabbadini claim, loss is embedded in the representational strategies of cinema as well as our individual and cultural engagement with film in general, then the identification of a distinct era of trauma cinema may seem somewhat arbitrary. This is particularly pertinent given the relationships established elsewhere between trauma and modernity (see Benjamin ([1935] 1969), as well as trauma and the cinema (see Kirby 1988: 112–31; Kaplan 2005: 24; King 2011: 33). Indeed, the very experience of watching a film – the essence of cinema – is intrinsically shaped by loss. Unlike genres defined by the industry and recognized by the mass audience, but like other film movements of the past, trauma cinema, therefore, transcends national boundaries, distinct time-frames and traditional approaches to genre thus calling into question whether it is even possible to provide a distinct definition. Nevertheless, it remains possible to identify certain visual characteristics and formal properties that enable a type of trauma cinema to be categorized as a movement within film history, even if trauma is inherently part of the medium itself. Consequently, my first contention is that Nolan's filmmaking can be understood as a distinct form of trauma cinema.

As one of the first scholars to critically engage with a distinct formulation of trauma cinema, Janet Walker bases her definition of what constitutes a trauma film on a criterion that is, first and foremost, oriented around a film's thematic content that often deals with a 'world-shattering event or events of the past, whether public, personal, or both' (2001: 214). On this basis, much of Nolan's work would seem to conform to Walker's taxonomy given his embrace of character histories that are frequently portrayed via flashbacks and other temporal slippages. Along these lines, Walker also stresses the importance of a film's representational strategies and narrative form when she says that:

> The stylistic and narrative modality of trauma cinema is nonrealist. Like traumatic memories that feature vivid bodily and visual sensation over 'verbal narrative and context', these films are characterized by non-linearity, fragmentation, nonsynchronous sound, repetition, rapid editing and strange angles. And they approach the past through an unusual admixture of emotional affect, metonymic symbolism and cinematic flashbacks.
>
> (2001: 214)

Elsewhere, Walker says that, unlike the classical Hollywood form of realism, trauma films draw on a range of 'innovative strategies' (2005: 19) in keeping with the modernist avant-garde for 'representing reality obliquely, by looking to mental processes for inspiration, and by incorporating self-reflexive devices to call attention to the friability of the scaffolding for audiovisual historiography' (2005: 19). Walker goes on to draw a parallel between the types of films she considers to be part of trauma cinema and the criteria for post-traumatic stress disorder (PTSD) outlined in the *Diagnostic and Statistical Manual of Mental Disorders* (DSM-IV-TR) (2000) according to which traumatic events are persistently re-experienced as intrusive distressing recollections manifesting in the form of dreams, flashback episodes, hallucinations and illusions (2000: 463).

Where Walker initially places an emphasis on the depiction of historical trauma, in the introduction to *Afterimage: Film, Trauma, and the Holocaust* (2003), Joshua Hirsch discusses examples of what he labels a 'post-traumatic cinema' that not only represent traumatic historical events but also attempt to 'embody and reproduce the trauma for the spectator' (2003: xi). Hirsch puts forward a theory of vicarious trauma as a way of addressing the impact of a group of documentaries including *The Death Camps* (1945), *Night and Fog* (1956) and *Mein Kampf* (1960) that depict the atrocities of the Holocaust and fictional films such as *Hiroshima Mon Amor*, which attempts to confront the absence of trauma as a structuring presence. Hirsch discusses the potential for film to relay trauma to a spectator through exposure to a filmed representation, which, as an indexical sign, positions them as a secondary witness to traumatic events. Consider, for a moment, the representational strategies employed during the break-in that occurs in a flashback at several points throughout *Memento* or the repeated visualizations of the deaths of Bruce Wayne's parents in *Batman Begins*. In these instances, a spectator can theoretically experience vicarious trauma induced by witnessing the physical reality of a traumatic event once removed. The theory of vicarious trauma that Hirsch develops is not only dependent on the denotive content of the films chosen for analysis, however, but also on their formal means of representation (Hirsch 2003: 19).

Drawing on Pierre Janet's distinction between 'traumatic memories' and ordinary or 'narrative memories' (cited in van der Kolk and van der Hart 1995: 160),[2] Hirsch proposes a framework for understanding the difference between realist and modernist modes of representation employed in cinema, suggesting that trauma films must attempt to reject the 'classical realist forms of film narration traditionally used to provide a sense of mastery over the past' (2003: 3) and instead adopt 'modernist forms of narration that formally repeat the traumatic structure of experience' (2003: 3). For Hirsch, the temporal structure of events recounted in conventional Hollywood realist narratives tends to adhere to the logic of narrative memory since both purports to provide the subject with a sense of mastery over time (2003: 20–21). In the 'tense' of narrative memory, for instance, he notes that 'one can call up an image of the past at will, make it present to consciousness, and insert it into the proper chronology' (2003: 21). A useful comparison in this context is a scene from *Memento* when Natalie asks Leonard to remember his wife. The spectator is prepared for the time jump when Leonard closes his eyes and the ensuing series of flashbacks coincides with his conscious recall. In contrast, traumatic memory or, what Hirsch calls, 'posttraumatic memory' is characterized by the collapse of linear chronology and the fragmentation of time (2003: 85). In effect, the past remains inaccessible to conscious recall while often thrusting itself abruptly into consciousness akin to Leonard's fleeting memory of the syringe discussed earlier.

By extension, where realist narration assumes an omniscient spectator – one who possesses an unrestricted view of time – post-traumatic narration is marked by patterns of cinematic abstraction that blur the subjective boundary between the past and the present, thereby transforming the spectator from a passive viewer to an active participant in its construction. Techniques that draw on existing tendencies evident in modernist art, for example, including reflexivity, subjectivity and ambiguity, have the effect of foregrounding the spectator's own relation to the screen. The indeterminable fate of Cobb's spinning top in *Inception* is perhaps the most salient example of this as the ambiguity of the film's ending calls attention to the spectator's desire for closure. Narration in these films is also frequently disjointed and chaotic with time becoming visible through flashbacks, proleptic flashes, parallel montage (intercutting between two geographically or temporally distinct scenes), ellipses and repetitions. Hirsch summarizes the combined effects of post-traumatic narration as a 'kind of failure [...] a collapse of mastery over time and point of view' (2003: 22). Building on Maureen Turim's analysis of the 'modernist flashback' contained within *Flashbacks in Film* (1989), Hirsch seeks to develop this discourse further by providing a specific example in the form of the 'post-traumatic flashback'.

Hirsch initially contextualizes Turim's distinction between the use of flashback in Hollywood film and the 'modernist flashback' by locating both within the discourse of trauma cinema (1989: 189). For Turim, the modernist flashback is noticeably different from the conventional use of the flashback in classical filmmaking suggesting that, where the latter functions to provide an image of the past, the former 'can make spectators more aware of the modalities of filmic fiction, of the processes of narrative itself. These manipulations of narrative temporality can serve to self-consciously expose the mechanisms of filmic narration' (1989: 16). Hirsch extends this distinction beyond a discussion of the spectator's relationship with a film's formal mode of representation to indicate how emphasizing the cinematic image as a construct might function as an attempt to *represent* the traumatic experience. He says that, in employing the 'modernist fragmentation of tense, restriction of mood, and self-consciousness of voice' (2003: 99), the post-traumatic flashback functions 'to create a disturbance not only at the level of content, by presenting a painful fictional memory, but also at the level of form' (2003: 99).

A flashback, post-traumatic or otherwise, cannot help but draw attention to the mechanisms designed to maintain the falsity of the fiction because of the way that it disrupts the linearity of a narrative. Nevertheless, Turim reminds us that various techniques have been employed to naturalize the more radical temporal manipulations such as 'locating them in the psyche or the storytelling capacity of a character within the fiction' (1989: 16). For Turim, the spectator is therefore caught in a dialectic of 'knowledge and forgetfulness' (1989: 17), one that mirrors their more general interaction with the cinema which, for a number of psycho-analytic theorists, is largely dependent upon a disavowal of the medium's artifice in favour of the 'impression of reality' created by it (Metz 1982: 140). I will go on to discuss these ideas in more detail in the following section but for now, the question remains as to whether the core function of the post-traumatic flashback has been diluted in favour of maintaining the illusion-making strategies of classic realist forms of film narration. Hirsch, for instance, claims that the post-traumatic flashback's shock value decreased as it 'entered the narrative repertoire of mainstream film' (2003: 110). Equally, Janet Walker's initial claim that trauma cinema is stylistically nonrealist implicitly suggests that classic realist film narratives do not employ the necessary aesthetic forms and representational strategies to communicate trauma. Nonetheless, these observations do not acknowledge how porous the boundaries between these two modes are.

One only needs to consider the range of films discussed by Todd McGowan in his monograph *Out of Time* (2011) to understand the increasing cross-pollination of techniques and thematic approaches between mainstream cinema and art cinema. He suggests that a number of films released since the turn of the millennium – which often utilize nonrealist forms of representation including achronological narratives, loops, repetitions, parallel ontological worlds and labyrinth polyphonic plots – communicate a different type of spectator relationship. For McGowan, these films are structured around the individual's experience of time and trauma. In films such as *Irreversible* (2002), *21 Grams* (2003), *Eternal Sunshine of the Spotless Mind* (2004) and *2046* (2004) McGowan suggests that trauma is experienced by the spectator within the narrative at the level of content through the breakdown of relationships, bereavement, violence and so on. However, beyond these basic commonalities, McGowan argues that each film's formal properties – which include a variety of structural loops, overlaps and literal repetitions – also create a vicarious traumatic experience for the spectator. He argues that by repeatedly returning the spectator to a traumatic encounter, these films remind us that 'no amount of time allows us to escape the hold that loss has over us' (2011: 14).

In these films, time is malleable rather than constant, thereby paralleling the spatialization of time that McGowan associates with the increasing development of digital technologies. For McGowan, the digital revolution and the attendant immediacy associated with the production and consumption of data (now a ubiquitous aspect of contemporary life) have produced significant changes in human thought and attitudes towards time. McGowan summarizes this notion when he says the following: 'Digital technology eviscerates the experience of authentic temporality, leaving contemporary subjects adrift in the experience of an eternal present' (2011: 25). The digital era, in other words, signifies a shift away from the phenomenological experience of time in process, recognized by St. Augustine, towards a culture of instant gratification. As a distinctly temporal medium, cinema possesses the capacity to demonstrate what McGowan refers to as a 'different form of temporality' (2011: xi). A consideration of these complex film narratives demonstrates an emphasis, not on time as a linear progression, but rather on the repetition associated with the temporal logic of trauma.

The Limits of Representation: Cinema and Psychoanalysis

The capacity of film to capture the experience of trauma is set into question by the limits of representation. Trauma is, by definition, beyond the scope of language and representation – that is what makes it unconscious. Hence, in principle, a *representation* of trauma seems somewhat contradictory. As the French psycho-analyst Jean Laplanche puts it, what is repressed is 'de-signified' meaning that 'it loses its status as representation (as signifier) in order to become a thing which no longer represents (signifies anything) other than itself' (1999b: 90). In effect, any element that exposes the unconscious can only be a signifier that gestures towards that which is de-signified (Laplanche [1987] 1989a: 45). For example, in Sigmund Freud's famous account of the Wolf-Man ([1918] 1955a), he postulates that the patient's childhood memory of his parents engaging in *coitus a tergo* in the afternoon is reawakened when he sees a nursery-maid washing the floor on her hands and knees. This is not in itself a 'representation' of the unconscious but merely reveals an underlying unconscious fantasy by replicating the position of the mother *a tergo*. In short, *representations* can only *indicate* an underlying unconscious trauma; they cannot *directly* represent that trauma. Perhaps, then, it is wiser to suggest that trauma cannot, in its *totality*, be represented. Nevertheless, it seems that art, at least to some degree, can provide an insight into the structure of the traumatic experience.

To understand the role of trauma within Nolan's films it is important to first emphasize that there remains an intimate and ongoing association between cinema and psychoanalysis. This connection is notable for several reasons not least because both originated in the last decade of the nineteenth century when, in 1895, the Lumière brothers screened their very first films in the basement of a Parisian café and, during the same year, Freud published his first major text on psycho-analysis, *Studies on Hysteria* ([1895] 1957). The coincidence that cinema and psychoanalysis share a date which marks the beginnings of both has been readily cited by film theorists who see this historical link as evidence of the indisputable association between the two (see Gabbard 2001; Lebeau 2001; Sabbadini 2003). However, more than this, a dialogue exists between cinema and psychoanalysis that stems from an understanding of the unconscious and of dreams.

In Sigmund Freud's early thought, what distinguishes the unconscious from consciousness and pre-conscious is that the subject cannot simply translate unconscious material such as irrational wishes and immoral/antisocial urges into consciousness without some form of traumatic disruption (see Freud [1900] 1965b). As such, for Freud, we can only encounter the unconscious via dreams, jokes, accidents or slips and through a process of free association (see Freud [1901] 1960a, [1905] 1960b). Of these, Freud suggests that it is primarily through dreams that a path to understanding the unconscious can emerge, as it is the privacy of the dream that attests to the prospect of the subject freely expressing unconscious desire as a form of wish-fulfilment ([1900] 1965b: 118–19). However, contrary to the popular belief that the purpose of dreams is primarily the fulfilment of wishes, Freud rejects the possibility that dreams can provide direct access to what is unconsciously desired. Instead, Freud suggests that, since external institutions such as religion and the law regulate the social order, the subject also possesses an internal authority – later referred to by Freud as the 'superego' – which distorts the dream by creating obstacles that prevent the realization of repressed desires (see Freud [1923] 1961a). This is to say that, despite the content of the dream being known only to the dreamer, their unconscious desire is still held accounta-ble to existing external social norms and values in such a way that the dream itself becomes distorted through a process Freud terms 'dream-work' ([1900] 1965b: 179). Such distortion not only reveals the impossibility of satisfying our desires but also that there is something inherently traumatic about desire itself that requires it to manifest in the unconscious in a disguised form.

As Freud conceives it, the distortions that occur at the level of the dream make analysis necessary and it is for this reason that Freud refers to the *interpretation* of dreams, rather than the dream itself, as the 'royal road' to the unconscious (see Freud [1900] 1965b: 608). Equally, if the interpretation of dreams provides access to the unconscious then cinema, which not only reproduces the relative physical immobility and passivity of dreaming while also exposing the subject to images that are beyond our conscious control, also has the same potential (see Baudry

1974; Metz 1982). Consequently, as we sit in the cinema our engagement with the images on-screen functions to connect us to the film in the same way that we connect with our dreams because each engages with what can be termed unconscious desire. It is through this connection that it is possible to suggest that the cinema offers us a site where we can engage in a form of dreaming in public, a concept echoed in the popular description of the cinema as the 'dream factory'. Crucially for McGowan, while the association of cinematic images with those produced by dreams is important, the cinema is unique among all other art forms because, unlike literature, painting or theatre, it 'marginalizes conscious will and privileges unconscious desire' (2015b: 8). McGowan suggests that while each of these forms engages the subject at the level of consciousness, they do so without necessarily activating the unconscious. In contrast, he argues that in both dreams and the cinema, the position of the subject is built upon the possibility of embracing the freedom associated with unconscious desire. Put simply, like dreams, cinema functions to express unconscious desire in ways that the social codes of everyday life do not permit. However, McGowan goes on to highlight that the price of this freedom comes at the expense of a confrontation with trauma. This remains one of the fundamental discoveries of psychoanalysis that separates it from not only the history of philosophy but also common sense, both of which assume that our happiness is the unquestioned aim of all our actions. As a theoretical tool, psychoanalysis reveals that the unconscious is structured according to a logic of desire which seeks to reject that which would be beneficial for the subject in such a way that ultimately sustains the necessity of desire as a constitutive part of the subject. As such, the encounter with our unconscious desire, whether in dreams or the cinema, is always traumatic.

If we understand that our access to the unconscious begins with a traumatic disruption and that, by extension, this entails an encounter with desire, then watching a film – which translates unconscious desires into concrete images – can also be a traumatic experience. Along these lines, even though the filmmaker and the spectator(s) are separate subjects and no single subject desires the same as another, the comparison between dreams and the cinema is maintained because films address the spectator as a social subject within a broader network of desires which are embedded within the social order. This is to say that while it would be presumptive to assume that a homologous subject exists in relation to film viewing, every film – regardless of subject or genre – is produced to arouse the subject's desire (McGowan 2015b: 9). Of course, desire is by no means straightforward and the existence of exploitation cinema and pornography, as well as numerous variations of the horror genre, are, in different ways, a testament not only to the heterogeneity of the audience but also to a vast variety of tastes. But, even in these examples, which frequently aim to disturb the spectator, desire is manifested through the subject's own unconscious desire *to be* disturbed. On this basis, every film can be interpreted using psychoanalysis as even those films that seek to disturb the spectator do so within an economy of desire whereby the realization of desire exists outside of the social order and as such, remains perpetually deferred. Film, then, can be an articulation of collective, unconscious desires that conflict with social norms, revealing an inherent encounter with trauma. It is for this reason that film theorists such as Christian Metz suggest that film is a powerful medium that offers us invaluable insights into the structure of the unconscious and the nature of the human psyche (see 1982).

A Traumatic Encounter with Jacques Lacan: Interrogating the Real

According to Lacan, the fundamental structure of the unconscious is a three-way combination of what he calls the Imaginary, the Symbolic and the Real ([1953] 1982). Much of Lacan's earlier psychoanalytic contributions focused on the registers of the Imaginary and the Symbolic whilst placing a limited amount of importance on the Real. However, Lacan's later writing is marked by a distinct change in emphasis as his account of the Real evolves to become a more central part of his theory alongside other concepts such as the gaze, the Thing (das Ding), the *objet petit a* and *jouissance* (enjoyment). The Real is perhaps best understood as that which remains outside the registers of the Imaginary and Symbolic beyond language and meaning (Lacan 1977d: 167).[3] By way of example, consider for a moment the death of a loved one. Like the Real, grief resists expression in language. Instead, the individual's own personal emotions manifest through a series of non-verbal affective symptoms including sadness, sorrow, fatigue, shock, anger, guilt and anxiety. Richard Armstrong notes in *Mourning Films* that

> it is not difficult to read death as an aspect of the Real, our profoundest fear yet impossible to speak. And like the Real, grief, the consequence of death for those left behind, lacks sense or meaning. We struggle to mediate grief through a symbolic system which for Lacan is already inadequate to the expression of human desire. So grief manifests itself in affects, which are too inexpressible, too uncontainable, too awful for verbal articulation.
>
> (Armstrong 2012: 11)

In Lacan's own discussion of the Real, he refers to it as 'the essential object which isn't an object any longer, but this something faced with which all words cease and all categories fail, the object of anxiety *par excellence*' ([1978] 1988a: 164, original emphasis). The point of indeterminacy where language ceases to function responds to Lacan's articulation of the Real as that which is un-representable or 'impossible' (1977d: 167) and it is this resistance to symbolization that lends the Real its traumatic quality. Along similar lines, the Slovenian philosopher Slavoj Žižek refers to the Real as 'something that persists only as failed, missed, in shadow, and dissolves itself as soon as we try to grasp it' (1989: 169). He goes on to say that 'this is precisely what defines the notion of traumatic event: a point of failure of symbolization – it can be constructed only backwards, from its structural effects' (1989: 169). Žižek's own theoretical stance emerges from Lacan's initial conception of trauma as a '*missed* encounter with the Real' (1977d: 55, emphasis added), which, as missed, cannot be represented, only repeated. The implication of this understanding points towards the temporal logic of trauma as one of perpetual return, something that manifests in Nolan's films through the spectator's desire to continually revisit his most complex enigmas.

Even though Lacan describes trauma as a 'missed encounter' (1977d: 55) with the Real, the capacity to conceptualize and depict the Real does exist in art and culture. For instance, in *The Return of the Real* (1996), the American art critic Hal Foster discusses Andy Warhol's *Death in America* (1963), a series of prints that explores the relationship between the media and violence. In his discussion, Foster places an emphasis on the way repetition is symptomatic of trauma. He suggests that the silk-screen technique that allowed Warhol to endlessly duplicate images of car wrecks, dead celebrities, electric chairs, mushroom clouds and so on 'serves to *screen* the real understood as traumatic' (1996: 132, original emphasis). However, he goes on to note that, 'this very need also *points* to the real, and at this point the real *ruptures* the screen of repetition' (1996: 132, original emphasis). Crucially, Foster is arguing that it is because the image is repeated that it becomes diluted of affect and is therefore no longer experienced as traumatic. However, at the same time, technical flaws in the process of reproduction such as blemishes from handling, tears and empty corners of the canvas disclose the mechanical way in which the prints were made, thereby exposing an altogether separate point of identification for the spectator's gaze. These instances or what Foster terms 'visual equivalents of our missed encounters with the real' (1996: 134), allow the subject to almost touch the Real, which 'pokes' (1996: 136) through the screen of repetitions. Along these lines, Warhol's repetitive images function as both a defence against trauma *and* an invocation of it. Likewise, Nolan's films function in a similar capacity as they frequently acknowledge the spectator's gaze through the visibility of mechanisms traditionally designed to mask the falsity of a film's fiction while, simultaneously, immersing the spectator in the illusion of the narrative event. In addition, his films are sustained by a compulsiveness that requires the spectator to return for repeated viewings. Moments such as the fleeting references to Leonard's time in a mental institution in *Memento*, whether Dormer (Al Pacino) intentionally meant to shoot his partner in *Insomnia* and Cutter's (Michael Caine) closing narration in *The Prestige* are just a few examples that produce a frustration in spectators who find themselves repeatedly returning to the text in the search for answers. In this way, much like the characters in these films, the spectator remains frozen in time.

Like all art, cinema then also possesses the capability to envisage the Real. Indeed, the combined effect of the visual and aural stimuli makes cinema a particularly appropriate medium through which to encounter the Real. For example, Emma Wilson argues that, of all the art forms, cinema has perhaps embraced the Real the most. She says, '[f]ilm at its most devastating is not an escape from reality, but an encounter with the Real' (2003: 10). The significance of the Real for film theory is Lacan's own emphasis on the visual. This is because film is, above all, a visual medium. Indeed, closely related to the field of vision, the traumatic Real is inseparable from Lacan's discussion of the gaze, although there is an elemental distinction between the *cinematic* gaze i.e. the 'look' of the camera and the gaze according to Lacan. The cinematic gaze differs from the 'look' as unlike the 'look', which defines what 'I' see, the gaze pre-exists my subjective perspective since 'I' am always-already looked at from all sides (Lacan 1977d: 74–75). Or, as McGowan puts it, '[t]he gaze is not the look of the subject at the object, but the point at which the object looks back' (2003: 28–29). The gaze prompts an encounter with the Real since it forces the spectator to confront their own subjectivity by drawing attention to the systems of representation that usually operate to conceal the mechanical nature of film production. When this happens, the spectator is reminded that the film is not a window into a private world but rather a product of labour created with ideological meanings for mass consumption. In essence, the spectator is aware that the film is a fiction but is willing to disavow this truth for the sake of maintaining the cinematic illusion, a sentiment similarly echoed in the final moments of Nolan's film *The Prestige*. In what are perhaps the most important lines of the film and more generally a defining example of Nolan's approach to filmmaking, Angier (Hugh Jackman) says to his rival, 'you never understood why we did this. The audience knows the truth. The world is simple, miserable, solid all the way through. But if you can fool them, even for a second, then you can make them wonder'.

I Desire, Therefore I Lack

According to Lacan, desire is constituted around a lack that emerges from the fundamental division of the subject ([1978] 1988a: 221). This split occurs, Lacan argues, with the child's separation from the mother and their entry into language or to the Symbolic ([1949] 1977e: 2). From one perspective, it is from the moment the child begins to speak that they become separated from the Imaginary – a realm of complete harmony with the mother in which all the child's needs are met – and become subject to the laws of the Symbolic (Lacan 1977d: 28). What occurs during this split is the repression of the child's desire for the mother, which, according to Lacan, attempts to compensate for the 'lack' that the subject experiences due to its separation from the mother (1977d: 193–96). Within this framework, this lack propels the subject into perpetually seeking new ways to compensate for what is missing through various stand-in objects. It is important to acknowledge that even though Lacan often describes lack in terms that seem to invoke a material object, he contends that desire cannot be derived from an object, choosing instead to emphasize the importance of objects as symbols, symptoms and signifiers. As he explains in *Seminar IV*, it is an 'object that is nowhere articulated, it is a lost object, but paradoxically an object that was never there in the first place to be lost' ([1986] 1992: 58). For Lacan, there are no objects of desire. Rather, it is because desire cannot be fulfilled that desire remains. What this means is that every object is an insufficient substitute for the wholeness of being that the subject seeks because lack is a constitutive element of subjectivity. As he puts it in *Seminar II*, '[t]his lack is the lack of being properly speaking. It isn't the lack of this or that, but the lack of being whereby the being exists. This lack is beyond anything which can represent it' ([1978] 1988a: 223). In other words, every desire regardless of its distinguishing features is motivated by the inherent lack in our condition as subjects that points back towards the experience of separation. Consequently, the individual is seemingly destined to repeatedly acquire a series of objects even though or rather *because* these objects mask the subject's inherent inability to recapture what was lost.

Of course, this is not to say that our desires cannot be realized but rather that there is an elemental distinction between how desire is *realized* and how desire is *satisfied*. Put simply, while there are objects that one may desire that can be obtained, as many individuals will testify, realizing one's desire does not result in an end to desire. Instead, desire is sustained and perpetually deferred as part of a continuous displacement from object to object at the level of the unconscious. This is what Lacan refers to when he writes 'desire *is* a metonymy' ([1957] 1977b: 175, original emphasis). Indeed, the repeated failure to obtain the lost-object requires that Lacan provide a distinction between two types of object that relate to the register of desire. For Lacan, the object of desire is altogether separate from the object *cause* of desire or what he terms the *objet petit a* or the *objet a*. While the object of desire is reducible to what is desired, this is to say an object through which the subject attempts to realize its desire, the *objet a* serves to trigger the desire of the subject and yet, at no time is this object attainable. Instead, the *objet a* is the lost-object which points towards the traumatic loss experienced upon the subject's entrance into the Symbolic. The *objet a* functions as an obstacle that separates the subject from the object of desire, thus propelling the continuous search for new objects which, in turn, ensures that desire is sustained through the perpetual absence of the object that one seeks or the presence of an obstacle barring access to it (see McGowan 2015b: 6).

The problem then, as McGowan indicates in *Psychoanalytic Film Theory and The Rules of The Game*, is that as subjects of desire we don't really want what it is that we think we want, and it is this revelation that returns us once more to trauma. He comments:

> All of the self-help books that exist in the world exist because we really can't help ourselves. Instead, we choose a path that will prevent us from fulfilling our desire, no matter how hard we try to continuously realize it [...] We are self-sabotaging beings [...] [and] because we are self-sabotaging beings, we cannot avoid the experience of trauma.
>
> (McGowan 2015b: 43–44)

For him, the act of self-sabotage allows the subject to perpetuate desire, thereby sidestepping the characteristic dissatisfaction that would occur upon the realization of desire. He says, '[o]ur self-destructiveness is not a pointless activity that we might remedy. It instead constitutes the basis for our capacity to enjoy. Through self-sacrifice, we create the loss that we enjoy' (McGowan 2015b: 56). In *The Prestige*, for example, Angier's continuously shifting search for the lost-object (enacted by his movement from one object to another) demonstrates the lengths that one will go to in order to facilitate an encounter with trauma. In effect, it is our ability to self-sabotage that derails us from the path to what we desire, which, in turn, endows us with the potential to embrace the experience of enjoyment. However, this enjoyment is, as McGowan points out, 'inextricable from loss, and there is no enjoyment without loss' (2015b: 56). The notion that a subject can enjoy trauma might seem somewhat counterintuitive at first. However, according to McGowan, while we otherwise seek to avoid traumatic events these occurrences do provide us with a 'degree of relief' (2011: 44) and ultimately inaugurate our being as desiring subjects. For McGowan, a traumatic event offers the subject temporary respite from the experience of daily life while, at the same time, pointing back to the lack at the centre of the subject as desire.

The discourse of desire orbits around trauma because we are seemingly driven to repeat the traumatic moment of original loss that is central to subjectivity. Such repetition often manifests in the form of failure, which, unlike success, foregrounds the possibility of having to return time after time to eventually succeed. But given that we are, as McGowan notes, 'self-sabotaging beings' (2011: 44) failure itself functions as the necessary barrier to success in such a way that sustains desire. Furthermore, even when we do eventually succeed, our attention frequently turns to something else and yet when we fail, the failure provides a core around which our thoughts and memories return. The central point Nolan's films continue to explore is that selfhood is intimately tied to traumatic loss. Trauma initiates our being as desiring subjects by marking us as lacking, and this lack accompanies the subject who repeatedly seeks – and fails – to re-experience the wholeness that preceded the traumatic loss. The relevance of desire has dramatic ramifications for the analysis of film when one considers that *every* film mobilizes desire, although as McGowan points out, 'most films do not sustain the logic of desire throughout the narrative. Instead, they retreat from the deadlock of desire [...] into a fantasmatic resolution' (2003: 36). In other words, while watching these films the cyclical nature of desire is often denied as the spectator acquires the object of desire at the expense of the *objet a*, thereby achieving a sense of closure. In contrast, Nolan's films offer a more complex rendition of desire in line with the conventions of what McGowan labels 'atemporal cinema' (2011) whereby desire is often perpetually deferred. In their movement away from linear time towards repetition, the films associated with atemporal cinema repeat the failure of desire, thereby dismantling our conventional understanding of temporality.

By destabilizing conventional relations of chronology, atemporal films highlight the failure in the spectator's relation to what they desire and thus encourage them to embrace the repetition attached to trauma. Here, one is immediately reminded of Freud's account of the *Fort-Da* game described in *Beyond the Pleasure Principle* in which an infant stages and attempts to master the traumatic experience of maternal loss by making a toy disappear and then reappear. Freud's analysis of the child's habitual behaviour points towards an understanding of the individual's need to master a traumatic event by returning to it so that they might transform it from a passive experience into an active one. Freud observed that the game entertains the child thereby functioning as a temporary distraction from their feelings of separation and yet the child continues to play the game again and again. Instead of lessening the experience of loss, the game accentuates the urge to overcome it. In other words, the repetition of loss reiterates the impossibility of integrating it, a repetition that, as Freud described it, represents the failed outcome of working-through a traumatic event. In the context of cinema, I believe that the pattern of repetition evident in the chronicle of the *Fort-Da* game clearly parallels the spectator's encounter with the majority of Nolan's films evident even when we examine those that are considered by a number of academics to be the furthest removed from his filmmaking such as *The Dark Knight* trilogy, a series of films that seems to be the least representative of his style. Unlike the experience of classical cinema, in which the spectator enjoys an apparent sense of mastery that is based upon their ability to anticipate future action based on their knowledge of conventional cues and signifiers, these films confound their ability to predict the direction of the narrative or obtain a sense of mastery and control over the events unfolding before them by withholding narrative closure. In this sense, one of the ways that these films reproduce the experience of trauma in the spectator is by providing a discontinuous experience of time that emulates the temporality of trauma.

Narrative Desire

This complex exploration of trauma is consistent throughout the majority of Nolan's films as they frequently opt to defer the spectator's desire by lacking narrative closure. For instance, in *Memento*, the spectator can never know fully whether Leonard was responsible for his wife's death. Equally, Cutter's monologue during the final moments of *The Prestige* hints at a hidden layer to the film that the spectator is seemingly unaware of. In *Inception*, the fate of Cobb's spinning top remains unknown and so the question of whether he remains in a dream or returns to reality is left open to interpretation. Clearly, Nolan's approach to narrative construction defies convention, which dictates that there should be a three-part movement from a state of equilibrium through disruption and finally a new equilibrium in which the fundamental conflict at the centre of the narrative is brought to a resolution. For Barbara Creed (2000), this elemental structure attempts to resolve the subject's underlying sense of lack by returning them to a state of wholeness, but it should be clear by now that Nolan's willingness to confront the spectator with the trauma of his or her desire demonstrates his ability as a filmmaker to point out the fundamentally illusory nature of this endeavour. Nevertheless, Creed emphasizes that the concept of lack is central to all narratives that invariably seek to fill a lack. She writes:

> All stories begin with a situation in which the status quo is upset and the hero or heroine must – in general terms – solve a problem in order for the equilibrium to be restored. This approach sees the structures of narrative as being in service of the subject's desire to overcome lack.
>
> (Creed 2000: 79)

Similarly, Mark Jancovich suggests that the concept of lack can be understood as part of the wider construct of narratological discourse, which binds the spectator to the film through a careful balance of loss and recovery (1995: 139–40). Significantly though, Jancovich concedes that despite a formative sense of closure that accompanies a large majority of texts produced in line with the fundamental tenets of classical narrative cinema, the subject's lack remains. He says, 'the sense of lack can never be filled, so narrative is ultimately unable to achieve complete resolution. The text provides substitutes for the missing object, but can never finally portray the moment of wholeness and completion' (1995: 139–40). Thus, it would appear that the very form of narrative bears witness to the lack inherent in being.

If according to Jancovich, the resolution offered by the traditional three-act model fails to restore the subject's lack, then an emphasis on open-ended narratives will *stress* lack as a constitutive element of identity formation. This is because, in life and by extension in film, all actions tend to be geared towards a desired outcome meaning that a beginning must, in some sense, be determined by an end. Or, if we use the analogy of desire, what we desire stems from somewhere although the point of origin may not be apparent to us until we get what it is that we think we want. Accordingly, the present moment is only endowed with significance because of the way in which we retroactively provide meaning to our actions. In film, given that the movement towards narrative closure aims to overcome lack, when the closure is limited or in some cases denied, the structuring power of desire becomes apparent via the inability to comprehend the past. It is precisely at the moment the film rejects closure that it *speaks* to the audience by acknowledging their desire and confronting them with their own complicity in the reception and understanding – or lack thereof – of the film. These moments then, which embrace the failure of the subject's assumed mastery, provide an encounter with the Real, which, according to McGowan, is 'what spectators desire when they go to the movies' (2003: 29). This theory gains traction in Nolan's films such as *Memento*, *The Prestige* and *Inception* whose narratives overtly contribute to the impression of a lack that strips the subject of their position of mastery. These films demand that repeated viewings occur to try and comprehend their ambiguities, possibilities and even contradictions.

Unlike the majority of classical narrative cinema, which provides the spectator with a sense of mastery through acquiring the object of desire, by resisting a logically and emotionally satisfying conclusion these films sustain the spectator's desire through a process of displacement and deferral. At a very basic level, questions are often left unanswered, the fates of major characters remain unknown and fundamental issues are unresolved. We are drawn to the process of uncovering these gaps in the narrative because what is hidden from us indicates the possibility of some secret enjoyment. Consequently, the degree of repetition that occurs – both physically, in the form of re-watching the film, and mentally, in the form of remembering it – functions to confer some form of meaning upon the text. However, returning to a film fails to provide the necessary enjoyment that one seeks. This is because exposing the secret (thereby obtaining the object of desire) necessarily destroys the desirability of the object and so we must seek another that might replace it. This is precisely why those who claim to have found solutions to even the most complex enigmas contained within Nolan's films fail to grasp that in doing so, they misunderstand the nature of desire which is most interested in reproducing itself.

Though we might imagine that our search for the *objet a* may eventually succeed, the reality is that this search will always fail. This is because we exist in a closed loop of desire in which desire remains unfulfilled, perpetually repeating itself in such a way that points towards the enjoyment of this failure. This paradoxical logic requires a further distinction between desire and the drive. Whereas desire operates according to the logic of displacement and dissatisfaction, the drive is organized in relation to an understanding that desire is a repetitive movement in which enjoyment emerges through failing to acquire the object of desire (Žižek 1999: 304). Within the dynamic of desire and the drive, the enjoyment embodied in the *objet a* draws a significant comparison to the structural experience of trauma. The repetition associated with the circular movement of trauma and desire is at once the source of our enjoyment as well as our pain. McGowan comments that '[e]njoyment is always traumatic enjoyment. Though we don't enjoy every trauma, we never enjoy without trauma' (2015b: 55). Equally, for McGowan, this understanding of the intimate relationship between trauma and desire extends to the cinema. He remarks that:

> There is no desire free of trauma, which is why desire is often repressed. But film enables us to encounter the trauma of our desire and to enjoy this encounter [...] Trauma in the cinema is not only traumatic; it is also enjoyable. The genius of film lies in its ability to subject us to a traumatic disruption we can enjoy.
> (McGowan 2015b: 164)

Accordingly, cinema can provide the spectator with the opportunity to experience an encounter with the traumatic Real by allowing them to momentarily confront their failed mastery precisely at the point they are accounted for within the film itself.[4] In many films, this confrontation is often elided in favour of sustaining the possibility of some form of 'fantasmatic resolution' (McGowan 2003: 36). However, in Nolan's films, the intersection between trauma and desire is frequently foregrounded in ways that point towards the spectator's active rather than passive role in the experience of his films. What this suggests is that the traumatic disruption is not only visible at the level of the diegesis, in terms of the content and formal structure, but also in relation to the spectator's own vicarious experience of trauma, and this is why Nolan is one of the most important directors of the twenty-first century and his films are an appropriate choice for psychoanalytic interpretation.

NOTES

1. Freud's initial topographical model of mind outlined in *The Interpretation of Dreams* identified three distinct levels: the unconscious, pre-conscious and conscious. In *The Ego and the Id* ([1923] 1960) Freud revised the existing model by replacing the previous terms with the id, ego and superego. In this structural model, the id, which is present at birth, consists of largely of instinctual drives operating at the level of desire. The id's self-gratifying urges are offset by the superego which functions according to social and moral authority of law and order. The outcome of the interaction between the id and superego is the ego, which can be aligned with reason and self.

2. Unlike narrative memory, which is characterized by the integration of past events through the process of conscious recall, traumatic memories remain fixed and are repeatedly re-lived through involuntary processes such as intrusive thoughts, nightmares and flashbacks (Janet [1919] 1976).

3. Lacan's account of the Symbolic order primarily refers to the social and linguistic realm according to the law of the father, also designated as the 'name of the father' (1988a: 230). Accordingly, the notion of the Symbolic constitutes the subject's relations to itself, culture and wider social and family networks. From a Lacanian perspective, it is the subject's acquisition of language which involves the passage from the Imaginary order to the Symbolic that provides the means for individuation and identity or, as Lacan puts it, 'it is the symbolic order which is constitutive for the subject' (1988a: 7).

4. Of course, this encounter is not prescriptive and there are, as numerous scholars have pointed out, an infinite number of positions for the spectator to adopt (see Bordwell and Carroll 1996). However, an awareness of alternative points of identification does not alter the fundamental structure of desire that underpins all of cinema.

Revisiting the Scene of the Crime: Repressing the Past in *Insomnia*

I could feel it right then, this is gonna catch up with me.

– Detective Dormer, *Insomnia*

In a bonus scene that was removed from *Insomnia*'s theatrical run but included as an extra on the film's DVD release, Detective Dormer (Al Pacino) confides in the hotel owner, Rachel Clement (Maura Tierney), that in his job he often deals with people who have lost someone. In his experience, he frequently finds that people are unsure of how to respond to loss. He says, 'A lot of them don't know how to feel [...] Everyone around them is acting like it's obvious what they're going through but they themselves, they don't know. They don't know what they're feeling. Sure they're sad. But, it's mixed up with a lot of other things'. He goes on to tell her that he himself felt embarrassed as a young boy when his brother died: 'it made me different' he remarks, 'Kids don't like to be different'. When people would ask him what had happened to his brother he would make up stories to avoid telling the truth: 'he broke his leg, he was visiting with relatives, anything but the truth. I figured my family moved around so much I could get away with it for a while [...] but there I was telling more and more lies'. At this point, Dormer trails off perhaps aware that the conclusion of his story involves recognizing that he was caught lying. Suddenly, his demeanour changes. Prior to this moment, he had seemed open and relaxed during their conversation but upon uttering these words he seems to recompose himself: his facial expression becomes more serious, his eyebrows furrow and the slight smile fades from his face. The camera then cuts to Rachel who stares at him for a moment as the silence between them lengthens before she eventually averts her gaze towards the floor.

During this deleted scene, Dormer and Rachel's non-verbal exchange is of significance as it marks a moment when Dormer seems to accidentally reveal his true self. Even at a young age, his willingness to deceive those around him by repressing the impact of a traumatic event hints at his ongoing desire to lie, which he continues into adulthood. The change in his body language represents an attempt to mask the realization that his admission might expose him to the truth of his own role in the death of his partner, Hap Eckhart (Martin Donovan), whom he shot while in pursuit of a murder suspect. Here, Dormer's repressed past returns to occupy the present in such a way that it momentarily threatens to reveal the unbearable truth at the heart of his identity. This brief scene, then, while admittedly not included in the theatrical release of *Insomnia*, nevertheless contains a number of key elements that this chapter will address in relation to the film under the broad framework of trauma, including the theory of repression and the bidirectionality of time in relation to a traumatic experience. I want to consider Nolan's treatment of trauma by analysing *Insomnia* in relation to the Freudian concept of *Nachträglichkeit* and its subsequent reformulation by Jacques Lacan as *après-coup* and Jean Laplanche as *afterwardsness* before locating the film within the broader context of Paul Sutton's paradigm of cinematic spectatorship.

Made in 1997, the original version of *Insomnia* features Stellan Skarsgård as Jonas Engström, a police detective who along with his partner Erik Vik (Sverre Anker Ousdal) is sent to a small Norwegian town to investigate the murder of a teenage girl (Maria Mathiesen). While in pursuit of a suspect, Jonas accidentally shoots his partner and attempts to cover up his role in the death. In doing so, Jonas begins his moral descent into uncertainty as guilt, confusion and shame are intensified by his inability to sleep. Despite some obvious omissions in the form of attempted rape, scenes of animal cruelty and the contrasting fate of the central characters, the subsequent remake of *Insomnia* by Nolan retains several of the key plot points from the original. In the film, Detectives Dormer and Eckhart are similarly sent to a remote destination to assist local police with their investigation into the death of a young girl called Kay Connell (Crystal Lowe). In a scene that parallels the original Dormer shoots his partner, but his intentions are less clear. In addition, the undercurrent of an internal affairs investigation alluded to prior to the death of Eckhart adds another dimension to the film not present in the original.

Whilst the film outwardly marks a stylistic deviation from those with which Nolan made his name in that it appears to be a relatively straightforward linear narrative, *Insomnia* remains thematically similar to the films that came before it. There is a varying focus on time, identity, guilt and self-deception that emerges in the critical discussions of the film but equally, what is rarely directly addressed by these commentators is the underlying theme of trauma that is also evident. Although Nolan's previous representations of the mind have been interpreted in relation to a more general psychological framework – in terms of the depiction of repression and traumatic memories in *Memento* for example (see Thomas 2003; Little 2005) – it appears to me that *Insomnia* can be analysed by embracing psychoanalytic concepts, in particular Sigmund Freud's notion of *Nachträglichkeit*. These ideas, which I argue are unique to Nolan's interpretation of the source material, are established in the film's title sequence, principally with the first image of the film, which will be examined in this chapter.

As the opening credits of *Insomnia* start, dark blood spreads outward on a white cloth in a series of receding close-ups as the film's title emerges from the depth of the image. Subsequent aerial shots of the Alaskan landscape are interspersed with the ongoing repetition of the imagery of blood-spreading and as each shot of the jagged glaciers transitions into a blank screen before segueing once more into the image of the white fabric, there is a sense that the visual transition between the shots represents the liminal state between waking and sleep. In this manner, the way the images of the glaciers become increasingly blurred foreshadows Dormer's (ironically a name that is similar to the French verb 'dormir', meaning to sleep) subjective mental state as continuously framed as trapped between the transitional states of waking and asleep. The sequence ends with an image of blood being dropped on to a white shirt cuff and an unidentified person who appears to be attempting to rub away the bloodstains. As the shots are so fleeting, the full measure of what has been shown only becomes apparent in flashbacks that occur later in the film. However, in these brief shots and the subsequent cut to Dormer analysing several crime scene photos, there is an implied visual association between the events. This relationship points towards a connection between the image of the unidentified person attempting to rub away the bloodstains and the criminal suspect who will become central to Dormer's investigation during the remainder of the film. We subsequently learn near the film's ending that, contrary to our initial assumption, what appears to be a criminal attempting to remove evidence is in fact Dormer in the process of framing a suspect during a prior investigation. Todd McGowan points out that it is this type of causal linkage seemingly present in the opening sequence that deceives the spectator by operating at the level of the 'deceptiveness of cinema' (2012: 82). He comments:

> The structure of the film creates a deception in which the spectator misinterprets the opening images, and this initial misinterpretation paves the way for a series of misinterpretations that end only when the film's conclusion enables the spectator to recognize them as such [...] the deception marks the beginning and occurs before any truth. The spectator begins the Nolan film with a mistaken idea of what has happened and what's at stake in the events. The movement of the typical Nolan film is not, as in most films, from ignorance to knowledge. Instead, the spectator moves from mistaken knowledge to a later knowledge that corrects mistakes. The beginning point is not a blank slate but an initial error.
>
> (McGowan 2012: 2)[1]

This reversal of what we have seen, the way in which Nolan later provides the images with a new and unexpected meaning as well as assigning it much more significance in the context of the film, is central to an understanding of the relationship between the spectator and screen as it marks the point at which the film *speaks* to the spectator. This sequence, which I argue reveals more than just the 'deceptiveness of cinema' (2012: 82) noted by McGowan, confronts the spectator by acknowledging their place within the text, thereby engineering a traumatic encounter with what Lacan refers to as the Real. I will return to the position of the spectator in more detail towards the end of this chapter, but for now, I want to consider Freud's early conception of trauma – specifically the concept of repression – before proceeding any further as this is a useful point of departure before examining Lacan's re-reading of Freud.

Repression

Alongside Josef Breuer, Freud's early writing on repression provided a foundation for many of the later developments in psychoanalysis. Freud's conclusion that hysteria and its somatic symptoms were caused by the repression of a traumatic event, namely childhood sexual abuse ([1895] 1957: 6), remains a landmark theory that continues to spark theoretical debates about what constitutes trauma and the complex role of internal and external factors in its experience (see Sugarman 2003; Busch 2005). For Freud, one of the principal concepts to emerge from what he initially termed the 'seduction theory' was that trauma does not simply originate from outside the psyche but is instead structurally internalized and subsequently awakened by potent reminders ([1895] 1957: 197). While Freud subsequently rejected his theory of seduction, a number of psychoanalysts have since returned to his early texts seeking to revise and re-evaluate many of the underlying ideas in line with a broader consideration of how trauma functions in relation to time (see Laplanche and Pontalis 1973: 404–08). Notably, Freud's fundamental thesis, which challenged the status of the original trauma by suggesting that the repressed memory of an event – rather than the event itself – is invested with significance retroactively, has been revived as a key theoretical principle for understanding the temporal logic of trauma by Lacan and Laplanche (see Lacan [1953] 1977a: 30–113; Laplanche and Pontalis 1973; Laplanche 1999a: 260–65).

Repression is described by Freud in terms of *Nachträglichkeit* (an extension of the German adjective *nachträglich* meaning 'later' or 'afterwards'), a vague term that has been variously translated as 'belatedness', 'afterwardsness' (Laplanche cited in Caruth 2014: 27) or *'deferred action'* (Freud [1895] 1950: 356, original emphasis). The theory indicates that actual experience, memories or impressions can be repressed in the unconscious and subsequently revised, gaining more potency in the context of later events (see Laplanche and Pontalis 1973: 111–12). For example, an incident that may not have been traumatic when it occurred during childhood may become profoundly traumatic in the present through deferred affect and belated understanding. For Freud then, trauma is seemingly registered retroactively. Thus, unlike trauma theory[2] that tends to assume unconscious trauma is merely dissociated in line with a continuous movement from the present into the future (see Holmes 1990; Bonanno and Keuler 1998; Rofé 2008), through the operation of *Nachträglichkeit* time becomes visible. It is the retroactive act of recall that thrusts a moment from the past into the present, thereby exceeding the conventional logic of time as a series of succeeding 'now' moments.

After his abandonment of the seduction theory, subsequent references to *Nachträglichkeit* occur primarily in relation to Freud's extensive case of the 'Wolf-Man' ([1918] 1955a). Through his interpretation of the Wolf-Man's dream, Freud concluded that the patient, while still very young, must have seen his parents engaged in sexual intercourse. The scene itself bore no significance at the time of its occurrence due to the child's inability to understand the nature and meaning of their interaction. Nevertheless, its effects were deferred until the patient was able to understand it ([1918] 1955a: 37–38, 45). Freud explains the process:

> At the age of one and a half the child receives an impression to which he is unable to react adequately; he is only able to understand it and be moved by it when the impression is revived in him at the age of four; and only twenty years later, during the analysis, is he able to grasp with his conscious mental processes what was then going on in him. The patient justifiably disregards the three periods of time, and puts his present ego into the situation which is so long past.
>
> (Freud [1918] 1955a: 45)

Crucially for Freud, between the ages of one and two, the primal scene means nothing to the patient. Only later, at the age of four, does the memory become imbued with traumatic meaning because of some unconscious association or other traumatic event and transformed through the dream-work. Freud suggested that the subject's initial experience of trauma only acquires traumatic meaning through the introduction of a second trauma. It is the secondary event that effectively re-activates the earlier memory, revealing its traumatic origin. Reflecting on Freud's analysis, Jean Laplanche and Jean-Bertrand Pontalis write that 'the subject revises past events at a later date (*Nachträglichkeit*) and that it is this revision which invests them with significance and even with efficacy or pathogenic force' (1973: 112). They go on to state that '[i]t is not lived experience in general that undergoes a deferred revision, but, specifically whatever it has been impossible on the first instance to incorporate fully into a meaningful context. The traumatic event is the epitome of such unassimilated experience' (1973: 112). To understand this in the context of *Insomnia* it is necessary to consider how the events of the film are connected. To do so, it requires examining the causal link implied during the title sequence between the death at the centre of the current investigation and Dormer's decision to frame a character referred to as Wayne Dobbs during a previous assignment. While we are given no indication of the duration between Dormer's indiscretion and Kay's death we can assume that, due to the (imagined) vision of her murder shown briefly during the opening sequence and the parallels between the actions of the suspect – Walter Finch (Robin Williams) – and Dobbs, these separate events are connected in Dormer's mind. We can also assume then that the (imagined) death of Kay reconstructed from the images contained within the coroner's report acts as the unconscious signifier that revives the effect of the earlier memory of Dormer's actions in the previous case.

As the image of blood-spreading occurs from the outset of the film during the opening credits, there is a potential to dismiss the images as a cinematic tool designed simply to mislead the spectator.[3] However, the combination of the non-diegetic sounds of a plane experiencing turbulence increasing in volume included over the images of Dormer planting evidence, as well as the initial shot of Dormer opening his eyes at the climax of these sounds, suggests that the opening could be considered to be a representation of Dormer's subjective state of mind as he drifts in and out of consciousness. This reading is further supplemented by the subsequent shots of the Alaskan landscape, which become increasingly blurred before transitioning back to the blood-spreading motif. However, this reading of the opening sequence is problematic primarily as it relies heavily on claims that are difficult to substantiate with the visual evidence of scenes from the film. For instance, Nolan conflates any sense of subjectivity by manipulating the conventional use of eye-line match cuts. In the history of film, eye-line match cutting conventionally uses two shots to establish spatial continuity. The first shot usually begins with a character looking off-screen, followed by a second shot that indicates what the character is looking at or in many cases, who the character is talking to. In *Insomnia*, Dormer is shown looking screen left (Figure 1) and the subsequent shot of the landscape (Figure 2) provides a causal link between these two shots. However, the nature of this cut on action is immediately undermined as a plane comes into view from screen right as part of the same continuous shot (Figure 3). We can assume that from the (now) diegetic sounds of the plane's engine heard during the initial shots of the film, Dormer is on the plane shown in Figure 3, therefore making the point of view shot redundant. From a technical perspective, Nolan employs a form of manipulation involving a disruption of conventional editing techniques.

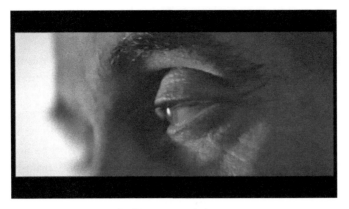

FIGURE 1: Dormer looking screen left, *Insomnia*.

FIGURE 2: Subsequent shot (implied POV) of the Alaskan landscape, *Insomnia*.

FIGURE 3: A plane comes into view from screen right as part of the same continuous shot, *Insomnia*.

Therefore, the distinction between subjectivity and objectivity has been, perhaps deliberately, distorted.

It is ultimately unclear whether the imagery of the blood and the panoramic shots of the Alaskan landscape are interlinked through Dormer's subjective perceptions or whether, like many of Nolan's films such as *Following*, *Memento* and *The Prestige*, the opening shots merely act to foreshadow the ensuing events of the film. This is not to dismiss the interpretation of the opening sequence offered here, but rather it is to say that there is perhaps another clearer explanation related to *Nachträglichkeit*, one that is more easily identifiable within the confines of the film's narrative. If we assume, as McGowan does, that the opening sequence acts as a cinematic cypher leading the spectator down a false path, then it is also possible to consider the opening as existing non-diegetically with only a tenuous link to the fictional world of the story. What this means is that if the notion of *Nachträglichkeit* is to be applied to the representation of trauma in *Insomnia*, we must look elsewhere within the diegetic realm of the film (post-title credits) to determine the unconscious trauma. Continuing McGowan's thread of analysis – and assuming that the opening sequence merely foreshadows the events of the film – when the blood motif first appears as Dormer tries to sleep, the subsequent images of the murder victim that appear momentarily on-screen are part of the cinematic diversion designed to deceive the spectator into associating the blood motif with the criminal under investigation. A single shot of an unknown individual attempting to remove some bloodstains, repeated from the film's opening, further enhances this conjectural reasoning. However, more tellingly, considering the framing device of Dormer attempting to sleep, the emphasis placed on Detective Eckhart during the remainder of this sequence is worth further analysis.

Three ensuing scenes that culminate in the blood-spreading motif appear to be fragments from earlier in the film, which includes shots of Eckhart but is either fabricated or the same events seen from a slightly different angle. These scenes not only question the reliability of memory, but they also establish a clear connection between the imagery of the blood and Eckhart.[4] The final scene from this sequence seems to support this reading as the moment Dormer discovers he has shot Eckhart is repeated on-screen, suggesting that it is Dormer's role in the shooting that acts as the signifier that prompts his recall of the initial incident. Dormer's situation then demonstrates the process of *Nachträglichkeit* in the sense that the original memory (planting false evidence) resides in a region of the mind repressed from his daily experience. The memory, which had not been available as part of conscious recall, nonetheless emerges in the second stage of the traumatic process when triggered by the experience of an ancillary trauma (Eckhart's death) causing the initial memory to irrupt into the present moment. The signifier of the unconscious trauma then imposes itself repeatedly on Dormer's psyche in the form of the blood-spreading motif that occurs on a few different occasions throughout the film and acts as a reminder of the repressed memory. The structural function of trauma in this sequence is similar to the case of Emma Eckstein, noted in Freud's early treatise on the *Project for a Scientific Psychology* ([1895] 1950) and *The Aetiology of Hysteria* ([1896] 1962a).

Freud's account of Emma is predicated on an understanding of trauma that is founded upon the relationship between two events. As an adult, Emma, whose symptoms included a phobia of going into shops alone, ascribes the cause of her response to an event which took place at the age of 12, but which occurred when she was aged 8. At age 12, Emma experienced an anxiety attack whilst in a shop where she witnessed two employees, one of whom she knew, laughing at her clothes. In his analysis, Freud surmises a link between this event and a previous memory, which, at age 8, involved Emma being sexually assaulted by a shopkeeper. At the time this event failed to register as meaningful to her having taken place prior to an understanding of the sexual nature of the attack. However, the initial memory later emerges as an after-effect of the onset of puberty in the form of psychosomatic symptoms that enable a reinterpretation and re-evaluation of the initial event. What needs to be emphasized in the context of an analysis of *Insomnia* is the structural mechanics of trauma as opposed to, in this instance, the sexual meaning retroactively attributed to the experience of trauma. In the case of Emma and *Insomnia*, the structural similarities between the deferred nature of their experiences of trauma highlight how Nolan can create an audio-visual expression of an abstract mental process.

Après-coup

It is worthwhile at this stage to consider the way in which Lacan extends Freud's notion of *Nachträglichkeit* as *après-coup* (meaning 'after the blow' or 'after the shock'). In doing so, it is possible to incorporate the earlier reading of the opening sequence as a representation of Dormer's subjective state of mind, while acknowledging McGowan's argument that the sequence operates at the level of the 'deceptiveness of cinema' (2012: 82). In his discussion of the Wolf-Man, Lacan theorizes that the primal scene is reconstructed based on its traumatic effect on the patient during analysis ([1978] 1988a: 176). It is the significance attached to the recollected experience – in this instance witnessing the act of intercourse between his parents – in the present as opposed to the presumed impact of the event in the past that enables the primal scene to emerge in the guise of the dream and take on its status as trauma. Of course, as trauma, the event must be repressed, thereby constituting the nucleus around which symptoms will form. Where Freud considered the progressive and regressive movements of *Nachträglichkeit* to be interdependent, Lacan's account of *après-coup* indicates that a psychoanalytic theory of trauma is not reducible to either a linear determinism that privileges the subject's history or an inversion of time whereby the future determines the past. Instead, there is a dialectical relationship between the two directions, which stresses the bidirectional progressive and regressive temporality of trauma. This is underlined by the editor-in-chief of the *International Journal of Psychoanalysis* Dana Birksted-Breen, who writes that:

> One movement cannot be separated from the other because retroactive resignification is developmental progression. For there to be progression there also has to be this kind of retrospective resignification). The forward movement necessitates a backward movement at the same time and, equally, the continual incorporation and restructuring of the past necessitates the ability to move forward.
>
> (Birksted-Breen 2003: 1509)

Likewise, according to Laplanche, what distinguishes the notion of *après-coup* or *afterwardsness* from *Nachträglichkeit* is the importance of a third factor (1999a: 260). Laplanche stresses Lacan's understanding of *après-coup* whereby the emphasis is not on the initial event or the corresponding second event but rather the reciprocal relationship *between* the two events. Discussing the case of Emma, Laplanche even goes so far as to suggest that no event in and of itself is fundamentally traumatic. He remarks:

> It may be said that, in a sense, the trauma is situated entirely in the play of 'deceit' producing a kind of seesaw effect between the two events. Neither of the traumatic events in itself is traumatic; neither is a rush of excitation. The first one? It triggers nothing: neither excitation or reaction, nor symbolization or psychical elaboration [...] If the first event is not traumatic, the second is, if possible, even less so.
>
> (1976: 41)

For Laplanche an event only becomes traumatic through an engagement with the structures of the unconscious, which retroactively makes the event traumatic. This process of constructing the past out of the present reverses the cause and effect relation inherent in time's arrow,[5] albeit temporarily. Ultimately then, when applied in the context of *Insomnia* it is not the original event of planting evidence that causes Dormer's trauma, nor the death of Kay Connell, and nor is it his involvement in the subsequent death of Detective Eckhart. Equally, whilst the repeated reminders of Eckhart's death (hallucinations, flashbacks and so on) appear to be signifiers connected to the unconscious trauma, these moments are also not to be considered the primary focus for his experience of trauma. Rather, an understanding of trauma emerges from the way in which all these events are de- and re-translated in relation to Dormer's own identity, which manifests by way of a pattern that shapes the unconscious motivations of his actions. The key to understanding this pattern of de- and re-translation emerges from a broader consideration of Dormer's actions within the film and central to these is his reasoning for concealing his role in Eckhart's death.

In the context of the narrative, Dormer's decision to implicate Kay's murderer in the death of Eckhart, thus temporarily exonerating himself, represents an extension of his desire to disavow the truth that stems from his decision to frame Dobbs in the events that precede the diegesis. Discussing the nature of Dormer's decision to lie about Hap's death, McGowan points out that, 'there is no clear reason for [Dormer] to lie in this situation. The dense fog in the area hampered visibility and would fully justify the claim that the shooting had been accidental, even if Will had in fact shot Hap purposely' (2012: 74). Similarly, J. L. A. Garcia writes that '[t]he detective was justified in firing to hit a fleeing suspect who had just shot one of the Alaskan policemen pursuing him, and hit Hap only by mistake' (2006: 103). This course of action then is borne out of an unconscious desire to lie that is manifested throughout the film, suggesting that Dormer's actions are a response to the failure of the justice system. In effect, Dormer seeks to enforce the law and yet he cannot do so without invoking the failure of those he is held accountable to. His *unconscious desire to lie* is, therefore, the by-product of a system that fails the victims of crime. It is reasonable to suggest that, without this unconscious desire to lie, he would not have planted evidence. Likewise, the ensuing triggering event of either Kay's or Eckhart's death would not have acquired traumatic meaning if unconsciously, they had not been linked to Dormer's initial indiscretion. Furthermore, the frequent appearance of hallucinations, flashbacks and so on related to the events of the film make little sense as traumatic signifiers in themselves. Instead, these can be considered as being part of an unconscious desire to break the cycle of trauma through a form of self-punishment that might lead to the truth.

Though Nolan deviates from the overt pro-filmic manipulation of narrative timelines associated with *Following* and *Memento*, in structural terms, *Insomnia* can still be understood in relation to how the narrative explores the mechanisms of trauma. The key to understanding the film's structural relationship to trauma resides in comprehending the cinematic deception that Nolan induces in the spectator from the outset of the film. According to McGowan:

> The structure of the credit sequence perpetuates a similar deception in the film's relationship to the spectator. The juxtaposition of the bloodied white fabric and the plane flying over the Alaskan wilderness leads the spectator to associate the fabric with the crime that Will is going to investigate, not with his own act of fabricating evidence. In this way, Nolan links the necessary lie of the police investigation with the deceptiveness of cinema (and specifically cinematic editing).
>
> (McGowan 2012: 82)

As the meaning of the opening scene is deliberately edited in a way to render it both misleading and unclear, we misunderstand the nature of what is presented to us. In this way, the fragments of information presented can be referred to as what Maureen Turim labels a 'lying flashback' (1989: 168). For Turim, the conventional use of the flashback acts to reveal a narrative truth; however, the flashback may also be used to question the authenticity of what is presented by undermining the truth. Such is the case with the flashback in Alfred Hitchcock's *Stage Fright* (1950). She remarks that 'it presents a version of events that is later shown to be not the way these events happened' (1989: 168). Similarly, in *Insomnia*, the film subsequently corrects our judgement in a scene where the fleeting images of the bloodied white fabric are explained when Dormer confesses to planting evidence. Considering this information about the past, the spectator is encouraged to retroactively revise the unconscious assumptions engineered by the film's lying flashback. In effect, the confession re-writes the information available to the audience, thereby having a retroactive effect. In doing so, the recurrence of the blood-spreading motif throughout the film becomes a structural signpost that frames the narrative in relation to trauma theory by communicating the bidirectional dimension of *après-coup* for both Dormer and the spectator.

The continued repetition of the image throughout the film aligns Dormer's unresolved experience of the traumatic signifier with the spectator's unawareness or misplaced understanding of the trauma's source. In this way, the temporal disjunctions of deferred action are integrated into the narrative structure replicating Dormer's cognitive function, thus inviting the spectator to experience *afterwardsness* vicariously. The importance of this scene is underscored by Nolan as part of the director's commentary available on the film's DVD release. He remarks that the imagery of the blood

> is crucial to the understanding of the narrative and what the narrative of the film represents because to me, at this point, you realize that you're really seeing the last act of the story, not the whole story and that everything that is really going on with this guy [Dormer] relates to something that happened before the film even began. That to me was a very interesting notion narratively speaking

[...] beginning the film with this blood imagery and then coming back to it at
this point helps get that across.

(Nolan, 2002)

In the film, the flashbacks are used to show Dormer's past, but these are a mixture
of subjective point-of-view shots and images presented as if an observer were
looking onto the events. In this way, the spectator is positioned as both Dormer
himself, in an attempt to understand the past, and as bystanders of the traumatic
experience. The absent or rather, misunderstood trauma at the heart of the story
distorts the narrative, prompting the spectator's involvement to repeat the mechanisms of deferred action by going back to re-examine the past while simultaneously
attempting to understand its bearing upon the present. The viewing experience is,
therefore, an opportunity to experience *afterwardsness*. Even more, as the film is
fixed but the viewing of it is not, I am suggesting that seeing the film again renders
its meanings differently; therefore, (re)watching the film is similar to a psychoanalytic experience. This is, in many ways, what I argue to be the essence of Paul
Sutton's spectatorial model of cinematic *afterwardsness*.

In his writing, Sutton adopts the concept *après-coup* to theorize a different
form of spectator engagement with cinema. Sutton theorizes that the spectator
remakes films as part of their ongoing engagement with the text both during and
after the cinematic experience. For Sutton, what this means is that the experience
of watching a film embodies the bidirectionality of *afterwardsness* described by
Laplanche insofar as the spectator subsequently possesses a 'remade and remembered' (2004: 386) version of a film later constructed from memory. More than
this though, Sutton contends that '[n]ot only is a spectator left with memories
from, and of, the film after it has ended, but any number of (frequently traumatic)
enigmatic signifiers or messages may have been unconsciously recorded requir-
ing subsequent de- and re-translation' (2004: 386). These enigmatic signifiers
perform the same essential function for Sutton as they do for Laplanche in the
sense that they are especially consequential for the formulation of the subject.
Following a Laplanchian model, subjectivity is constructed via the process of
auto-translation whereby the spectator, overwhelmed by the 'sheer volume and
traumatic intensity of the visual and aural stimuli' (2004: 386), subsequently
enters a process of reconstruction and re-translation (auto-translation) that is
required to decipher the messages received via the screen. The implications of this
spectatorial paradigm for the articulation of identity are made clear by Sutton
when he says:

These memories, enigmatic signifiers, 'fragments', the de-translated remnants
of one's cinema history are re-translated and remade, engendering a remaking

of oneself around these fragments in a process of 'auto-translation', what might also be thought of as a kind of re-narration.

(Sutton 2010a: 81)

This view of spectatorship proposed by Sutton resonates with Nolan's own film-making since, much like Nolan's films to date, the model requires the spectator's active engagement with the film to generate meaning.

In the context of *Insomnia*, the revelation that what we initially interpreted to be the original scene of the crime was, in fact, an earlier miscarriage of justice enacted by Dormer, forces the spectator to reconstruct the film's story and re-evaluate the character's subsequent actions according to this new narrative information. In line with Sutton's conception of cinematic *afterwardsness*, the film's narrative structure thus indicates that meaning can only be constructed retroactively. Up until the point in the film when Dormer finally reveals the meaning of the blood-spreading motif, *Insomnia* had been organized around a void or narrative deception (albeit one that the spectator was unaware of) that we can only fully understand in reverse. It is the void in the film which therefore functions as a stabilizing and structuring signifier similar to the function of what Lacan describes as *le point de capiton* (translated in English as quilting point or anchoring point) – places where the 'signified and signifier are knotted together' (1977c: 268).

Configured by Lacan as a point in the signifying chain at which 'the signifier stops the otherwise endless movement of the signification' (1977c: 303) and, consequently, generates the illusion of fixed meaning, *le point de capiton* provides a momentary sense of cohesion and consistency for other signifiers, albeit retroactively. As Slavoj Žižek argues, when writing about Ernesto Laclau and Chantal Mouffe's *Hegemony and Socialist Strategy* (1985), the 'floating signifiers' of our language are 'structured into a unified field through the intervention of a certain "nodal point" (the Lacanian point de capiton), which "quilts" them, stops their sliding and fixes their meaning' (2008: 95). In *Insomnia*, the moment that Dormer reveals his role in the case against Dobbs functions as a nodal point in the film as it has the dramatic effect of reshaping our perception of the narrative and conferring upon it a sense of closure while appearing to legitimize or, at the very least provide a rationale for, Dormer's own actions throughout. What this effectively does is foreground the distinction between desire and the drive whereby desire is built upon an investment in the possibility of obtaining the lost-object (and thus the ultimate experience of *jouissance*), whereas the aim of the drive is in the endless repetition of the drive itself. The drive, according to McGowan, 'locates enjoyment in the movement of return itself – the repetition of loss, rather than in what might be recovered' (2011: 11). Based on this distinction between desire and the drive, the construction of *Insomnia*'s narrative can be understood as negotiating the interplay between the two. On one hand, Dormer's admission of guilt forces us to retroactively reconsider what we have seen, thereby enacting the temporal structure of the drive and yet, at the same time, his confession allows us to *feel* as though we have acquired the lost-object. When Dormer confesses, the spectator mistakenly elevates this moment to the status of the lost-object since it gives the narrative shape and meaning. However, in doing so, the object of desire is necessarily missed because it merely points back to the void inherent in our existence.[6]

NOTES

1. The initial misinterpretation that occurs during the film's opening sequence can be related to '*proton pseudos*', a concept outlined by Freud in the *Project for a Scientific Psychology* to refer to 'false premises and false conclusions' ([1895] 1950: 352).

2. The term 'trauma theory' is first mentioned in Cathy Caruth's *Unclaimed Experience: Trauma, Narrative and History* (1996: 72). However, Judith Herman argues that the antecedents of this theory and the beginnings of clinical understandings of trauma can be traced to Jean-Martin Charcot, a French physician who, in the late nineteenth century, began the first systematic study of trauma (1992: 10).

3. In a typical mainstream film, credits are conventionally signalled at the beginning or the end of the text. However, there is some debate as to how to establish where credits begin and end as Lesley Stern (1995) points out. She writes:

   the difficulty of locating where the film 'proper' starts can be seen if you try to ascertain the differences between a pre-credit sequence, a diegetic credit sequence (where credits are superimposed over moving images, a slice of narrative action) and an autonomous non-diegetic segment (where titles are superimposed over a background that is frequently though not invariably fixed and abstract).

   (1995: 128–29)

   Based on this distinction, *Insomnia* would appear to be a diegetic credit sequence operating as a 'slice of the narrative action' (1995: 129).

4. A momentary shot of Dormer attempting to scrub away Eckhart's blood from his shirt bears a significant symbolic parallel to the initial shot contained within the opening sequence of Dormer attempting to remove bloodstains accidentally dropped onto his own shirt whilst trying to plant evidence. In both instances, it is the same act that represents an attempted disavowal of the truth and it is this revelation that provides evidence of the potential essence of the trauma.

5. According to the second law of thermodynamics, time's arrow is unidirectional (see Coveney and Highfield 1990).

6. This is perhaps why the film concludes with only a partial sense of resolution, thereby demonstrating a resistance that aligns the film with desire. The ending is only partial because the spectator does not witness Ellie (Hilary Swank) relay her findings about Dormer's past indiscretions to the police. Erin Hill Parks has also suggested that during the final moments the fate of Dormer's legacy remains ambiguous. She says, 'Ellie, meanwhile, is poised to decide who she will be. She can continue to be a moral and honest police officer, exposing the truth about Hap's killing, or she can choose to remain silent and preserve, or even save, [Dormer's] professional reputation. It is unclear what she will do, and the final scenes of an open landscape emphasise the multiple possibilities available' (2010: 80).

Batman Begins, Again: The Temporality of Trauma in *The Dark Knight* Trilogy

Should I just bury the past out there with my parents, Alfred?

– Bruce Wayne, *Batman Begins*

Years after the murder of his parents, Bruce Wayne (Christian Bale) returns to Wayne Manor having been dismissed from Princeton University. Directionless and lacking purpose, he nevertheless informs his butler Alfred (Michael Caine) that he won't be staying beyond the primary reason for his homecoming, which is to attend the appeal hearing of the man responsible for killing his parents. Despite Alfred's offer, Bruce declines to take up residence in the master bedroom of Wayne Manor, preferring instead to stay in the room he grew up in as a child. A little confused, Alfred reminds Bruce that the estate now belongs to him to which he responds, 'No Alfred, it's my *father's* house', Alfred interjects, 'Your father is dead', 'and this place is a mausoleum', Bruce forcefully replies. 'If I have my way, I'll pull the damn thing down brick by brick', he adds. It is clear from Bruce's vocal resentment as well as his immediate association of the mansion with a mausoleum that he views the house as a painful reminder of his loss. However, later in *Batman Begins* when the mansion is under attack by Ra's Al Ghul (Liam Neeson), Bruce's attitude has seemingly softened somewhat in response to his growing respect for his father's legacy of philanthropy.

During the assault on Wayne Manor, a number of shots depict the building's destruction as Bruce laments the demolition of the estate. He says, 'What have I done Alfred? Everything my family, my father built', to which Alfred responds, 'The Wayne legacy is more than bricks and mortar sir'. Here, Alfred's acknowledgement of the mansion's symbolic value offers Bruce comfort by emphasizing the transcendent nature of his parent's legacy, which he suggests extends beyond the trauma of their deaths. During the film's conclusion, this sentiment is returned to once again demonstrating not only a sense of circularity but also of change. Among the ruins of the mansion, Bruce's childhood friend Rachel (Katie Holmes) asks him what he will do with the rubble. He replies in such a way that points towards his acceptance of the past remarking that he will, 'Rebuild it, just the way it was brick for brick'. However, as Rachel walks away, Alfred proposes that they make some improvements to the foundations of the grounds with the implication being that such enhancements pave the way for the construction of the Batcave in the caverns of the estate. Bruce's agreement, alongside the ensuing epilogue featuring the newly promoted Lieutenant Gordon (Gary Oldman), cements his ascension to the role of Batman which paradoxically functions to perpetuate the memory of his parents' deaths while also acting to try and come to terms with this traumatic event experienced during his childhood.

In many respects, it is this emphasis on the defining moments in the formative years of Bruce Wayne's childhood and adolescence that separates Nolan's version of Batman from the one established in Tim Burton's 1989 film – and from almost every other cinematic incarnation of the character. Where the sequel *The Dark Knight* deviates somewhat from the stringent emphasis on Bruce's past, *Batman Begins* is unique in the Batman canon insofar as it is principally concerned with these moments and their associated effects on Bruce's subsequent search for his identity. Will Brooker, for instance, argues that the uniqueness of *Batman Begins'* narrative emerges through the rearrangement of familiar elements taken from a range of different source materials in a novel way (2012: 65). He suggests that Nolan and co-writer David S. Goyer built their story around selected moments from, among others, the comic books *Batman: The Dark Knight Returns* (1986), *Batman: Year One* (1987), *The Man Who Falls* (1989) and *Batman: The Long Halloween* (1996–97), while at the same time inventing new scenes and characters to narrate the story of Bruce's loss, training and transformation into Batman (2012: 48–74). By focusing on the details of Bruce's childhood and adolescence as integral to the development of his decision to adopt the persona of Batman, Nolan and co-writer David S. Goyer were able to present audiences with a fresh perspective on the mythology of the character, which I argue hinges upon the spectator's vicarious experience of trauma.

With this in mind, this chapter aims to accomplish three main things. The first is to propose that *Batman Begins* illustrates the temporal directionalities of trauma initially described by Sigmund Freud and subsequently developed by Jacques Lacan and Jean Laplanche from within the film i.e. from the position of the protagonist. Second, I argue that the spectator negotiates a complex interaction with other pre-existing Batman cultural texts and events including the tragic death of Heath Ledger in 2008. Third, the chapter concludes by arguing that the cyclical temporality of trauma evident in the structure of *Batman Begins* extends beyond the film to include the trilogy. Here, I offer a number of competing interpretations of the ending to *The Dark Knight Rises* in relation to Nolan's presentation of trauma, the most convincing of which suggests that even if Bruce Wayne survives the bomb blast at the end of the trilogy, his subjectivity remains tied to the trauma of his parents' deaths. Taken together, these separate but overlapping strands of analysis draw attention to the multi-layered presentation of trauma in Nolan's filmmaking that extends beyond his non-franchise films produced to date.

Batman Begins

As a point of departure, it is useful to reiterate the defining features of Freud's theory of *Nachträglichkeit*. In principle, the notion refers to the way a *recollected* event, the *memory* of an event rather than the event itself, is invested with significance or may become traumatic retrospectively (Laplanche and Pontalis 1973: 112). The most common example cited to explain the theory is that of a child who experiences an event which at that time does not have any meaning but is later revised in the context of a second event during which the initial event becomes traumatic. In this context, it is particularly apt that *Batman Begins* opens with a young Bruce Wayne (Guy Lewis) playing in the grounds of his parents' mansion before accidentally falling into a disused well where he is attacked by a swarm of bats (Figure 4). The subsequent cut to an older Bruce Wayne during his self-imposed imprisonment in a Bhutanese jail at some point in the future reveals that this opening sequence, which culminates in the swarm, was, in fact, a dream.

According to Cathy Caruth in her study of trauma, *Unclaimed Experience*, trauma is 'the response to an unexpected or overwhelming violent event or events that are not fully grasped as they occur but return later in repeated flashbacks, nightmares, and other repetitive phenomena' (1996: 91). Understood in light of this statement, both the initial bat swarm and the murder of Bruce Wayne's parents are clearly marked as traumatic events. But, it is through the retroactive logic of *après-coup* that it is possible to comprehend the representational nexus between these two moments in Wayne's childhood. That is, the *original* traumatic signifier (the bat swarm) had initially been rendered unavailable as part of conscious recall only emerging in his nightmares. According to Freud's logic, while the original signifier has been repressed in the unconscious region of the mind, when control of consciousness is withdrawn during sleep, the emotional intensity of the original event is often unconsciously revisited in the form of a nightmare. The re-enactment of the original signifier during sleep represents an expression of desire from the ego (rather than the id) to 'transform the memory-trace of the traumatic event into the fulfilment of a wish' ([1933] 1964a: 29). In effect, dreams that contain the repetition of trauma are the result of the mind's attempts to master the traumatic memory, particularly as, in this instance, the original signifier has not been allocated meaning. It seems that it is this lack of understanding that prevents the original signifier from being integrated into a coherent narrative during lived experience. What is important to understand here is that, while Wayne's dreams expose him to the (repressed) original signifier, it is not until he is subjected to a second trauma, in this instance the murder of his parents, that the original signifier is reconfigured as being traumatic and is subsequently accessible during lived experience. The *second* signifier retroactively constitutes the meaning and potency of the *first*. This is a significant temporal mechanism in Lacan's re-reading of Freud's theory of *Nachträglichkeit* and one that is presented by Nolan in *Batman Begins* as the temporality of trauma communicated in the film points towards the bidirectionality of time.

This relatively linear series of events in the film – the bat swarm followed by the deaths of Bruce Wayne's parents – is separated by a sequence that functions to underline the bidirectional links between past, present and future. During this sequence, the young Wayne attends the opera *Mefistofele* with his parents, and at one point he is confronted with actors performing on-stage as dark winged creatures. The violent motions of the creatures trigger an intrusive memory of the earlier bat swarm, which is expressed as a series of momentary and fragmented images viewed from his subjective perspective. The way that this sequence is cut together as a rapidly edited montage of images combined with the aural quality of Wayne's panicked breathing functions clearly to convey the *original* (past) encounter of the bat swarm as being a (present) distressing experience. Added to this, the other formal techniques employed by Nolan such as the close up of Wayne's face (Figure 5) and the abrupt sound breaks generated by the contrast between the operatic score and the screeching bats encourage the spectator to experience his distress vicariously.

Wayne's anxiety during the opera stresses the structural complexity of trauma since the experience helps connect all the separate incidents through an unconscious association with the fear felt during the *original* event – the bat swarm attack. This is because Wayne's discomfort and fear during the opera had led him to ask his parents if they could leave the theatre early. Unbeknownst to him at the time, it is this action that will lead to their deaths at the hands of an opportunistic armed robber who confronts them in an alleyway as they leave. In terms of an understanding of the temporal logic of trauma put forward here, while the younger version of Bruce Wayne does not make the connection explicit, thereafter the film returns to these three moments – the bat swarm, the opera and the murder of his parents[1] – using both visual and aural cues to provide us with an insight into what the older Bruce Wayne considers to be the source of his suffering. Take, for example, his first encounter with the organic form of the nerve toxin subsequently released over Gotham City during the film's climax. Moments before inhaling the smoke, Wayne's mentor Ducard (also played by Liam Neeson) encourages him to 'journey inwards' and, as he breathes in, a montage of the swarming bats (Figure 4), his younger self at the opera (Figure 5) and the moment that his father was shot (Figure 6) appear rapidly on-screen accompanied by the sound of

FIGURE 4: A momentary glimpse of the swarming bats,
Batman Begins.

FIGURE 5: Young Wayne at the opera, *Batman Begins*.

FIGURE 6: Thomas Wayne is shot attempting to protect his wife,
Batman Begins.

the screeching bats emphasizing the importance of these events as being the central constituent parts of Wayne's identity.

Within this triad of memories, the scene at the opera is therefore crucial to understanding how the narrative bears out the temporal logic of trauma. This is because Wayne's experience as the single survivor of the criminal act that killed his parents is determined by his ability to blame himself because he retrospectively acknowledges the immediate causal connection between his desire to leave the theatre and his parents' deaths moments later. Following his parents' funeral, he says, 'It was my fault, Alfred. I made them leave the theatre. If I hadn't gotten scared'. Implicit in this connection is Wayne's awareness that all of these events are somehow interconnected and related to his actions. Even though there is no singular moment of realization that materializes for Wayne whereby he consciously connects the deaths of his parents to his encounter with the bat swarm, it is clear that it was the re-emergence of his fear associated with this moment that resulted in his anxiety during the performance which, in turn, triggered his desire to want to leave the theatre resulting in their deaths. By contextualizing Wayne's experience at the opera within the wider personal framework of his parents' murders, it becomes clear that the defining unconscious trauma of Wayne's life is one that, contrary to the established Batman canon, predates him witnessing his mother and father being killed. To understand the temporal logic of trauma in *Batman Begins*, the experience of Wayne's parents' murders – despite their centrality to the mythology of the character – cannot be conceived of as being the *original* unconscious trauma. Rather, it is necessary to understand their deaths as part of the nexus of events that allows the memory of the bat swarm to emerge and acquire traumatic significance in the context of his parents' deaths.[2]

My analysis of the temporal logic of trauma in *Batman Begins* must also account for the complex narrative structure of the film, which during the first 40 minutes, presents three separate points in time that continuously overlap. The film's structural organization is important because an understanding of the intersection between trauma and memory depends, in part, on the spectator's ability to recognize temporal and spatial shifts in the film. Or, put another way, to understand trauma and memory the spectator requires an awareness of the visual and aural codes that distinguish the *past* from the *present* in the film. In *Batman Begins*, the opening sequence removes these markers of time. Specifically, the transition from Wayne's encounter with the bat swarm as a young boy to his imprisonment as an older man confronts our conventional understanding of causality because, not only has a large amount of time been elided in an instant, this scene retroactively reconfigures the opening as existing in the distant *past* as opposed to the (assumed) *present*. Even more significant than this is that this single cut frames *all* the subsequent visualizations of his childhood and adolescence as memories meaning that, in the context of the film, neither the character nor the spectator experiences trauma directly. For example, we are not shown the murder of his parents as it occurs chronologically in Wayne's life. Instead, and more importantly for the argument being presented, both the spectator and Wayne are restricted to experiencing the murder of his parents through what amounts to be an *atemporal* repetition of the incident. Correspondingly, as these events are framed as flashbacks, the traumatic experience is unassimilated because it remains as part of a continual cycle that seeks to return the character and the spectator to an *absent* moment that exists, diegetically speaking, *outside* of time and only in memory.

In the context of trauma theory, Caruth characterizes this type of incident as a 'missed experience' (1996: 62). She says, '[t]he shock of the mind's relation to the threat of death is thus not the direct experience of the threat, but precisely the *missing* of this experience, the fact that, not being experienced in *time* it has not yet been fully known' (1996: 62, original emphasis). For Caruth, it is specifically because the unconscious trauma is missed that it functions as an encounter with the Real. For, if the subject does not experience trauma, they are unable to encode it into language. As the unconscious trauma remains outside the symbolic order of language, resistant to expression, the Real is this very absence – the impossibility of a signifier that could represent the unconscious trauma. In *Batman Begins*, the night Wayne witnesses his parents' murders is a *missed* experience in the sense that it is 'experienced too soon, too unexpectedly to be fully known and is therefore not available to consciousness until it imposes itself again, repeatedly, in the nightmares and repetitive actions of the survivor' (Caruth 1996: 4). Even as an adult Wayne cannot move past the moment of his parents' deaths because the nature of the traumatic experience means that it is fundamentally *atemporal*. Consider, for example, the use of music during this sequence and at other points in the trilogy as another means through which trauma is transmitted.

During the final moments of the scene following the death of his parents, a soprano vocal sung by a choir boy from the non-diegetic score, 'Barbastella', is heard. Significantly, during a scene following Wayne's initial return to Gotham for the trial of the man who murdered his parents, he tentatively handles a gun that he intends to use to avenge them. While there are no overt visual reminders of his parents' deaths, the imagery of the gun is accompanied by the same soprano vocal sang by the choir boy from earlier in the film. In the second instance, the musical motif provides an aural link to the earlier sequence and as such provides an insight into Wayne's subjective state of mind. Furthermore, the film's composer, Hans Zimmer, digitally manipulated the length of the note to represent the idea that Wayne is frozen in time at the moment of his parents' deaths (Williams n.d.). The vocal also reappears at two points in *The Dark Knight Rises* demonstrating a sense of atemporality that I will return to later in this chapter.

In *Batman Begins*, Wayne's anguished response to his parents' deaths is implicitly tied to his own psychological reaction to the bat swarm, which is exacerbated by the experience of fear he felt during the opera. That he encouraged his parents to leave the theatre early is an action that significantly deviates from the previous versions of this narrative, and it is a creative decision that further compounds the character's sense of guilt (see Darius 2011: 108; Langley 2012: 21). For example, in Tim Burton's *Batman*, his parents' deaths take place after they leave a movie theatre as a number of people are shown to be exiting at the same time. Similarly, in the animated television series *Batman: The Brave and the Bold* (2008–11), a young Bruce Wayne is shown to be jubilant having enjoyed a filmed version of *The Mask of Zorro*. Therefore, in *Batman Begins*, Nolan and Goyer present a reworking of the constituent parts of Wayne's trauma, which provides an understanding of how *après-coup* structurally organizes Wayne's earliest memories.

Until this point, my analysis of *Batman Begins* has been largely focused on the representation of trauma in relation to specific events while only hinting at the relationship between them. Therefore, it is worthwhile to consider in more detail the way in which Laplanche views Lacan's notion of *après-coup* (itself a re-reading of *Nachträglichkeit*) as *afterwardsness* by dismissing the inherent traumatic fixation of individual events, preferring instead to consider the relationship *between* these events as part of a constant process of de- and re-translating what Laplanche refers to as 'enigmatic signifiers' ([1987] 1989a: 125). In his account of psychoanalytic subjectivity, Laplanche argues that these 'enigmatic signifiers' or messages are unconsciously implanted by the other[3] during the subject's infancy before he or she is equipped to understand them. For Laplanche, the enigmatic quality of these messages stimulates the development of the child's own unconscious which is propelled by the continual de- and re-translation of these messages, a process that Laplanche refers to as 'auto-translation' (1989b: 247). This process of auto-translation offers us an alternative means to not only approach the interaction between the principle traumatic events in *Batman Begins* but also to examine the paradigm of cinematic spectatorship put forward by Paul Sutton based upon the Laplanchian reworking of Freud's notion of *Nachträglichkeit*.

In the context of *Batman Begins*, Paul Sutton's theory of cinematic *afterwardsness* is valuable because it rearticulates (or more accurately re-translates) the *original* trauma of the bat swarm as the *repressed* enigmatic message implanted in Wayne's unconscious when he encounters them during his childhood. Sutton explains in his essay 'Prequel: The "afterwardsness" of the sequel' that:

> As Wayne negotiates this process of 'autotranslation', he 'takes up' the identity of Batman and 'leaves behind' a version of Bruce Wayne. Wayne's unconscious in this account is formed, in part, as a result of his encounter with the bats as a

child; they represent the repressed 'enigmatic message', which requires continual de- and retranslation (around which his identity coalesces). When he becomes Batman, Wayne finally achieves a retranslation that fits its context.

(Sutton 2010a: 150)

As Sutton points out, the enigmatic message of the bats is subsequently de- and re-translated, remaining occasionally untranslated (repressed), throughout the remainder of the film (2010a: 149).[4] This process of auto-translation is experienced simultaneously by the character and the spectator due to the way that Nolan restricts our knowledge of the key events in Wayne's life by framing them as flashbacks during the film's opening 40 minutes in what appears to be, at first, a multi-stranded narrative. This formal technique, which is also accompanied by other strategies such as eyeline-match cutting and point-of-view shots, functions to emphasize our alignment with Wayne's subjective state of mind and as a result, communicates an understanding of trauma that is grounded in the temporal organization of the film in terms of the logic of *afterwardsness*.

Beyond the film's narrative structure, the process of de- and re-translation associated with the enigmatic message of the bat swarm extends to reflect Sutton's theory of the spectator's 'cinematic unconscious' (Sutton 2004: 386) in a way that foregrounds the spectatorial experience as both active and creative. By revising the trauma at the heart of the character's mythology to reflect Wayne's compound fear of bats, Nolan successfully re-translates the spectator's memories from, and of, the comics, the graphic novels and the previous films in the franchise. Sutton comments:

> *Batman Begins* renders the untranslatable of the earlier films translatable; it provides a new context of significance for the emergence of Batman while at the same time retranslating or remaking the four previous films of the Batman cycle. Thus *Batman Begins*, which charts the *before* of these earlier films, *afterward* effectively remakes them.
>
> (Sutton 2010b: 150, emphasis added)

Reflecting on Sutton's essay, Martin Fradley suggests that *Batman Begins* possesses an 'uneasy temporal relationship' (2013: 22) with the previous feature-length on-screen iterations of the character. He says, '[d]espite its aggressive promotion as a radical break from the earlier films, *Batman Begins* can be variously understood as a remake of Burton's 1989 film, a prequel to the Burton-Schumacher series, or a stand-alone movie' (2013: 22). He goes on to say that '[t]he viewer's encounter with *Batman Begins* thus provides an ontological recontextualization of the earlier films, re-translating and rewriting the viewer's memories of previously fixed narratives' (2013: 22). As a prequel, *Batman Begins* ultimately lays claim to being 'original' while at the same time existing as a literal sequel. This is an effect of the film's relationship to the other pre-existing texts that produces a conscious *afterwardsness* effect for the spectator who, aware of the cultural context of Batman, is required to effectively rewrite their knowledge of the past considering a renewed understanding of the present.

Coming Full Circle

The temporality of trauma in *Batman Begins* is, in many ways, cyclical. The film opens with Wayne's experience of fear felt during the bat swarm attack at the bottom of a disused well and it culminates in his return to the same well in what functions as a metaphorical return to his past. The scene begins with the literal repetition of the extreme low angle shot taken from the bottom of the well during the opening sequence (Figure 7). In this instance though, it is significant that Wayne is sealing the well (Figure 8) as for several scholars this symbolic moment attests to the acceptance of his traumatic past (see Pheasant-Kelly 2015: 99–119; McGowan 2015: 164–74). However, while this moment may indicate the resolution of Wayne's fear associated with the bat swarm, what complicates the resolution offered at the end of *Batman Begins* is the nature of the extended trilogy, which demonstrates that Wayne's entire adult life has remained bound to the defining moment of the bat swarm he encountered as a child. For instance, in the final third of *The Dark Knight Rises*, the imagery of the disused well returns in the form of a subterranean prison (Figure 9).

During this scene, a well-like opening reveals a circle of light that offers the hope of freedom to the prisoners held captive underground. Only one person has ever succeeded in climbing out of 'the pit' and Wayne's own repeated attempts to escape using a safety rope prove unsuccessful. Instead, he is told by a fellow prisoner (Uri Gavriel) that his failure lies in his inability to embrace the fear of death that the fall would otherwise provoke were it not for the harness protecting him. It is significant that when Wayne finally attempts the climb without the safety rope, a cloud of bats bursts from the cliff face beside him suggesting, at the very least, a metaphorical return to his *original* trauma that extends beyond the diegetic realm of *The Dark Knight Rises* and to the spectator's own 'cinematic unconscious' (Sutton 2004: 386) memory of *Batman Begins*. Jacqueline Furby notes:

> Whether the bats are real, or symbolic of the primal nature of his fear at this moment is unclear, but his leap is successful. He reaches across the abyss, and climbs from the pit. So, there is a sense throughout all three films that [...] Wayne is caught in that eternal moment of the flight of bats that has shaped his destiny but prevented him from moving forwards with his own life.
>
> (Furby 2015: 257)

FIGURE 7: Wayne falling down the well, *Batman Begins*.

FIGURE 8: The well in the process of being sealed, *Batman Begins*.

FIGURE 9: Wayne attempts to escape 'the pit' without the use of a safety rope, *The Dark Knight Rises*.

What this moment implies is that, even though at the end of *Batman Begins* Wayne is shown nailing planks of wood over the well's opening, his trauma cannot be healed, nor can it be avoided in the simplistic way suggested by the symbolic gesture of covering the hole. Instead, the residual trauma associated with the bat swarm is continually subject to the process of de- and re-translation throughout Wayne's life[5] functioning to perpetuate the figure of Batman while, simultaneously, embracing and distancing himself from the memory of his parents' deaths.

In many respects, Wayne's complex relationship with the identity of Batman is encapsulated in the closing moments of *Batman Begins*. During the climax of the film, Lieutenant Gordon raises the question of escalation to Wayne as Batman in their quest to rid Gotham of crime. He says, '*[w]e* start carrying semi-automatics, *they* buy automatics [...] *we* start wearing Kevlar, *they* buy armor-piercing rounds' (Nolan and Goyer 2005: 149, original emphasis). In this scene, the film displays a self-reflexive awareness that implies Batman's existence is part of the problem he attempts to eliminate. Yet, what the film's ending (and that of the trilogy taken as a whole) concludes is that the figure of Batman is a necessary symbol that functions to not only defer Wayne's desire but also that of the spectators. In Nolan's reinvention of the Batman series, Wayne seeks to bring justice to Gotham, but this is seemingly outweighed or at the very least matched by his own vested interest in the continuation of Batman's vigilantism as a form of self-punishment attached to his experience of traumatic loss. At the level of the diegesis, Wayne's attachment to the identity of Batman actively perpetuates crime rather than eradicating it, while also exacerbating the type of criminality drawn to Gotham. His actions as Batman, therefore, act as the obstacle that prevents him from embracing the traumatic loss associated with his parents' deaths, meaning that he can effectively sustain the essence of his desire for justice *ad infinitum*.

Outside of the diegesis, the spectator also experiences a similar deferral of desire as even though Batman can defeat his foes and in rare instances retire, there remains an ongoing desire for his continued existence that is matched by both the character and the spectator. In many ways, this is because, as Justine Toh points out, the Batman brand is a commodity text that the authors and rights-holders are required to sustain. Consequently, the streets of Gotham are never clean. She says, '[a] safe Gotham City, its criminal elements eradicated, is bad for Hollywood's business because it renders obsolete a franchise about the Dark Knight's agitations for justice' (2010: 137). However, there is a fundamental difference between how this desire to perpetuate the identity of Batman is perceived. For the character, the desire to adopt the persona of Batman is presented as being secondary to his primary motivation to restore justice in Gotham. But, as we have already established, this is somewhat ironic as his efforts to cleanse the city of crime propagates more crime, thereby revealing that what sustains his desire is his investment in the identity of Batman. In contrast, the opposite can be said of the film's spectators whose primary object of desire is to witness Batman enacting his own form of vigilante justice. However, this is ultimately mediated by the unconscious awareness that if he were truly successful, he would no longer be needed. In this sense, what sustains Wayne's desire for justice is the figure of Batman but what sustains the spectator's desire for Batman's presence in Gotham is the failure of justice. This is why, rather than offering the spectator a sense of closure, Nolan elects to sustain the legacy of Batman at the end of *Batman Begins* by hinting at the arrival of the Joker in Gotham.

For audiences and critics, because *Batman Begins* ends with Lieutenant Gordon's concerns about the escalation of crime in Gotham City and the emergence of a new type of villain, this scene was constructed as a clear indication of a planned sequel. But, at the time, Nolan was more interested in investing the diegetic world with a continuity that extended beyond the screen and into the minds of the spectators. He says, '[i]n leaving it open-ended – which we always wanted to do – it wasn't about sequel baiting. It's much more about sending the audience away with all these characters living on in their minds and spreading outwards and upwards' (Nolan and Goyer 2005: xxiii). Similarly, during the closing montage at the end of *The Dark Knight* Batman resigns himself to becoming a villain to hide the truth of Harvey Dent's (Aaron Eckhart) death. The film ends with the capture of the Joker (Heath Ledger) and Batman as a fugitive on the run thus maintaining the continuity of the diegetic world off-screen. However, this ending is also imbued with an extra-textual dimension in the context of the tragic loss of Heath Ledger, who died from an accidental overdose of prescription drugs in 2008. Given the extensive news coverage of Ledger's death in the months preceding the release of *The Dark Knight*, a viewer subsequently watching the film was likely aware of the posthumous nature of his performance. Consequently, the ending of the film is infused with a loss that transcends the fictional events portrayed on-screen.

Unlike *Batman Begins* and *The Dark Knight*, where both seem to end with the perpetuation of Bruce Wayne/Batman as an enduring character dichotomy, approaching *The Dark Knight Rises* in the context of trauma is complicated by the matrix of Nolan's brand identity alongside the industrial and commercial concerns surrounding the film's production as the final part of an *authored* trilogy. This is because, as an authored trilogy, Nolan's series of films can achieve a sense of closure that the comics and the previous on-screen iterations of the character cannot due to the ongoing institutional pressures for commercialization.[6] As a consequence, the ending of *The Dark Knight Rises* is neither in keeping with the mythology of the character nor does it function according to the temporal logic of trauma established in the previous two films. By initiating Wayne's protégé John Blake (Joseph Gordon-Levitt) as a replacement for Bruce Wayne during the closing moments of *The Dark Knight Rises*, the indication is that Wayne can relinquish the identity of Batman at a time when justice has ultimately not been restored in Gotham. The final montage implicitly suggests that Wayne can, at the very least, escape his trauma or perhaps even overcome it by saving the city, thereby upholding his father's legacy. Admittedly, this reading is complicated by the ending of *The Dark Knight* and the beginning of *The Dark Knight Rises*, which does respectively show Wayne saving the city, therefore fulfilling his father's legacy, but subsequently becoming a recluse who resides in the memories of his parents and Rachel. I want to suggest that the reason for this is bound to the notion of sacrifice. While Wayne sacrifices the identity of Batman at the end of *The Dark Knight*, his identity as 'Bruce Wayne' remains. This is important because, unlike the symbol of Batman, which Wayne repeatedly suggests is transferrable,[7] it is 'Bruce Wayne' who is defined by trauma, and therefore, sacrificing one identity does not resolve the other.

The Failure of The Dark Knight Rises

During the climactic sequence of *The Dark Knight Rises*, Batman successfully escorts a nuclear bomb out to sea using the Bat-plane where it explodes at a distance that is safe enough to protect the residents of Gotham. However, what is implied by this act is Batman's death due to the apparent lack of an autopilot system. Significantly though, the subsequent montage reveals that Wayne fixed the autopilot on the Bat-plane, thus potentially enabling his escape from the bomb blast. Perhaps the most conclusive evidence of Wayne's survival is Nolan's decision to reveal Wayne at a café in Florence during a scene that re-animates Alfred's self-confessed fantasy expressed earlier in the film. Depending on the spectator's preferred reading, the shared silent exchange between the two men implicitly suggests that Wayne survived the explosion (further evidence of which manifests in the renewed rooftop bat-signal, the instructions provided for Blake and significantly the missing pearls belonging to Bruce Wayne's mother) or, as some have speculated, this scene is a form of wish-fulfilment on Alfred's part.

It is tempting to view this scene as a form of wish-fulfilment given the close visual parallels between how it is originally presented and replicated in the second instance. For example, the framing, composition and colour palette is largely duplicated albeit with minor variations. Furthermore, as the end sequence is shot from Alfred's subjective point of view this undermines its own structure as an objective reality, especially when considered in relation to Alfred's own experience of trauma regarding Wayne's apparent death. In either case, the film posits Wayne has escaped his trauma through self-sacrifice or through geographical displacement. What is important to note here is that Wayne's 'death' and subsequent rebirth is spatial, rather than temporal. What I mean by this is that Wayne's shift from Gotham City to Florence represents a geographical cure – a physical, spatial removal from the place associated with loss – rather than a psychological one. In an interview that precedes a compendium of the screenplays to the trilogy Nolan says:

> For me, one of the most important bits in *The Dark Knight Rises* is when Alfred says, 'I never wanted you to come back to Gotham'. Talk about when he left. It's surprising and it's shocking, but there's a real logic to it [...] Gotham is his parents. Gotham is his tragedy. He cares deeply about it and doesn't want to leave it behind but, at the same time, it's a prison. It's the prison of his past.
>
> (Nolan 2013: x)

To imply then, as Nolan does during the climactic scenes of the film, that Wayne can escape or even overcome his trauma, is to locate his past within a specific spatial region as opposed to embracing the temporal logic of trauma. At the simplest level, this is communicated by the choice of location as the city of Florence which shares a close association with the Renaissance, literally meaning 'rebirth'.

As Batman apparently sacrifices himself during the final moments of *The Dark Knight Rises*, Wayne's appearance in Florence symbolizes his own rebirth as 'Bruce Wayne' without Batman. Furthermore, the presence of Selena Kyle (Anne Hathaway) who is shown wearing Wayne's mother's pearls, a significant symbol[8] associated with the deaths of his parents that he had locked away, preserving them in a vault and as such, in his (repressed) past. Todd McGowan notes:

> By showing Bruce living out Alfred's fantasy, Nolan offers the perfect Hollywood resolution. The hero retires with the romantic partner at his side. And yet, here the conventional ending cannot but disappoint because it illustrates the extent to which Bruce has misunderstood the nature of his own subjectivity. His subjectivity does not reside in the identity of Bruce Wayne who has permanently left the Batman's mask behind. It resides in the mask itself, in the truth that appearance allows to emerge. The mask is the truth of the subject because it manifests the past trauma. This is the case for both Batman and Bane in the film: both wear a mask in response to a trauma that has *scarred their being irreparably, and the promise of life without the mask, like the promise of life beyond trauma, is an ideological lie.*
>
> (McGowan 2012b: n.pag., emphasis added)

From a commercial perspective, seeing Wayne on-screen at all following the explosion ensures the possibility of a hypothetical future collaboration between

Nolan and the actor Christian Bale returning to *The Dark Knight* franchise. But in psychoanalytic terms, for McGowan, Nolan's decision to have Wayne relinquish the mask of Batman points towards the promise of life beyond the traumatic experience, thus breaking the cyclical movement of time associated with the temporality of trauma. However, the paradoxical logic of this decision becomes evident when we consider that for Wayne, his attachment to the Batman identity will never, and can never, stop. This is because the death of his parents is a traumatic experience that he has never been able to, and ultimately will never fully assimilate because the temporal logic of *afterwardsness* is one of perpetual return. As such, McGowan's reading of the ending to *The Dark Knight Rises* suggests that Nolan undermines a conventional understanding of the temporality of trauma because he purports to show a 'Bruce Wayne' without Batman, a character dichotomy that cannot exist because of the intrinsic and irreparable traumatic loss at the heart of Wayne's existence.

The Dark Knight Returns?

How then can we reconcile the ending of *The Dark Knight Rises* within the wider context of Nolan's filmography, which, as has been discussed, frequently presents the subject's relationship to trauma as defined by the continuous repetition of loss? There are two ways to debate the ending that may offer varying degrees of satisfaction for both the spectator and the scholar of Nolan's films. The first, and perhaps most plausible given the textual information presented, is that Wayne cannot survive the bomb blast because the resolution of his psychological journey and the redemption of Gotham City are predicated on his self-sacrifice. Wayne can be aligned with what Claire Sisco King refers to as the role of 'sacrificial victim-hero' (2011: 2), a male protagonist who nobly gives up his life so that others may be saved. This term provides a frame of reference for understanding the film's final presentation of trauma as it is only through his redemptive death that the traumatic loss of his parents can be re-inscribed with new meaning. Working along these lines, Wayne's sacrifice, much like Detective Dormer's (Al Pacino) during the final moments of *Insomnia*,[9] is a viable alternative to his survival because, as King points out, it 'affords its victim new meaning and new life, offering a posthumous narrative that resonates closure and redemption' (2011: 17). The retrospective activation of meaning associated with the sacrifice of these protagonists is one that can be related to *afterwardsness* since, according to King, 'the act of sacrificial death is itself a traumatic one' (2011: 17). Therefore, the character's death revises their traumatic history in line with the temporality of trauma outlined so far. This is to say that their sacrifice re-writes the lost (repressed) trauma altering its meaning in the process. As such, where the temporal logic of *afterwardsness* is one of perpetual return, the redeeming qualities of self-sacrifice are the only other means by which past trauma can potentially be alleviated.

Alternatively, another theory would suggest that Wayne survives the bomb blast, but his survival continues to perpetuate the closed loop of trauma that is largely consistent with Nolan's other films. According to this theory, Wayne's existence is principally predicated upon the look of an other. Simply put, even though he seems to have escaped his traumatic past by leaving Gotham behind, his complicity in acting out Alfred's self-confessed fantasy responds to his own failure to lead a life that is separate from what someone else had wished for him. Through the look, Wayne becomes an object for the other and at this moment his ability to transcend the unconscious trauma is usurped. By conforming to Alfred's fantasmatic image of his life established earlier in the film, Wayne's existence is seemingly bound to the fantasies of an other. Accordingly, Wayne's struggle to lead a life free from trauma emerges from his inability to locate and sustain a distinct sense of self that is wholly or at least in part, independent of the other. In this instance then, it is significant that Wayne's final appearance in the film is constituted through the lens of Alfred's desire because, in these fleeting moments, which can be interpreted as Nolan's attempt to envision a post-traumatic state, Wayne exists as an extension of someone else's experience rather than as an individual. As a consequence, Wayne's identity remains intimately tied to pre-existing social abstractions and as a result, he retains the traumatic kernel of the Real, the traumatic kernel that structures his existence. It would appear that while Batman can exist without Bruce Wayne, Bruce Wayne cannot exist without Batman.

NOTES

1. Further references to Bruce's parents also appear in *The Dark Knight* and *The Dark Knight Rises* although these are not depicted visually in the form of flashbacks but are instead restricted to verbal accounts, photos and aural cues contained within the narrative.

2. This is in keeping with several other analyses of the character that suggest Wayne's experience of his parents' deaths is one that bears the hallmarks of a traumatic experience (Langley 2012: 35–54).

3. By 'other', Laplanche is referring to a concrete other, this is to say a physical other, as opposed to the Lacanian big Other associated with the Symbolic Order (see Evans 1996: 136).

4. Notable appearances of the bats occur during Wayne's training with Ducard in the Himalayas and again when he encounters a single bat in Wayne manor along with the ensuing swarm that engulfs him at the site of his *original* trauma.

5. Further examples include both the death of Rachel (Maggie Gyllenhaal) and the fate of Harvey Dent/Two-Face (Aaron Eckhart) in *The Dark Knight* perpetuate Wayne's survivor guilt, which stems from his inability to save or protect his parents.

6. Even when Wayne retires as Batman in both the comics and the film *Batman Forever* he frequently returns to the role in a way that points to the ongoing continuity of the character.

7. Despite Bruce's belief that 'Batman could be anybody' it is clear from both the comics and the on-screen versions of the character that only those who have suffered a similar traumatic loss are permitted take up the cowl. For example, in *The Dark Knight Rises* it is revealed that Blake too was an orphan. Elsewhere, in the comics, Jason Todd is an orphan, whereas Tim Drake is only allowed to enter Bruce's inner circle after the death of his mother. Similarly, Jean-Paul Valley and Terry McGinnis are enlisted albeit after the deaths of their respective fathers.

8. As a cultural symbol the pearl can also be understood as an analogy to trauma. A pearl is formed inside a pearl oyster (i.e. a mollusc) because of a parasite penetrating the shell. The mollusc proceeds to secrete layers of nacre to protect itself (see Read 1991: 256). Each pearl can, therefore, be thought of as the repressed trauma buried or masked. The resulting pearl (or work of imagination or art) has a smooth and untarnished exterior, which hides a painful seed at its centre.

9. Detective Dormer's death is signalled as being a sacrifice because he 'saves' Ellie (Hillary Swank) from following his own path of corruption by telling her to hand in the evidence that will incriminate him in the death of his partner, thus causing his existing convictions to be overturned.

Looking for the Secret: Trauma and Desire in *The Prestige*

I knew an old sailor once, he told me he went overboard, got tangled in the sails. They pulled him out, but it took him five minutes to cough. He said it was like going home.

– Cutter, *The Prestige*

At one point in *The Prestige*, Christopher Nolan's film about the rivalry between two magicians in Victorian-era London, Alfred Borden (Christian Bale) warns a young boy (Anthony De Marco) about the danger of revealing the secret to his magic trick: 'They'll beg you and they'll flatter you for the secret, but as soon as you give it up, you'll be nothing to them. You understand? Nothing. The secret impresses no-one, the trick you use it for is everything'. This excerpt can be read as a more general reflection of Nolan's own attitude towards his audience who are often left without definitive answers to his most intricate narrative puzzles, thereby forcing them to return to each film to discover hidden meanings. However, this conversation can also be interpreted as an analogy for the psychoanalytic theory of desire, which can be readily applied to most of Nolan's films to date. As discussed in Chapter 1, in Lacanian terms, desire is animated by a quest for wholeness that stems from a fundamental lack that emerges during the early development of each human subject. This lack, established at the moment the child is divorced from a state of perfect harmony with the mother (the first love-object) and displaced into the realm of language, propels the subject into a perpetual search for an object that might compensate for the subsequent feelings of loss. Crucially, however, since this lack is framed as the desire to return to some impossible form of pre-natal oneness with the mother, the desire remains inherently unsatisfied. As Slavoj Žižek notes, '[d]esire is the metonymic sliding propelled by a lack, striving to capture the elusive lure: it is always, by definition, "unsatisfied"' (1992: 228). By identifying the 'lure' of the secret behind an illusion in relation to desire, Borden correctly recognizes the essence of desire, which is to sustain itself by obstructing its own fulfilment. If,

71

as Borden says, the magician chooses to reveal the secret then the circuit of desire is ostensibly complete. However, in accordance with a Lacanian understanding of psychoanalysis, upon obtaining the object of desire (in this instance the secret) we do not experience the necessary conditions for desire's satisfaction. Instead, the object simply leads on to something else in what is effectively an endless chain of signification. This is precisely why Borden rails against exposing the secret of an illusion because he is aware that, in doing so, the spectator's investment in it is necessarily shattered, and they will simply turn their attention elsewhere.

This brief exchange between Borden and the young boy in *The Prestige* is indicative of the film's preoccupation with the complex dynamics of desire, which frequently intersects with trauma. This chapter suggests that it is the central character's obsession with obtaining the lost-object that points towards the experience of traumatic loss which, in turn, can be ultimately traced back to the lack that defines us all. Beyond *The Prestige*'s thematic exploration of these ideas, the intersection between trauma and desire also manifests at the level of form through a pattern of visual and narrative repetition. With these ideas in mind, the purpose of this chapter is threefold. First and foremost, the chapter draws attention to the metonymic function of desire by placing an emphasis on the death of Angier's (Hugh Jackman) wife, Julia McCullough (Piper Perabo) as an encounter with the Real. Second, this chapter provides a detailed account of the film's shot-to-shot pattern of editing and composition to argue that it relies on a series of visual and structural repetitions to represent traumatic signifiers. Finally, this chapter concludes by outlining the links between the overarching structure of the film and the temporality of trauma by examining the connections between the narrative and the structure of a magic trick. These three strands of analysis inform the chapter's central contention that *The Prestige* communicates the structure of the traumatic experience both structurally and stylistically through a process of thematic, formal and visual repetition that is linked to what Jacques Lacan defines as being a 'lack or gap in the structure of the Other' (1977c: xi).

Much like *Insomnia*, *The Prestige* – Nolan's fifth and perhaps most critically underrated film – has been largely ignored by scholars.[1] Based on Christopher Priest's novel of the same name, the film centres on the relationship between two stage magicians, Robert Angier and Alfred Borden. Initially partners, the death of Angier's wife during a performance leads to a deep division between the two men and subsequently an intense rivalry. From a thematic perspective, the film overtly draws attention to the idea of duality and repetition through the physical doubling that takes place in various forms throughout (see Tembo 2015: 201–18). The central characters not only act as doubles of each other, but ultimately have their own physical doubles giving rise to a series of complex questions about identity and the self. For instance, it is revealed that Borden is one of a pair of twins who have concealed their identities since birth to perform their signature trick: 'The Transported Man' (in which a person disappears into an apparently empty doorway and reappears instantaneously through another unconnected to the first). At another point in the film, Angier initially uses another man to play his double in an attempt to replicate Borden's trick before ultimately commissioning technology from Nikola Tesla (David Bowie) that enables him to clone himself, a strategy which eventually leads to his apparent murder at the hands of *a* Borden.[2] In addition, aside from the physical doubling that takes place throughout the film, Angier also possesses a double identity[3] and the deaths of the protagonists' wives are mirrored by the magicians' own respective demises: Julia by drowning, Sarah (Rebecca Hall) by hanging.[4]

The emphasis on duality and repetition within the narrative is also evident at the level of *The Prestige*'s form as Nolan uses the framing device of two diaries. In recounting the magicians' thoughts and actions, the diaries demonstrate how each man constructs his own sense of self apart from, and in relation to, the other. However, more than this, the diaries also function as a narrative technique that permits the flashbacks, flash-forwards and repetitions that organize the narration. Such techniques not only disrupt the linear progression of the narrative, thereby illustrating the temporality of trauma, but the provision of multiple narrators also adds further complications to the spectator's understanding of the plot as the film addresses compound layers of time and space. Essentially, Angier is reading Borden's notebook in the diegetic past whereas *a* Borden reads Angier's diary in the diegetic present. However, such a simplification of the structure fails to address a third plot thread that bookends the film involving the disappearance and reappearance of a caged bird accompanied by Cutter's (Michael Caine) structural breakdown of a magic trick. This scene not only functions as an appropriate allegory for the presence of the physical doubles in the film but also acts as an outline of the film's structure that sheds light on the relationship between the trick and trauma. It is the film's complex narrative, then, that outwardly promotes the necessity for repeated viewings and, therefore, reveals how the traumatic experience can be understood in relation to *The Prestige*. However, it is also the thematic content of the film expressed through the arrangement and organization of repeated elements including a recurrent pattern of shot-to-shot editing that equally communicates the structure of trauma.

Desire Is a Metonymy

In *Book XI* (1977d), Lacan offers an account of repetition that emerges primarily from Sigmund Freud's writings in *Beyond the Pleasure Principle* ([1920] 1955b), namely that of the 'repetition compulsion' (*Wiederholungszwang*) and the case study of the *Fort-Da* game. According to Freud, the compulsion to repeat constitutes a formative moment in working-through trauma. When subject to a traumatic experience, Freud argues that an individual repeatedly returns to the memory to retroactively master the event. Such repetition, he argued, is a result of the subject's inability to locate the trauma as either reconciled with the present or put into the past as part of a coherent narrative. Freud's central example of traumatic repetition compulsion is the *Fort-Da* game invented by his grandson.

The game involves the child repeatedly throwing a wooden reel on a string over the edge of his cot and subsequently retrieving it accompanied by the sounds 'o-o-o-o' ('fort'/gone) and 'da' (there). In his observations on the *Fort-Da* game, Freud suggests that the child's compulsion to repeat is a re-enactment of the trauma associated with the departure of the mother and his attempt to come to terms with her absence. By repeatedly staging the trauma, Freud contends that the child transforms a passive experience into an active game, thereby achieving a sense of mastery over the emotions attached to the event. However, what Lacan proposes deviates from the Freudian interpretation of the *Fort-Da* game as he suggests that 'the exercise with this object refers to an alienation, and not to some supposed mastery' (1977d: 239). According to Lacan, the mother is not simply reducible to the wooden reel. Rather, the reel functions as a 'symbol of lack', or what Lacan calls the *objet petit a* (the object-cause of desire) (1977d: 103).[5] For Lacan, the wooden reel not only functions as a signifier for the loss of the mother but more broadly as an indicator of the metonymic function[6] of the *objet a*. Here, it is the experience of loss that sets the metonymic process of desire in motion and in this context the game is significant not only in terms of what is lost but also because of the emergence of the subject's desire within a system of substitutions that are in the expression of language (presence/absence). Whether following Freud's reading of the game as a substitute for the absence of the mother or Lacan's reading of the game as the child's entry into language, the appearance and disappearance of the wooden reel ultimately recalls the fundamental structure and characteristics of trauma.

The importance that both Freud and Lacan attribute to the figure of the mother in their respective engagements with the *Fort-Da* game is largely consistent with the prevailing theoretical foundation of psychoanalysis, which dictates that the subject's desire is principally framed as a response to the infant's separation from the mother. It is during the transition from the pre-Oedipal phase to the Oedipal Complex, however, that the overwhelmingly patristic nature of psychoanalysis, with its emphasis on the Law of the Father, begins to emerge. Freud, for example, argues that the subject's initial identification with, and desire for, the mother was displaced upon the child's recognition of the mother's lack (constituted by Freud as the absence of a penis). The discovery of her physical castration, attributed to an act perpetrated by the father, positions the mother as a passive victim of the controlling and commanding father whose 'law' the child subsequently internalizes as the superego. Along similar, albeit slightly divergent lines, Lacan conceives the child's entry into the Symbolic Order (the realm of language and culture) not by way of a literal castration but rather a symbolic castration that is understood primarily as an effect of language. It is Lacan's rejection of the anatomical literality of the penis in favour of a linguistic model that emphasizes the privileged position of the phallus (a symbol of power and patriarchal authority), which, according to him, calls attention to women's negative entry into the Symbolic Order. For Lacan, women's relation to the phallus is one of lack as language and culture are intrinsically patriarchal or phallocentric in their construction, indicating that the ways through which women can articulate an authentic vision of female desire are inherently restricted – hence his famous axiom that 'The Woman does not exist' ([1975] 1998: 69). In both Freud and Lacan's theoretical configurations of early psychosexual development, patriarchal authority in all its permutations seems to occupy a more central role, whereas women are relegated to passive and inferior positions.

Subsequent feminist reworkings of these psychoanalytic theories have contested the minimization of women within the role of the subject's formation by postulating that all subjects, regardless of sex, are defined in relation to a lack caused by symbolic castration. Kaja Silverman, for instance, offers an alternative to the traditional understanding of castration by suggesting that the chief reason women's bodies are located as the site of lack is no more than a means to disavow the prevailing feelings of male inadequacy derived from the prospect of female power and authority (1992: 46). In contrast, for Silverman, both male and female subjects are symbolically castrated at the point of entry into the realm of language meaning that the inherent lack is shared by *all* subjects. By attempting to dissolve the boundary of sexual difference between men and women, such theories have not only had the effect of elevating the status of the female body within critical discussions of subject formation, but they have also helped to account for the paradoxical position that women occupy within a patriarchal society and psychoanalytic thought. For example, according to Lacan, women can occupy the position of the object of desire (upon which heterosexual male fantasy is written) and, altogether separately, be the cause of man's desire (*objet a*). But, crucially, expressions of female desire cannot emerge within the constraints of phallocentric society. Taken to their logical extremes, these ideas find a restrained parallel in Nolan's films, which often marginalize women's experience at the expense of male-driven narratives that focus on troubled men. When female characters do appear, they frequently do so in one of a limited range of guises including as the impossible object of heterosexual male fantasy such as Leonard Shelby's (Guy Pearce) absent wife in *Memento* or as a woman who enjoys too much and so must be punished like Miranda Tate (Marion Cotillard) in *The Dark Knight Rises*. In these films, the quest to locate the lost-object (frequently framed in relation to a woman) is inevitably revealed to be unsatisfying and perpetually out of reach with the implication being that the object of desire is always positioned in such a way that encapsulates an altogether deeper primordial desire for unity with the mother.

In keeping with the vast majority of Nolan's other films to date, then, it is the death of a woman that constitutes the central loss around which the narrative of *The Prestige* is primarily organized. In this instance, it is the passing of Angier's wife that acts as the initial catalyst for the rivalry between the two protagonists that dominates the plot thereafter. Early in the film, it is established that the twin brothers, alongside Angier, began their respective careers as 'plants' in the audience for a renowned stage magician. Each night *a* Borden and Angier would be 'randomly' selected to participate as aids in the construction of an illusion during which the magician's assistant (a role played by Angier's wife) is bound at the wrists and ankles before being lowered into a tank full of water. On one tragic occasion, *a* Borden appears to tie a more complex knot (the Langford Double) that Julia could not slip underwater and, as a direct result, she drowns.

What is at stake in this sequence is the possibility of encountering the Real, in the Lacanian sense, of the impossible unknown at the heart of trauma. The Real, for Lacan, represents a 'missed encounter' (1977d: 55) which, as missed, cannot be represented, only repeated. In this sequence, the distress of Julia's death is signalled to the spectator throughout its occurrence due to the visual and aural design of the scene that includes fast-paced editing and an absence of non-diegetic sound. But, it is also repeated immediately afterwards through a dramatic re-enactment that shows Angier's own painful attempts to relive the incident in what amounts to a perpetual cycle of self-destructive repetition associated with unconscious trauma.[7] As a consequence, the spectator not only bears witness to Angier's experience of loss but also to the pattern of repetition that figures among the after-effects of a missed encounter with the Real. In the film, Angier re-enacts her death because the experience is so violent and sudden that it is repressed and subsequently manifests in alternate forms. Equally, for the spectator, repeated visual cues and numerous references to Julia's death occur throughout the film in such a way that indicates how the unconscious traumatic signifier extends outwards beyond the bounds of the story itself to encompass the spectator's vicarious response.

The sequence begins with a fleeting shot of Julia's body floating lifelessly in the tank of water (Figure 10) before cutting to the back of a mysterious figure who stands hunched over a sink with his head fully submerged underwater (Figure 11). The film returns to the stage performance to show Julia momentarily struggling while immersed in the tank before returning once again to the man who hurriedly withdraws from the sink gasping for air. As he falls to the floor it becomes apparent that the man is Angier but, significantly, it is only through the spectator's retroactive reconstruction of the sequence that his actions can be partially understood. By deliberately withholding his identity, Nolan initially makes it unclear what is going on. However, it is when Angier is revealed that the spectator can understand this scene as his attempt to recreate the moments leading up to his wife's death. During the remainder of the sequence, Angier sits quietly sobbing on the floor while a further short-lived memory of her death appears on-screen followed by another (Figure 12) before concluding with a final shot of him sat alone with his head in his hands. Of significance throughout this sequence are the momentary glimpses of Julia's struggle. Not only do these shots make the psychological connection between her death and his re-enactment of it explicit, but they also function to highlight the role of time in understanding a structural account of trauma.[8]

At the start of this sequence, the first shot that follows Julia's death (Figure 10) ruptures the narrative timeline by momentarily returning us to the preceding events. This is further complicated by the subsequent shots of her struggle that either directly contradict the linearity of the framework put forward in the previous sequence or provide additional material and points of view.[9] Of note is the last image in this sequence that shows Julia struggling underwater (Figure 12). This brief shot was seen considerably earlier in the film during the initial depiction of her death, pointing towards the deliberate conflation of time as a series of linear instants. As such this sequence, and more generally the narrative, exhibits the structure of the traumatic experience in which the past is continuously repeated anachronistically in the present. This notion is aptly summarized by Todd McGowan who describes the pattern of repetition as that which disrupts linear time as it erupts into the present and compels the subject to repeat the past. He remarks:

> Time is not moving toward a different future that might free us from loss but returning us back to the experience of loss. Rather than being a movement forward, it is a movement of return. The temporality of the subject is the temporality of the repetition of a fiction, which circulates around a traumatic kernel rather than proceeding in a linear fashion toward the future or toward an ultimate truth. Time provides a venue for this repetition, from which there is no respite.
>
> (McGowan 2012: 115)

FIGURE 10: Julia's lifeless body floats in the tank, *The Prestige*.

FIGURE 11: An unknown person stands hunched over a sink with their head submerged underwater, *The Prestige*.

FIGURE 12: Julia struggling underwater, *The Prestige*.

In terms of the film's narrative trajectory, it is Julia's death that forms the basis for understanding the structure of the traumatic experience in *The Prestige* as the narrative is constructed around her absence both directly and indirectly. For example, the continued repetition of several camera set-ups and shot compositions attached to the stage performance during which she dies function as a structural signpost that frames the narrative timeline in relation to trauma by enacting a discourse of repetition upon the spectator that continually points back to the missed encounter with the Real. Narratively speaking, however, it is her absence from the story following her death that elevates her to the position of the lost-object or the *objet a*.

Here it would be wise to avoid confusing the *objet a* (the object *cause* of desire) with the object *of* desire (the desired object) (Lacan 1977d: 62–69). The distinction is important as the object *cause* of desire is constituted as the *objet a* by its placement *outside* the structure of the Symbolic Order, whereas the object *of* desire exists *within* of the structure of the Symbolic insofar as it is at least seemingly obtainable. According to a Lacanian reading, it is not until Julia dies that she becomes the object *cause* of desire and takes on value for the subject when she is impossibly unobtainable. It is only through her death that Julia ceases to be an object *of* desire and is reconstituted as the object *cause* of desire. In a similar vein, Lacan's essay on *Hamlet* refers to the death of Ophelia as the moment where she is 'reintegrated' as an object *cause* of desire, 'won back here at the price of mourning and death' (1977d: 24). In *The Prestige*, the course of events that brings Angier's rivalry with the twins to a climax can be read along similar lines as it is possible to account for all of Angier's acts on the basis of the death of his wife and her reconstitution in grief as the *objet a*. For example, in one of the scenes following Julia's death, *a* Borden attends her funeral during which Angier repeatedly asks him to reveal what type of knot he tied in the moments leading up the incident. *A* Borden, either through ignorance or denial, is unable to provide him with a definitive answer and so Angier sets out to force him to remember by threatening him with a loaded pistol. Upon their next meeting, *a* Borden is once again incapable of providing him with the answer that he seeks, and so Angier shoots him, thereby setting in motion the chain of events that will lead to his own death and *a* Borden's imprisonment and execution.

It is important to consider why Angier must know whether Borden tied the Langford Double. What justification is strong enough to push Angier towards committing murder? After all, regardless of which knot one of the twins tied, Julia's death remains a tragic accident. The film doesn't answer this question directly, but it is possible to speculate about a potential interpretation based upon a Lacanian understanding of desire. Angier's desire to know whether Borden knew what type of knot he tied seems to emerge from his belief that the truth of the situation is kept from him. Even though Angier was present when the knot was tied, he misses the shared silent exchange between *a* Borden and Julia which seems to indicate the latter's willingness to attempt an escape from the more complex knot. As *a* Borden ties the rope around her wrists he hesitates slightly and looks into her eyes. She glances up at him momentarily sharing his gaze before nodding, almost imperceptibly. He subsequently seems to alter the type of knot that he was tying although it remains ultimately unclear as to whether he chooses to use the Langford Double or reverts to a safer option. The reason for this central ambiguity arises from the lack of dialogue in their exchange. In this sense, there is something unknown and unknowable about this moment that produces a number of different possibilities, which both the spectator and Angier retroactively seek to understand.

The subsequent shift from Angier's frustration with the inaccessibility of the truth to the envy that he feels when witnessing Borden's family life highlights the metonymic displacement of desire as his desire is subject to a continual process of displacement from one object to another. Reflecting on seeing *a* Borden with his wife Sarah and their new-born baby, Angier says, 'I saw happiness, happiness that should have been mine'. Prior to this moment in the film, his primary motivation has been to understand Borden's role in the cause of his wife's death – thereby allowing him to try and overcome the anguish that her absence causes him while obtaining, at least superficially, some form of closure. But, at this point, his desire for knowledge is displaced onto the concept of the ideal family unit. Later in the film, when he is within reach of realizing this desire through his relationship with Olivia (Scarlett Johanssen), Angier's desire is displaced once again when he consciously distances himself from her by demanding that she leave him and join Borden to obtain his secret for 'The Transported Man'. After making this request, Angier attempts to kiss Olivia. Even though she retreats from his advance, it is his response to her rejection that illustrates the complex interplay between our conscious wishes and our unconscious desires. When Angier calls Olivia a 'good girl' he is seemingly aware that asking her to try and steal the secret of Borden's illusion will likely lead to problems with their own relationship. But, on the other hand, in doing so Angier unconsciously destroys the path to realizing his own desire by displacing it once more onto Borden's secret. When Olivia subsequently falls in love with *a* Borden, Angier confronts her saying that 'He's taken everything from me: my wife, my career, now you'. Olivia points out the intrinsic irony in this statement when she responds by noting that he initially sent her away, notwithstanding her protest.

Despite his obsessive pursuit of contiguous objects, Angier is largely out of touch with desire at the level of the unconscious. It is Angier's obsessive fixation on discovering the secret to Borden's illusion that highlights the extent of his displaced desire to continue mourning the loss of his wife. For example, during the previous exchange with Olivia, she reminds Angier that his pursuit of the secret to 'The Transported Man' will not bring his wife back from beyond the grave. Angier angrily retorts, 'I don't care about my wife, I care about his secret'. It is clear though that, regardless of his vocal outburst, Angier's actions betray his unconscious commitment to the object *cause* of desire, which is, in this particular instance, the memory of his wife.[10] What this means is that, even though the narrative of *The Prestige* is superficially built around Angier's search for the secret to Borden's signature trick, the object of his desire is not the method of the illusion but rather Borden's complete downfall. By extension, what prevents Angier succeeding is his unconscious desire to perpetuate the memory of his wife. This dynamic is communicated towards the end of the film in a scene where Angier, as his alter-ego Lord Caldlow, visits *a* Borden in prison after having adopted his daughter as his ward.

In a revealing exchange of dialogue between the two men, *a* Borden expresses how far their rivalry has come when he says 'This ain't a bloody competition anymore. This is my little girl's life. And don't you dare put her in the middle of this'. Angier responds by reminding *a* Borden of his own loss saying 'Oh, I know how hard it is to have someone so special taken away from you, don't I, Borden?' This fleeting reference to the death of Angier's wife, which Borden recognizes by pausing and shifting his eyes slightly, not only temporarily invokes his own (or his twin brother's) role in the event around which the entire narrative encircles, it also activates the spectator's memory of it, thereby cognitively returning them to the site of loss. In the following moments, Borden desperately attempts to try and stop Angier from taking his daughter away from him by finally offering him the secret to 'The Transported Man': 'This is what you're after. That's what this is about' he says. However, perhaps realizing that *a* Borden has finally reached a breaking point, Angier chooses not to look at the folded piece of paper upon which the secret is written but instead tears it into shreds. This action demonstrates that Angier is no longer invested in the secret because he obtains the object of his desire, which is Borden's undoing. Of course, as Lacan stresses, obtaining the object of desire negates the object's very appeal and so Angier tears the piece of paper up because at the moment of obtaining the object of his desire it is displaced once more on to the figure of Borden's daughter Jess (Samantha Mahurin).

Within this matrix of desire, Jess is positioned as a substitute for Julia, which is not to say that she represents a romantic interest in any way, but rather that she is a replacement for the absent love-object. In effect, what is at stake is the ownership of desire. By adopting Borden's daughter as his own, Angier seeks to subjugate and subsume her subjectivity by positioning her as the object of his desire. However, Jess is not the privileged object of desire beyond having the capability to transmit feelings of love towards her surrogate father. Therefore, it is the loving attitude that Angier desires: that is, to be loved by an other who can act as a substitute for the lost-object. Lacan writes, '[t]he love of the person who desires to be loved, is essentially an attempt to capture the other in oneself' (Lacan 1988b: 276). He says '[t]he desire to be loved is the desire that the loving object should be taken as such, caught up, enslaved to the absolute particularity of oneself as object' (1988b: 276). However, for Lacan, this kind of love is inherently impossible (as it is conventionally understood) because it represents an extension of the infant's constant yearning for a sense of wholeness attached to the first love-object. This understanding of desire as a metonym for the child's first desire, to return to the point of origin and restore a primal connection with the mother, indicates that desire is also a return of the repressed.

Freud first introduced the concept of 'the return of the repressed' as an involuntary process whereby previously repressed material is brought to conscious awareness ([1896] 1962a: 170). According to Freud, it is the insistent return of thoughts, memories and feelings deemed to be unacceptable or unbearable, which are the target of psychoanalytic analysis. Significantly, in this context, what has been repressed is the child's desire for the mother. The ensuing metonymic displacement of this desire might seem like a linear movement through time and space similar to the structure of language. However, in the same way that Lacan suggests a sentence's meaning is derived from the retroactive effect of applied punctuation ([1981] 1993: 262–63), the drive of metonymy involves a temporal movement that is at once a push forward towards the future and a pull back towards the past. What this effectively means is that even though the metonymy of desire is the primary motivating force driving the shift from one object to another, each displacement is merely a substitute for the first love-object meaning that metonymy, like trauma, is temporally bidirectional.

At this point in *The Prestige*, even though Angier is apparently no longer burdened by the memory of his wife (the object *cause* of desire), her absence remains a constituent component of his subjectivity and a central aspect of the film's narrative construction. For example, at Julia's funeral, Cutter recounts the story of a sailor who was thrown overboard and nearly drowned. Later, as he and Angier dispose of the device used during the latter's version of 'The Real Transported Man' Cutter reminds him of the story. He says, 'I once told you about a sailor who described drowning to me', to which Angier responds, 'Yes he said it was like going home'. Cutter replies, 'I was lying. He said it was agony'. At this point in the film, Cutter's admission serves two functions. First, it modifies his initial words of comfort as a lie. Second, it results in an after-the-fact readjustment of Angier's emotional relationship to the pain that his wife suffered during her own death and, by extension, the anguish that each of his clones (inseparable from himself) has experienced too. In the following moments, Angier walks towards a water tank containing one of his clones. He gently runs his hand across the smooth glass surface before muttering to himself, 'no-one cares about the man in the box'. There is an irony present here as the gesture of caressing the glass hints at a shared connection between Angier and the deceased duplicates, which indicates that he alone *does* care about the man in the box as it represents an extension of himself. He is seemingly aware that each time he kills a clone in order to perform his version of 'The Real Transported Man' he commits what amounts to an act of self-mutilation that gradually erodes what is left of his identity. This sacrificial act, then, in some ways distances Angier from the memory of his wife while, at the same time, brings the two of them symbolically closer through a process of re-enactment and repetition.

The Aesthetic of Repetition

Referring to the Lacanian notion of desire as part of his basis for a discussion of narration, Peter Brooks (1992) suggests that repetition can undermine the forward movement of a text by simply reproducing events without any deviation from the original. Or, repetition can be productive by demonstrating the value of repeating events with enough difference to achieve some form of change and even growth or, in terms of a plot, narrative development. He says:

> Narrative [...] must make use of specific, perceptible repetitions in order to create plot, that is, to show us a significant interconnection of events. An event gains meaning by its repetition which is both the recall of an earlier moment and a variation of it. The concept of repetition hovers ambiguously between the idea of reproduction and that of change, forward and backward movement. Repetition through this ambiguity appears to suspend temporal process or rather, to subject it to an indeterminable shuttling or oscillation that binds different moments together as a middle that might turn forward or back.
>
> (Brooks [1984] 1992: 99–100)

Likewise, in her discussion of rhizomatic time and temporal poetics in *American Beauty* (2000), Jacqueline Furby notes that the repetition of various formal elements (including images, settings, colours, shapes and textures) anchors our interpretation of a film by appealing to what she refers to as 'human aesthetic rhythmic sensibilities' (2006: 28). Furby suggests that when certain formal elements are repeated with variations that emerge from meaning and context '[t]his temporal pattern speaks of a particularly human rhythmic design, and provides an escape from the "standardised, context free, homogeneous" clock time "that structures and times our daily lives"' (2006: 28). It is possible to suggest that this temporal pattern, which is evident in a variety of other art forms but obtains a particular visibility through cinema, affords the specta-tor the ability to transcend the inherent restrictions of 'clock time' in such a way that contributes towards their sense of immersion in what Furby calls a 'temporal environment that is sympathetic to human time and addresses the needs of the desiring subject' (2006: 28). Take, for instance, the title sequence of *The Prestige*, which shows a vista of black top hats scattered among fallen branches in a glade while Borden's voice-over narration poses the question 'Are you watching closely?'

The shot of the black top hats (as well as a variation of the accompanying voice-over)[11] is repeated several times most prominently mid-way through the film and once again during the climax. This circular pattern of repetition both affirms and denies the subject's desire, on the one hand demonstrating how we long for mastery – to attain full and complete knowledge – and on the other revealing the lack that constitutes the subject. In this example, it is Nolan's will-ingness to address the spectator both directly (via the voice-over narration) and indirectly (via the repetition of shot composition and camera movement) that poses a threat to the fictional integrity of the film. At the same time, he chooses to do so in a way that requires the spectator to become an active participant in the construction of the film, thus furthering their investment in the illusion of the images on the screen. The pattern makes us aware of and impels us to question the narrative by implying that there is something significant about the image of the hats that hides its true nature while, at the same time, refusing to provide the desired answer. Instead, at the simplest level, the initial image of the hats serves as a subsequent analogy for the underlying theme of duplicity and repetition in the film. The subsequent cut to an aviary containing multiple identical canar-ies continues this trend by setting up another pattern of visual repetition that is sustained throughout the film.

During this scene, Cutter appears to be narrating the three constitutive parts of a magic trick to a young girl whom we later identify as Borden's daughter. Throughout Cutter's monologue, Nolan intersperses several shots of *a* Borden watching Angier's version of 'The Real Transported Man', but of interest is the first glimpse of him sat in the audience (Figure 13). The introduction of *a* Borden presents him in a medium-shot framing his body in profile facing right. Signifi-cantly, this camera setup is repeated with slight variations throughout the course of the film beginning with when we learn about the origins of the magicians' rela-tionship as well as the primary reason for their subsequent rivalry. In the second example, the two men sit separated by a few rows in a theatre to conceal their

FIGURE 13: *a* Borden sat facing off-screen right, *The Prestige.*

involvement in the on-stage performance. Once again, the sequence begins with a shot of *a* Borden, now clean shaven, sat facing towards the stage (Figure 14) before the camera dollies right to Angier sat in another row (Figure 15). In the ensuing performance in which Angier's wife is accidentally killed, the framing and movement are once again duplicated but the two men have now switched places (Figure 16).

In their collection of blog posts, *Christopher Nolan: A Labyrinth of Linkages*, David Bordwell and Kristin Thompson observe that Nolan's stylistic choices here and at other points in *The Prestige* respond to both narrative cohesion and comprehension by subtly sustaining the film's general theme of duplicity and repetition (2013: 23). Even more than this though, the continued repetition of the angle congruent with the onlooker staring rightward off-screen at a performance seen at several other points in the film provides *The Prestige* with a certain structural stability or in Lacanian terms *le point de capiton*. As each repetition occurs, it reminds us of the previous iteration and in doing so provides a subtle link back to the central traumatic loss of the film.

Later in the film when each man attends the others' stage performance, a new pattern of composition emerges, albeit one that echoes the earlier camera setups in subtle ways. In these instances, Nolan restricts the spectator's knowledge of each magician's arrival until a key moment in the scene that requires the use of an upward tilt (rather than a dolly right) to reveal their presence. In the first example, *a* Borden is in the middle of his bullet catch routine when Angier, seeking the truth about Borden's involvement in Julia's death, obtains the unloaded prop pistol and inserts an object into the barrel. The camera initially focuses on the individual's

FIGURE 14: *a* Borden in a medium-shot framing him in profile facing right, *The Prestige*.

FIGURE 15: Angier sat in another row at the same performance, *The Prestige*.

FIGURE 16: The framing and movement of the previous shots are duplicated but the two men have now switched places, *The Prestige*.

hand movements (Figure 17) which, given the multiple warnings about the dangers of performing a bullet catch expressed in the film up to this point, should provide the spectator with an initial clue as to the identity of the volunteer. Nevertheless, it is not until the camera tilts upward that Nolan reveals a disguised Angier who subsequently points the now loaded pistol at *a* Borden (Figure 18).

Similarly, in the second instance, the spectator is once again restricted to the stage performer's range of knowledge when *a* Borden interrupts Angier's performance of the 'Vanishing Bird Cage'. For a second time, the camera focuses on the subject's hands (Figure 19) before tilting upward to reveal *a* disguised Borden (Figure 20). On this occasion, the individual's disfigured fingers are an immediate signifier of Borden's identity, which is perhaps why the tilt is comparatively quicker. Yet, the camera movement itself is a clear repetition of the earlier sequence. From a technical perspective, it can be considered that the formal repetitions evident throughout *The Prestige* draw attention to a visual pattern that emphasizes various forms of repetition compulsions described by Freud in his description of *Fort-Da*. Whether the form is static (framing), dynamic (camera movement) or a combination of the two, the deliberate repetition of a series of images, shots and framings creates a visual rhythm that emphasizes the importance of these events while indicating a sustained endeavour to extend the notion of duplicity and repetition beyond the thematic content of the film. This is certainly the case in these examples

FIGURE 17: An unknown figure inserts an object into the barrel of the gun, *The Prestige*.

FIGURE 18: The camera tilts upward to reveal a disguised Angier, *The Prestige*.

FIGURE 19: The disfigured hand of a Borden rests on top of the cage, *The Prestige*.

FIGURE 20: The camera tilts upward to reveal a disguised Borden, *The Prestige*.

which demonstrate connections across seemingly disparate sequences. However, on other occasions, the structure of a scene is repeated to foreground the spectator's restricted knowledge of events. For instance, during the twins' first performance of 'The Transported Man' Nolan cuts away from the finale of the trick meaning that the spectator does not witness the physical double that it produces (as a later extended repetition of the sequence reveals).

The scene opens with a shot of *a* Borden performing what is known as the 'Chinese Linking Rings' illusion in a small theatre. To begin with, the handheld camera moves unsteadily towards the stage before cutting to a static reverse shot taken from behind *a* Borden's body which shows a disguised Angier arriving at the venue. The subsequent shot/reverse shot exchange confirms the filmic space with Angier on one side of the auditorium staring rightward off-screen (Figure 21). As *a* Borden proceeds, the scene is complicated by a flash-forward to a series of shots interspersed throughout the performance that detail Angier's subsequent recollection of the illusion to Olivia (Figure 22). Once again, Nolan relies on the familiar pattern of placing the subject to the left of the frame looking off-screen right. But, of interest, in this case, is the final shot of the overall sequence, which reveals Cutter to be sat in the audience of the performance (Figure 23). This shot,

FIGURE 21: Angier looking off-screen right, *The Prestige*.

FIGURE 22: Angier once again looks off-screen right while recounting the trick from memory, *The Prestige*.

FIGURE 23: Cutter looks off-screen left, *The Prestige*.

as well as the subsequent shift to an altogether different location following the cut, is significant for a few reasons, chief among them being that the traditional shot/reverse shot dynamic is ruptured as the spectator is denied the subsequent reverse shot of the trick's finale which is implied by Cutter's glance off-screen left. The choice to deny the spectator a visual depiction of the final act at this stage of the film confronts their unconscious acceptance of the traditional shot/reverse pattern of editing, thus foregrounding what is absent. A conventional reverse shot showing the trick's conclusion would have ordinarily neutralized the potential threat to the security and coherence of the filmic space (and the unity of the diegetic world). Instead, by imagining the unseen reverse shot the spectator inadvertently becomes aware of the film's framing and so they are also momentarily aware of the limitations of the enframed image. In this regard, the first performance of 'The Transported Man' is particularly significant as unlike other examples in *The Prestige* where Nolan cuts from a scene prior to its formal conclusion,[12] the spectator is evidently aware of what is missing. This calls attention to the film's frame, thus forcing the spectator to confront their own subjectivity by acknowledging their presence as part of the film's construction.

As a rule, in *The Prestige* the anchor of axis or 180-degree line is principally focused around Angier and the eye-lines are largely consistent with his position. It is perhaps surprising, then, given this apparent emphasis that we are provided with a momentary glimpse of Cutter in the previous sequence when a cut to Angier's reaction would have been more logical given the prior shot/reverse shot dynamic. As it stands, the glimpse of Cutter seemingly functions to allow the subsequent discussion that takes place between Angier and Cutter in the next scene. Bordwell and Thompson suggest that such a decision to repeat the same camera setup with a different character functions to combine narrative coherence and production efficiency (2013: 27). Certainly, in this instance, the sequence's aesthetic construction serves to further the narrative by principally negating the necessity for superfluous exposition, which, in this instance, would involve the visualization of an altogether separate performance to facilitate the subsequent conversation between Angier and Cutter. However, if the glimpse of Cutter merely functions to enable the following exchange between the two men, then it is worth questioning why Cutter is shown at all when an additional piece of dialogue would have performed the same function. The reason for this line of enquiry is that Cutter's placement at what appears to be on first viewing the same performance not only ruptures the previous shot/reverse shot setup but also complicates the narrative flow when it is revealed that he is, in fact, watching an altogether separate performance.

The placement of Cutter on screen right in a position where Angier was similarly sat at the start of the sequence, combined with the diegetic sound of the ball bouncing continuously across the two separate shots, indicates a causality that reflects a linear set of events placing Cutter at the same performance. However, Angier's enquiry as to whether the audience applauded after the trick, remarked upon in the subsequent scene, indicates a distinct temporal difference between the two performances. Such a subtle manipulation of time and space may in most cases go unnoticed as in general, for the purposes of narrative cohesion, a filmmaker will maintain adequate spatial and temporal orientation to provide continuity across different shots. However, in this instance, the decision to include Cutter's appearance in the audience foregrounds the role of a phantom creator who organizes the shot-to-shot construction of the film. The diegetic sound of the ball bouncing across two distinct spatiotemporal dimensions combined with Cutter's look directed off-screen constitutes not only a denial of the frame as a limit but also a breach in linear time demonstrating a circular movement that requires the spectator to engage in a process of retroactive reconstruction to generate meaning.

Narrative Desire

As a fiction film, *The Prestige* allows us to bear witness to the relationship between the spectator and the screen in such a way that foregrounds cinema's transcendent capacity to temporarily liberate the spectator from the experience of lack inherent in being. However, just as for Lacan, the sense of lack can never be filled, so the film ultimately also fails to offer the sense of wholeness that the subject craves. Unlike classical narrative cinema, Nolan's motive in *The Prestige* is not to perpetuate the continued cloaking of the cinematic apparatus to provide such unity, but rather to generate a more active awareness on the part of the spectator. If the spectator is aware, on some level, that the images on the screen are constructed and controlled by an absent yet structuring presence, when the author becomes increasingly visible, as is the case with *The Prestige*, the viewing subject cannot help but reconsider their own relationship to the cinematic image. The experience of watching the film is therefore deliberately saturated with lack as it continually calls attention to its own production processes, albeit through the analogy of a magic trick.

The narrative of a trick, as it were, can be broken down into three stages allowing for comparisons to be made between the parts of a trick and the conventional three-act structure of Hollywood narratives (see Olson 2015: 55). In *The Prestige*, Cutter refers to these parts or acts as the pledge, the turn and finally the prestige. During the pledge a magician presents the audience with an ordinary object: 'a deck of cards, a bird or a man' he says. Then, during the turn, the magician 'takes this ordinary object and makes it do something extraor-dinary'. Finally, the trick concludes with what Cutter refers to as the 'hardest part': the prestige. He says, 'you wouldn't clap yet because making something disappear isn't enough. You have to bring it back'. At this moment, the trick concludes when the object reappears. However, the success of the performance is in part dependent on the skill of the magician who must employ the techniques of misdirection and sleight-of-hand during the transition from one stage to another to produce a dramatic climax. But, the success of the performance also relies upon an act of disavowal: the spectator pretends to believe in the illusion of magic, while at the same time, actively trying to discover the secret that produces their amazement. Rachel Joseph argues that the structural principles underpin-ning the magic trick mirrors the traumatic aspect of performance, both on-stage and on-screen, which entails both an unbearable excess and a missed event. She notes:

> The use of the word trick in the context of the magic show offers an important clue; the viewer expects to be deceived, and part of the fun is trying to figure out how the performer does the deceiving. More importantly, on a theoretical level the trick plays with vision: what the naked eye sees and what remains invisible. The trick enacts the trauma of appearance and disappearance.
>
> (Joseph 2011: 8)[13]

By making an object appear and disappear, a magician can momentarily fore-ground the void at the core of being which is quickly subsumed by the subject's desire for mastery. As such it is the secret – the invisible excess of the magician's performance – that is the barrier that prevents the spectator's fulfilment of desire. It is through both seeing and failing to see that the spectator removes the threat that the truth of the illusion poses, that of an encounter with the Real, and yet also generate the necessary (missed) encounter with the Real.

In *The Prestige*, the truth that the trick conceals is an encounter with the Real, one that, as missed, paradoxically cannot take place. Despite Cutter's insistence, as well as several other hints, the audience both sees and fails to see that Borden's act relies on a double due to a cognitive barrier between the method and the effect. As Cutter puts it during the closing moments of the film, 'you're looking for the secret – but you won't find it, because of course you're not really looking. You don't really want to work it out. You want to be fooled'. The film ends with Cutter's voice-over announcing that the spectator will not discover the secret of the trick, and thus the film. Consequently, Nolan succeeds in withholding the gratification associated with narrative closure. It is this desire for a coherent narrative resolution that once again points to the constituent parts of the traumatic experience as, in vain, the spectator seeks out the lost-object, the cause of desire, and yet it repeatedly eludes them time and time again revealing the underlying lack at the heart of existence alongside a fundamental inability to reconcile the traumatic experience.

Eric L. Tribunella suggests that the structure of all narratives – the movement from a beginning through to a middle and finally reaching an end – implicates the desire of the subject who anticipates that a conclusion will confer some form of meaning upon the text retroactively (2010). However, if, as is the case in *The Prestige*, the ending does not conclude in the desired manner then:

> [The] failure of the expected ending actually to appear represents a loss. The ending is 'had' in that the certainty of it makes a notion of beginning possible but, when the text or narrative sequence fails to end properly or does not end as the reader might expect, then it is as if the reader discovers that the end was in a sense never had. This experience of disappointment, of discovering that one does not have what one thought or expected, can be understood as a kind of loss.
>
> (Tribunella 2010)

Where spectators frequently perceive the diegetic world in such a way that allows them to reconcile the gaps between the real world and the filmed events by seeking a satisfactory conclusion, such an investment in *The Prestige* will inevitably lead spectators to speculate about the ending in a manner that points towards the existence of a truth that extends beyond what is presented on-screen. However, as the film expressly seeks to undermine the traditional focus on the screen by opting instead to highlight the effort that goes into constructing the fiction, such (false) wholeness is unobtainable. By the same token this is why, according to McGowan, those who merely disregard the film based on their ability to decipher the secret of Borden's illusion are inherently misguided (2012: 199). He suggests that dismissing the film because of the apparent simplicity of its plot is to do so at the expense of the labour involved in the process of its creation. Rather than hide the techniques that call attention to the cinematic apparatus, the film foregrounds its own narrative and visual composition through reflexive strategies that expose the parallel between the trick and trauma. In doing so the spectator can transcend trauma, albeit temporarily, through an enriched experience of the work of art that encapsulates both the spectacle of the story and a recognition of the sacrifice integral to the process. As such, *The Prestige* makes clear that the film's source of meaning, like the pathology of traumatic experience, is derived from the overall experience, not in the end towards which we are always travelling.

NOTES

1. Of those texts that do analyse *The Prestige* this chapter is particularly indebted to Todd McGowan's chapter in *The Fictional Christopher Nolan*, which examines the film in relation to temporality and art.

2. The principal reason for adding the prefix 'a' before referring to Borden is that it emphasizes the impossibility of distinguishing which Borden is responsible for the various acts committed throughout the film.

3. Early in the film, he tells his wife that he uses the name Angier because his family would not accept him being a magician. He is actually a wealthy aristocrat who goes by the name of Lord Caldlow.

4. There are several other parallels exhibited elsewhere in the film that emphasize the theme of duality such as the use of identical birds in the vanishing bird cage illusion and the relationship between Nikola Tesla and Thomas Edison whose own professional rivalry mirrors that of the magicians.

5. From this point onward the term *objet petit a* will be referred to as *objet a*.

6. Metonymy is frequently characterized as a mode of communication that corresponds to a linear conceptualization of words and phrases whereby one element is successively substituted for another based on a relationship of contiguity (see Lackoff and Johnson 1980: 36). For instance, in the following sentence – They don't make Hollywood's movies like they used to – the term 'Hollywood' (a suburb of Los Angeles, California) is used as a metonym for the entire US film industry.

7. This scene also foreshadows Angier's apparent fate as 'the man in box' seen during the film's opening sequence.

8. These scenes also embody the primal experience of an intrauterine space by drawing the spectator into an aquatic mode of perception composed of muted sounds inferentially consistent with the experience of being submerged underwater. In addition, while trapped in the tank and Julia's attempts to voice her distress are muted in a way that positions the experience as being beyond language and located firmly in the Real.

9. Such examples include an extension of the first shot that bridges the two separate scenes as well as the initial shot of Julia attempting to voice Robert's name which is presented from a different angle during the re-enactment.

10. Angier's inability to relinquish the memory of wife leads him to internalize her as the lost love-object so that his ego becomes the site of self-reproach. In this respect, Angier's pursuit of Borden's secret evidenced throughout the film is indicative of a particular response to trauma through the internalization of aspects attached to his memory of Julia.

11. This phrase is repeated by *a* Borden a further three times. First, when he shows Sarah's nephew a trick involving a double-sided coin. Once again when speaking to a prison guard and lastly in the moments leading up to his execution.

12. The film contains several examples where Nolan cuts away from a scene before the action concludes only to return to it later to reveal the remaining portion of the scene. For instance, Nolan cuts away after Angier tests the teleportation machine for the first time, during Olivia's confession to *a* Borden and during the film's opening montage of Angier's death and Cutter's description of the three stages of a magic trick. Crucially, however, all these sequences can be viewed as being self-contained as the spectator is unaware of the remaining part of the sequence until it is revealed later in the film.

13. The magic trick's structure of 'there' and 'gone' embodies the trauma of disappearance and return associated with the *Fort-Da* game.

The Dream Has Become Their Reality: Acting-Out and Working-Through Trauma in *Inception*

I feel guilt, Mal, and no matter what I do, no matter how hopeless
I am, no matter how confused, that guilt is always there.

– Cobb, *Inception*

In a revealing sequence towards the end of *Inception*, Cobb (Leonardo DiCaprio) is finally able to confront what amounts to a physical projection of his late wife Mal (Marion Cotillard) at the lowest level of the dream-world created within the film's narrative. It becomes clear from their brief exchange that Cobb's memory of his wife is tainted by feelings of resentment and anger derived from her decision to commit suicide, leaving him as a widowed father of two children. He says to her, 'I have to get back to them. Because *you* left them. You left *us*' (Nolan 2010: 196, original emphasis). However, in the same conversation, he later admits that his projection of Mal can never match the richness of who she was. He says, 'I can't imagine you with all your complexity, all your perfection, all your imperfection – You are just a shade of my real wife. You're the best I can do, but I'm sorry, you are just not good enough'. This exchange – the culmination of several interactions which take place throughout the film – bears a striking resemblance to the structure of a psychoanalytic session through which Cobb, like the patient, explores complex feelings and unresolved issues about themselves by working through their relationships with others. Indeed, by the end of this encounter, Cobb is apparently able to relinquish the memory of Mal in a moment that represents the catharsis that he seeks.

The belief that Mal's death is the sole reason for his inability to return to their children is the essence of what initiates the spectator's investment in Cobb's quest to reunite with them. However, as with *Memento*, this belief is based on a fundamental lie that Cobb tells others (including, by proxy, the spectator) to avoid confronting his responsibility for her death. When the truth is revealed, it has the retroactive effect of revising our perception of Cobb's actions throughout the film while also providing a new context for his interactions with Mal's projection. Prior to the emergence of his role in her suicide, Mal's repeated appearance throughout the film functions as a continual reminder of his loss by positioning Cobb as a victim of her selfishness. In contrast, however, after he reveals the truth of his involvement in her death, their prior encounters can be reinterpreted differently. When Cobb renounces the projection of his wife towards the end of the film, he does so because he has undergone a series of repetitions linked to the process of 'acting-out' (see Freud [1914] 1956) which has led to his ability to work-through his role in her death. In what follows, he seemingly succeeds in reuniting with his children by re-translating the memory of his role in his wife's suicide with the ideal of himself as a 'good' father. Ultimately, however, the final shot of the film – a small pewter cone spinning on a table top – casts doubt upon whether Cobb can return home or whether this is merely another delusion of his own making.

The ending of *Inception* is significant for several reasons, not least because of the impossibility of determining whether Cobb successfully exits the dream-world or not, but also because the scenes that presage this final shot emphasize the role that fictions or fantasy plays in relation to our own experiences of trauma. For instance, the lie that Cobb consciously tells others means that his wife's suicide is repeatedly unconsciously acted out in the dream-world. However, as the film progresses, he is encouraged to use the dream-world in much the same way that we, as spectators, utilize the fantasy space of the cinema: to help us work-through or navigate our day-to-day experience of reality. The fact that Cobb's ability to return to reality is based on a disavowal of a truth is just another means through which an additional parallel emerges between the character's circumstances and the spectator's experience – just as Cobb denies what he unconsciously knows to be true, the spectator too dismisses their underlying awareness of the falsity of the film's construction in favour of the therapeutic value it can provide.

In many ways, *Inception* represents an ostensible shift in Nolan's treatment of trauma as, unlike other protagonists prior to this point in his career, Cobb is seemingly redeemed at the level of the narrative through his ability to work-through his relationship to the unconscious trauma that forms the basis of his identity. He can achieve a catharsis of sorts by the end of the film, albeit one that is constructed from the fiction he uses to achieve it. To demonstrate this, the repetition of Mal's suicide (which occurs in various guises throughout) can be understood as part of the therapeutic process of acting-out the memory of his role in her death. By doing so, Cobb can work-through his attempt to recall the event within the dream-world so that he is able to redeem himself and return to their children. This process of 'working-through' (Freud [1914] 1958) painful memories finds a parallel in the way that dreams are positioned as being analogous to cinema as a means for the subject to engage with a fictional reality that can lay the foundations for transforming our understanding of who we are. Cobb's return to his children can also be located within a wider discourse surrounding a return to paternalism evident in a number of other cultural texts released since the turn of the millennium.

Acting-Out and Working-Through Trauma: Downwards Is the Only Way Forwards?

As we have seen so far, the story of loss pervades Nolan's entire filmography. Films as varied in style as *Memento* – in which a man with no short-term memory attempts to reconcile the loss of his wife by hunting down her apparent killer – to *Interstellar* – a film that negotiates loss through the figure of the absent father – repeatedly returns the spectator to the site of loss. In *Inception*, the experience of loss is embedded within the generic conventions of a heist movie. In the film, a group of criminals led by Cobb can perform a psychological form of corporate-espionage whereby they collectively enter a subject's subconscious or *unconscious* as I will henceforth refer to it in line with Freudian analysis, via a form of dream-sharing technology to either steal a secret (extraction) or plant an idea (inception). The underlying plot of the film concerns a businessman called Saito (Ken Watanabe) who has hired Cobb to 'incept' his competitor, Robert Fischer (Cillian Murphy), the heir to an energy conglomerate, with the idea of breaking up his father's company. In return, Saito offers Cobb the guarantee of returning to the United States and most importantly, to his young children – Phillipa (Claire Geare/ Taylor Geare) and James (Magnus Nolan/Johnathan Geare) – whom he was forced to leave having been implicated in the alleged murder of his wife.

To begin with, the opening prologue depicts Cobb literally on the shore of his unconscious, in what the characters of the film refer to as limbo, trying to find Saito in an event that takes place towards the end of the film's diegetic action. The subsequent cut to Cobb's failed attempt at extracting a secret from Saito's mind not only transports the spectator to a period decades earlier, but also presents them with the different layers of Saito's dream-world ranging from a lavish cocktail party in a Japanese castle, to a dilapidated hotel room and urban streets filled with rioters. That Saito is introduced as an aged man before the film cuts to reveal his younger self also foregrounds the way the film will cross spatial and temporal divides in a way that points towards the subjective nature of time. These opening scenes, set within a dream, function to introduce the spectator to the central concept of shared dreaming, thus pointing towards the function of cinema for the collective audience. The subsequent inception of Fischer that takes place during a flight from Sydney to Los Angeles adds further complexity to our understanding of the narrative as Cobb and his team enter a dream within a dream within another dream, each individual layer supported by a separate narrative thread.

Beyond the formal structural organization of the narrative, which primarily takes its cue from the nature of the nested dreams central to the inception of Fischer, the film's timeline is also guided by Cobb's conflicted psychological response to his role in his wife's death, which shifts between acting-out and working-through. In psychoanalysis, the distinction between acting-out and working-through initially emerges in Freud's essay 'Remembering, repeating and working-through' ([1914] 1958). Freud considered the former to be an unconscious process through which repressed memories are repeated as certain actions ([1914] 1958: 150), whereas he suggested that the latter refers to the analysis undertaken during psychoanalytical treatment to overcome resistances that inhibit a patient's recovery. Dominick LaCapra (1994) has made a further distinction between acting-out and working-through related to the Freudian discourse surrounding melancholia and mourning. For LaCapra, melancholia is characterized by compulsively acting-out a trauma that resists closure, whereas the process of mourning is characterized by working-through a trauma as something that belongs to the past (1994: 65). Melancholia, he says, is 'an arrested process in which the depressed and traumatized self, locked in compulsive repetition, remains narcissistically identified with the lost object' (1998: 44–45). In contrast, '[m]ourning brings the possibility of engaging trauma and achieving a reinvestment in, or recathexis of, life which allows one to begin again' (LaCapra 1999: 713). Elsewhere, he notes that:

> Working through is an articulatory practice: to the extent that one works through trauma [...] One is able to distinguish between past and present and to recall in memory that something happened to one (or one's people) back then while realizing that one is living here and now with openings to the future.
>
> (LaCapra 2001: 22)

Understood in this sense, in *Inception* the notions of acting-out and working-through help to account for the compulsive repetitiveness of slight variations of events that are oriented around Mal's suicide.

In a series of flashbacks that occur throughout the film, we learn that the couple, who had been experimenting with the nature of nested dreams, spent so long in the world they created that Mal chose to take limbo to be their reality. Recognizing that she had suppressed her knowledge of the truth, Cobb planted the idea that Mal was dreaming by means of inception. This idea was planted so deeply in her unconscious that it took hold of her so that, even when she awoke, she continued to believe that their reality was a dream. In a desperate attempt to 'wake up', Mal subsequently committed suicide in the real world. However, before killing herself she framed Cobb for her murder to try and force him to join her by filing a letter with their attorney[1] expressing fears for her own safety and falsely accusing Cobb of making death threats. These actions, borne out of a misplaced desire to coerce him into killing himself in what Mal perceived to be a dream, prevent his return to their children while simultaneously serving as a potent reminder of his own actions which, while based on love, led to her death. Although Mal's death occurs in an event that precedes the diegesis, Cobb's projection of her continually appears throughout the film as the physical manifestation of his memory indicating that it is only by confronting or acting-out the past in the first instance that one is able to work-through it and move beyond it. Mark Fisher goes so far as to describe the projection of Mal as 'a trauma that disrupts any attempt to maintain a stable sense of reality; that which the subject cannot help bringing with him no matter where he goes' (2011: 42). For instance, during Fischer's dream, memories associated with Mal's deaths(s) are employed as barriers to the successful completion of the team's mission, thus initially preventing Cobb's return to reality. At the first level of Fischer's dreamscape, a freight train associated with the couple's initial suicide in limbo threatens to disrupt the group's plans. At the second level, an aural trigger of a champagne glass breaking and a set of curtains reminiscent of those visible during Mal's suicide in 'reality' function as temporary obstacles that point towards the past trauma(s) of her death(s). Elsewhere, the spectator is also forced to revisit and repeat Mal's suicide which is communicated not only via a conventional flashback but also as a (re)lived experience. As such, the spectator encounters the memory and setting of Mal's suicide(s) through numerous repetitions. Consequently, Nolan depicts the psyche of Cobb as defined by the pathological response of acting-out his role in the death of his wife.

Fundamentally, then, the guilt attached to the loss of Cobb's wife can be situated within the ongoing critical discourse surrounding Freudian theory, particularly Freud's distinction between the processes of mourning and melancholia. In his essay 'Mourning and melancholia' ([1917] 2001), Freud contrasts the latter to what he refers to as the normal process of mourning by suggesting that while the former enables the individual to gradually detach from their memories of the lost-object, the melancholic expresses an inability to resolve the grief associated with their loss which is therefore repeated *ad infinitum*. For Freud, this repetition is in part owing to a certain ambivalence or rather a dialectic between love and hate for the object that was present before it was lost ([1917] 2001: 256). This ambivalence informs the principle distinction between mourning and melancholia and is central to understanding the melancholic's continued investment in what was lost. In this sense, the narrative of *Inception* predominantly dramatizes the shift from melancholia to mourning as theorized by Freud. Take, for example, Cobb's ambiguous feelings towards the (lost) object of Mal, which is expressed as the inevitable consequence of his estrangement from their children.

Though *Inception* stresses Cobb's final decision to embrace the possibility of reuniting with his children during the film's conclusion, the incremental revelations surrounding his wife's suicide reveal that his attachment to Mal or rather *his* fantasmatic *image* of her, is where the film's underlying attempt to represent the structure of the traumatic experience can be found. Here, the phrase 'his fantasmatic image of her' requires an explanation because we do not actually witness Mal in the film's diegetic 'reality'. Instead, we are restricted to Cobb's memory or unconscious projection of her. As such, here the term 'fantasmatic' refers to the notion that her individual subjectivity is effectively rendered devoid of individual meaning beyond Cobb's perception of her. This is particularly problematic when considered in relation to Arthur's (Joseph Gordon-Levitt) statement when asked what Mal was like 'in real life' as he simply replies, 'She was lovely'. This is a striking contrast to Cobb's projection of Mal as a spectre who haunts his dreams and casts further doubt onto the true nature of his character. As the projection of Mal is an exclusive product of Cobb's own subjectivity and therefore an extension of his own ego, an understanding of trauma in the film emerges through the lens of desire. In *Inception*, Cobb's unconscious desire is expressed through Mal's repeated attempts to lure him away from 'reality' which, according to the logic of the film, represent *his* own unconscious and ultimately narcissistic desire to sustain the memory of her or at least *his* subjective version of her. Here, as Todd McGowan notes, the film exhibits a sophisticated awareness of the distinction between the object that causes desire and the object that one desires or what Lacan refers to as the *objet a* and the object of desire (2012: 167). In Chapter 4, this distinction proved to be useful when examining the role of another dead wife in *The Prestige*. Here, we can apply it to Cobb's wife in *Inception* to understand the repetition of desire and object loss linked to traumatic memories.

McGowan says that the goal of the heist, in both in the typical heist film and in *Inception*, is the object of desire. In contrast, he says the object-cause of desire is the barrier to this object, which is only maintained when what is desired remains inaccessible. In effect, desire is not stimulated by the object that the subject seeks but rather, by the obstacle that prevents the subject from obtaining it. McGowan remarks, '[t]hroughout the film, Mal plays the part of the obstacle that prevents any realization of Cobb's desire, but the film reveals that the obstacle is the real object' (2012: 167). Cobb's deferred return to his children foregrounds the true nature of his desire, which manifests in the continued repetition of actions associated with his role in Mal's death. Indeed, the memory of Mal's suicide is repeatedly acted out throughout the film by Cobb to perpetuate his memory of her, but also as an indicator of his own narcissistic desire to discover a meaningful way of working-through his own role in her death. The portrayal of Cobb's grief recalls Freud's suggestion that the melancholic introjects traces of the lost-object thereby preserving it within the ego where it is subject to a pathological form of self-punishment ([1917] 2001: 246). Or to put it another way, the subject is seemingly unable to relinquish the lost-object and so internalizes aspects of the other so that the ego itself becomes the cause of self-reproach.

In this respect, Cobb's paranoia and suicidal thoughts evidenced through-out *Inception* are indicative of the melancholic's response to trauma through the internalization of aspects attached to his memory of Mal. Consequently, without necessarily debating the merits of the various interpretations as to whether Cobb re-enters the real world or not, his alleged return to 'reality' during the film's climactic moments represents a shift from the position of melancholia to mourning as his reunification with their children is dependent on his ability to work-through the unconscious trauma and achieve what Tammy Clewell, referring to the work of Freud, calls a decisive and "spontaneous end"' (2004: 44). In contrast, however, Lisa K. Perdigao suggests that Cobb is 'ultimately unable to achieve the "spontaneous end" of grief that Freud describes' (2015: 120). She foregrounds the shared connec-tions between Cobb and the character of Leonard Shelby (Guy Pearce) in *Memento* arguing that they both engage in a form of 'hyperremembering' (2015: 120), a term she borrows from Clewell that describes a type of 'obsessive recollection during which the survivor resuscitates the existence of the lost other in the space of the psyche, replacing an actual absence with an imaginary presence' (2004: 44). For Perdigao, these characters are unable to successfully complete the process of grieving and so, 'indefinitely (and perhaps infinitely) become lost in a process of hyperremembering, sustaining a hyperreality that they, and the viewers, cannot escape' (2015: 121). This is nowhere more visible than during the film's ending, which highlights Cobb's predicament, as many argue, without providing the kind of closure anticipated within mainstream cinema – does Cobb return home to his children or is he forever trapped within the closed loop of grief?

An Elegant Solution for Keeping Track of Reality:
The Meaning of the Totem

Even though *Inception* continually invokes the memories of Cobb's deceased wife and the moment he was forced to abandon his children[2] – moments that manifest in the form of unmarked flashbacks, a sense of paranoia and Cobb's unrelenting confusion about what constitutes reality – the question of how to distinguish between reality and the dream-world within the film has frequently been emphasized by numerous commentators and scholars. The use of a 'totem' potentially provides some clarity regarding the boundaries between the interior dreamscape and the physical reality by reflecting a singularity known only to the character and in Cobb's case, the spectator. Take for example Arthur's totem, a loaded die that will only function according to his knowledge of the object's correct balance and weight. Ariadne (Ellen Page) recognizes that the totem represents 'an elegant solution for keeping track of reality'; however, this simple key to understanding the distinction between the character's waking perceptions and the dream world is problematized by Arthur's explanation which reveals that 'when you look at your totem, you know beyond a doubt that you're not in *someone else's dream*'. His description of how the totem functions indicate that the dreamer may be able to determine that they are 'not in someone else's dream' but this does little to ensure that they are not in their own dream, thus complicating a straightforward determination of whether a character exists within a dream or reality. The totem then, much like the meaning of 'Rosebud' in *Citizen Kane* (1941), is merely a cinematic signifier that provides an underlying structure for the film designed to place the spectator in the position of being guided by the desire for knowledge. The mystery of what constitutes a dream and what is reality is perhaps nowhere more explicit than in the film's final moments, which foregrounds the enigma.

Having successfully navigated the various dream layers of Fischer's mind, Cobb finally returns home to his children and takes out his totem – a small pewter cone once belonging to Mal – leaving it spinning on the table. According to the logic put forward by the film, in a dream, the top never falls whereas if it does, Cobb can conclude that he is awake, but this logic is a drastic oversimplification.[3] Seeing their faces, he turns away from the top as it continues to spin. A momentary wobble precipitates its fall but, before we can be sure of its downfall, the screen cuts to black failing to provide a firm conclusion in its final frame. The significance of this final scene for fans, critics and scholars in many ways returns us to the ending of *The Prestige* in which Cutter (Michael Caine) reprises his explanation of what elements constitute the structure of a magic trick. He says, 'Now you're looking for the secret, but you won't find it because, of course, you're not really looking. You don't really want to work it out. You want to be fooled'. Not only does Cutter's speech point towards an implicit level of interaction between Nolan and the spectator, more than this, it also foregrounds the spectator's willingness to invest in the fundamentally illusory nature of the fiction presented.

It would appear that for Nolan, we 'want to be fooled' as these moments, whether manifested in the mystery of a magic trick or the unknowability of Cobb's fate, provide a temporary liberation from the experience of lack inherent in being thus providing the spectator with a short-lived flight from reality or what McGowan refers to as the 'monotony of being' (2012: 107). However, Nolan is seemingly aware that the experience of transcendence comes at a price, which is often at the expense of a truth, something his films attempt to reveal. In both films, this truth resides not, for example, in the mystery of Tesla's (David Bowie) machine or in the fate of Cobb's spinning top, but rather in understanding that these puzzles are a form of misdirection that distracts the spectator from comprehending the truth. The truth of Nolan's films is not the diegetic events as they happen but rather the spectator's investment in the falsity of these events or as Will Brooker puts it, 'the answer to *Inception*'s key question, "whose subconscious are we going through, exactly?" – or simply put, *whose mind is it anyway?* – is always Nolan himself. His real trick is that we cared about the trick at all' (2015: xii, original emphasis). Likewise, McGowan points out:

> The great controversy over the ending of *Inception* is yet another one of Nolan's deceptions. The deception does not consist in making us think that Cobb has returned to the real world when in fact he hasn't, but in making the question of the reality of the final scene appear as if it is a – or the – central point of the film'.
> (McGowan 2012: 168)

Read in this manner, the film deceives the spectator by appearing to emphasize the importance of the distinction between the dream and reality when, in truth its real focus is *'the subject's relationship to trauma*, a relationship that the dream often facilitates and reality enables us to avoid' (McGowan 2012: 150, emphasis added).

The possibility put forward by the film's ending that Cobb can recover what was lost by working-through the meaning of the traumatic signifier subtly demonstrates what McGowan perceives to be the underlying message of the film, which presents reality or consciousness as a retreat from trauma. He notes:

> Reality provides solace because it has the effect of insulating us from our desire, while the dream demands that we follow the logic of this desire, no matter how traumatic its revelations might be. One wakes in order to avoid encountering the truth of one's desire manifested in the dream.
> (McGowan 2012: 150)

However, what McGowan is seemingly reluctant to acknowledge is the possibility that the encounter with trauma within a dream can function in such a way as to lay the foundations for *attempting* to work-through our relationship to the traumatic experience in reality. As the final sequence in *Inception* suggests with its focus on what was originally Mal's totem, the moment that Cobb turns away from the spinning top is the moment that, regardless of whether he exists in the dream or 'reality', he re-translates the memory of his role in her suicide with the reconciliation offered by working-through the traumatic experience. In contrast, McGowan notes that:

> Cobb works to do away with the traumatic repressed idea. He fills the space of this idea with another idea that is more palatable for the subject, an idea that the subject will no longer choose to forget. He is a psychologist who believes that he can cure repression, but his cure demands an incredible amount of psychic violence [...]. Even Ariadne has a horrified look when Cobb reveals that he performed inception on Mal and gave her the idea that led to her suicide.
> (McGowan 2012: 161)

Implicit in this act is Cobb's relinquishment of the memories associated with his wife's death and his attachment to the deceased, but as Mark Fisher points out, '[g]rief itself is a puzzle that can't be solved' (2011: 42) (see also Perdigao 2015: 120–31). Fisher goes on to note that Nolan's decision to collapse the figure of Mal, the antagonist of the film, with the object of grief functions to highlight the subject's experience of grief which, as he points out, 'isn't only about mourning for the lost object, it's also about struggling against the object's implacable *refusal* to let go' (2011: 42, emphasis added). Where McGowan and Fisher argue that *Inception* positions the grieving subject in a state of arrested development, I am arguing that the film's narrative communicates the transformative possibilities of acting-out and working-through trauma using a fictional reality. That the final shot emphasizes the ontological uncertainty of Cobb's return merely diverts the spectator's attention away from where the message of the film resides. Those spectators who invest themselves in the fate of the spinning top fail to realize that this is not where the message of the film lies. Instead, Nolan invites the spectator to reflect on the way that dreams function as a window to our unconscious desires which, while often the source of potentially traumatic neurosis, are frequently a path towards working-through the traumatic experience. To this end, it seems to me that what Nolan expresses in *Inception* is the close connection between our dreams and the cinema, a relationship that is dependent on our willingness in both arenas to project our innermost traumatic desires in the hope of finding a means to articulate them in such a way that affords us the ability to overcome them.

The Dream Factory

In many ways, Cobb's desire to repeatedly replay his role in his wife's death within the dreamscape evokes a broader consideration of the fundamental link between dreams and the cinema. Like the dream, the screen functions as a space on to which the subject can project their innermost traumatic fantasies and unconscious desires. Just as the dream facilitates Cobb's ability to act-out his own fantasmatic narrative in the fictional space, when viewing a film, the spectator is also encouraged to abandon their complicity with the social and moral codes of society in favour of playing out their own desire. In the same way that our dreams function to allow us to express our innermost desires without apparent reproach, so too does the cinema screen. Ian Alan Paul writes:

> Just as Cobb's dream-spaces are affected by his subjectivity, the space of the theatre is in many ways also the space of our own desires and subjectivities. In a dark room, the audience experiences the light of the projector presenting them with images and realities in an analogous way to how the characters in the film themselves dream. We are allowed to live experiences that are completely virtual both through our entanglement with the production of the film as well as through our innate desire to create and connect.
>
> (Paul 2010)

This meditation on the role of fantasy in the construction of individual subjectivity is reliant on a structure of 'fetishistic disavowal' or what the French psychoanalyst and student of Lacan, Octave Mannoni refers to as 'I know very well, but all the same' ([1969] 2003: 68). The individual knows that what they experience to be real is false, but they choose to believe it anyway or, to paraphrase the film's own expression, it is the truth they once knew but chose to forget.

In *Inception*, the film's ending shows that Cobb's (and the spectator's) experience relies on an act of fetishistic disavowal. His decision to abandon the spinning top is a testament to Cobb's willingness to disregard the possibility that he might still be dreaming in favour of reconciling with his family. Similarly, the spectator knows that the film is merely a play of light and shadows meaning that even if Cobb is, diegetically speaking, still dreaming, the top will inevitably fall after the cut to black because the spectator is experiencing a finite fictional narrative (see Olson 2015: 54). Nevertheless, they overlook this truth in the same way that Cobb does so that they can be wilfully duped by the diegetic reality that the film presents in favour of the therapeutic effect that the medium can provide. In this regard, Nolan provides a commentary on the connection between films and dreams by implicitly suggesting that the individual gains pleasure from the inherent gaps between what they perceive and what they imagine. As such, progressing through the various spatiotemporal layers of *Inception* entails filling these gaps. Paul remarks that:

> The structure of *Inception*, and perhaps the structure of all film, already implies an involvement on the part of the audience in the process of producing the story.

Through the use of the cut in editing and of various compressions in space and time, the mind of the viewer is always in a state of filling in the gaps. As we move between the different spaces and times of the plot, our own mind is generating arcing logics and filling in details in an attempt to create a cohesive whole. Through this process of production we are indeed making, as characters remind us several times throughout the film, a 'leap of faith' in order to make the film complete.

(Paul 2010)

This task extends beyond the diegesis because the cinematic experience does not end with the closing credits. Rather, in keeping with Paul Sutton's psychoanalytic conception of *afterwardsness* discussed in Chapter 3, the spectator subsequently possesses a 'remade and remembered' version of the film later constructed from memory (2004: 386). Like the subject's recall of the past, the spectator's mental image of a film evokes that which is no longer present and imbues it – albeit retrospectively – with a renewed significance resulting in the reconfiguration of the subject's sense of self and identity (see Sutton 2004).

At the level of the diegesis, Cobb's attempted re-translation of his role in his wife's death is perhaps the clearest iteration of the process of *afterwardsness*. Notably, Cobb's recollection and subsequent reworking of his memories through the active fantasy of reconciliation facilitate the revision of his own identity as a paternal figure of authority. Within this model, the structure of *afterwardsness* describes a notion of subjective composition whereby identity is positioned as a state of 'constantly becoming' enabling the individual to come into being through a continual process of bringing memories into the present (see Bergson [1911] 1983: 298–344). This negotiation of the self is therefore played out in relation to an understanding of time that is constructed from subjective experience. For instance, in his analysis of time, Henri Bergson contends that there are two models of duration: 'homogeneous' and 'heterogeneous' ([1889] 1910: 237). Where the former refers to a quantitative measurement of time, the latter refers to our experience of time as subjective and organic, varying from moment to moment. Bergson stresses that 'heterogeneous' time is irreducible to 'homogeneous' time by placing a particular emphasis on *durée*, that is, an individual identity obtained over the passage of time. Bergson argues that this experience of 'becoming' cannot be captured through isolated moments of time but is visible when considered as part of a wider continuum of experience.[4] The present moment then, and by extension, our enduring sense of self, emerges in relation to a *subjective* reality constructed from the cumulative experience of the past rather than one that is in any way *objective* according to an ontological criterion of value. What this means is that our identity and our experience of *a* 'reality' is, in large part, determined by our willingness to emotionally invest in what we subjectively perceive to be 'real' often despite our awareness to the contrary.

In *Inception*, Cobb can reshape and reinterpret the past in a way that facilitates his return to *a* subjective 'reality', and he takes this 'reality' to be the real world because he is able to see his children's faces. But, as McGowan points out, their faces are 'no more an assurance of reality than the totem' (2012: 169). Instead, Cobb's belief in his children's faces as a guarantor of 'reality' is predicated on an act of fetishistic disavowal in that the successful working-through of the traumatic signifier and the ensuing transition from a state of melancholia to one of mourning is contingent on the construction of a redeemed vision of his identity as a 'good' father. According to Nicola Rehling, this reinstatement of paternal authority is consistent with the increasing prominence of the relegitimization of traditional ideals surrounding fatherhood that is a response to a time of heightened anxiety in contemporary culture and society. She writes:

> In the last few decades, fears about how absent fathers damage their children have been endlessly articulated in the U.S. and British media, as well as neo-conservative and neo-liberal political rhetoric, with the supposition that only a restoration of paternal authority will heal male pain and, by extension, the ailing social body.
>
> (Rehling 2009: 61)

Notable examples of this type of film include *Road to Perdition* (2002), *Finding Nemo* (2003), *The Day After Tomorrow* (2004), *War of the Worlds* (2005), *Taken* (2008) and *Man of Steel* (2013). In these films, the threat posed to paternalism is not rendered as a radical opportunity to overhaul the associated oppressive ideology of patriarchy, but rather as the frightening loss of stability and protection alongside a nostalgic longing for the past. Therefore, these films frequently envisage a return to traditional conceptions of fatherhood through men who are redeemed by their ability to sacrifice themselves for others or, alternatively, can re-establish both patriarchal law and order via traditionalist and regressive forms of male violence (see also Hamad 2011: 249–50).

In *Inception*, the loss of paternalism is negotiated by Cobb who sacrifices his own desire to sustain the idealized projection of his own wife in favour of returning to his children. These paternal issues are paralleled by Cobb's attempted inception of Fischer, which also seeks to reconcile a father-son relationship through deception. For Fischer, the traumatic signifier is exposed as the failure of paternal love when it is revealed that the last word his father said to him on his deathbed was 'disappointed'. Fischer interprets this remark as his father's final statement of rejection believing that he had failed to live up to his high expectations. However, during the film's climax, Cobb re-translates this memory imbuing it with a new (albeit false) meaning by literalizing an aspect taken from one of Fischer's most cherished childhood memories, in which he and his father shared the enjoyment of playing with a homemade pinwheel. The significance of this memory to Fischer is revealed when his father accidentally breaks a framed photograph capturing the moment and when Eames (Tom Hardy) later discovers the same photo in Fischer's wallet. Despite its obvious importance to Fischer, he tells his godfather 'Uncle Peter' (Tom Berenger) that the photo and, by extension the moment, is not significant to his father as he was the one to put the framed photo beside his bed. Consequently, when the pinwheel is revealed to be contained inside his father's safe at the lowest level of Fischer's unconscious, it obtains a (false) measure of significance through the implicit suggestion that it was a memory that his father also valued. This (false) revelation cements the idea that Fischer was not a disappointment, allowing him to work-through his unresolved issues with his father and adopt an identity divorced from the image of his father.

Fischer's reconciliation with his father is ultimately a false reconciliation represents a fundamental rejection of his own identity. McGowan, for instance, suggests that Fischer's (false) reconciliation with his father is a betrayal of himself that foreshadows Cobb's own reunion with his children at the end of the film (2012: 163). In this sense, it subtly points towards the inherent unreliability of any resolution that the film presents. By reuniting with his father Fischer is betrayed by a false idea that not only contradicts his best financial interests but also undermines his own agency through the successful falsification of a meaningful emotional bond, which subsequently forms the basis for his renewed sense of self. Equally, Cobb's decision to abandon the melancholic state that has preserved his wife within his unconscious emerges from his investment in a certain image of himself as a father and as such, the supreme figure of paternal authority. This process of self-(re) formation then relies on the subject's willingness to (re)constitute their identity based on a fiction which, as we have seen, can contain memories of experiences that are subject to continued revision and even knowing falsification. This becomes visible not only at the level of the diegesis through the act of inception itself but also in terms of the spectator's engagement with the film.

In *Inception*, the relationship between the spectator and the film is indicative of what John Beebe, a psychiatrist and practising analytical psychologist, considers to be a more general perception that 'there are films which induce an unexpected new consciousness in many who view them [...] in addition to wanting to be entertained, the mass audience is in a constant pursuit, as if on a religious quest, of the transformative film' (1996: 582). For Beebe, cinema is, therefore, an important catalyst for change providing stimulation for growth, transformation and the process of individuation in which self-development can occur. However, what these accounts do not take into consideration, and what *Inception* foregrounds, is that these experiences are often built upon a false affect that engenders a double bind making us think or feel two things at once ('I know very well, but all the same'), while at the same time exerting a fascination with the fiction that ensnares our attention and in many cases alters our identity. In their essay on narrative, myth and psychology in *Batman Begins*, *The Dark Knight* and *Inception*, Krešimir Vukovic and Rajko Petkovic emphasize this process in the latter; they note:

> Nolan warns that what we take for granted is often fictitious, but it is fiction that has the power to affect our emotions and identity on an unconscious level that we tend to ignore. The act of inception affects not Fischer, but *us* as viewers as *we* let *our* minds be shaped by a fictitious reality, whether that of dreams or films.
>
> (Vukovic and Petkovic 2013)

What Nolan reveals in *Inception* is the broader interaction between the spectator and the film, which extends beyond the internal structural logic and thematic emphasis on working-through the past to understand the present. From the psychoanalytic perspective, what the film offers is a self-reflexive commentary on the interplay between fictions, whether that may be films or dreams and reality. Just as dreams lay the foundation for subsequently working-through the traumatic experience, film provides us with a dream-world that we, as spectators, utilize to help us work-through or navigate our day-to-day experience of reality.

Inception, therefore, communicates a type of spectatorship based on the experience of what Joseph Bevan in his article for *Sight and Sound* refers to as an 'escapist entertainment' built on the blurred lines between fiction and metafiction (2012).[5] It is here, at this amorphous boundary that Bevan draws attention to the transformative aspects of Nolan's films noting that, '[he] seems to suggest that it's a human being's ability to fictionalise himself – to practise a performative morality, to make themselves into whatever they need to be – that redeems them' (2012). For Bevan, this redemption involves a choice that recognizes the priority of falsity in the process of individuation, he says: 'In *Inception*, Cobb's renunciation of his dream inamorata is a choice between one lie and what might possibly be a further lie: the catharsis of the unification with his children' (2012). Elsewhere, McGowan convincingly argues that Nolan's entire film catalogue is dependent upon various forms of deceit but more recently he has suggested that the false hero, a figure who ends up betraying the spectator's confidence, is at the heart of what he considers to be Nolan's central filmmaking project of depicting the primacy of the false (2015). Referring to *Inception*, McGowan remarks, 'the spectator invests in the quest by hero Cobb to return to his children only to discover that this quest is itself deceptive' (2015: 172). In doing so, 'the film uses the falsity of Cobb and his quest to highlight the psychic priority of the false world of dreams for the *divided subject*' (2015: 172, emphasis added).

Given that Cobb's identity is fundamentally split at the level of the diegesis, his projection of Mal is at once a manifestation of his role in her death and, by extension, the barrier that prevents him from attaining a (false) sense of unity. Cobb's return to reality, then, is reminiscent of the way that cinema enacts the spectator's desire for wholeness. This process involves, for Christian Metz, an engagement with two systems of identification: primary and secondary. Where the former refers to the spectator's identification with the look of the technical apparatus (i.e. camera, projector), the latter refers to the way that the spectator projects their own ego onto the on-screen while, at the same time, introjecting character representations within the psyche of oneself (1982: 49, 56). In effect, according to Metz, the experience of watching a film is a continual process of projection-introjection or presence-absence (1982: 48–53). The oscillating mechanisms of projection and introjection begin in early infancy, but continue to be enacted through the subject's broader relationship to society and culture including art, literature and the media (see Wright 1984: 80–104). Consequently, in *Inception*, where Cobb functions as the primary point of identification for the spectator, his decision to abandon the unconscious projection of Mal in favour of his return to 'reality' not only permits the reconstitution of his identity as a father at the level of the diegesis but also temporarily satiates the spectator's desire for wholeness and fulfills the spectator's quest for some profound meaning. In this way, cinema offers the spectator the illusion of overcoming the inherent lack in being that determines their relations to others as well as the self by framing the object of desire (in this case a unified self) as being attainable. However, as has been argued earlier in Chapter 4, desire is never satisfied and so the lack in the subject remains – something that cinema exploits and Nolan indulges with the cinematic signifier of the spinning top. Given this context, Cobb's ability to work-through the continued repetition of the memories associated with his role in Mal's death potentially represents a fundamental betrayal of his desire to act out her presence at the expense of his ability to achieve a sense of wholeness which of course is not possible since wholeness, for Lacan, is illusory (1977d: 1–7).

Broadly speaking, what cinema permits is the spectator's willingness to invest in the possibility of transcending the inherent division that confronts the subject, a division that according to Lacan, returns the subject to the trauma of its emergence. In doing so, the spectator can – albeit *temporarily* – occupy a position of fantasmatic completeness. In contrast and in keeping with Nolan's other films, *Inception* reveals that the truth of the subject's existence becomes visible because of the fundamental role that the traumatic experience plays in the constitution of our identity, rather than despite it. However, when Cobb turns his back on the memory of Mal he overcomes the traumatic kernel within his unconscious at the expense of a temporary experience of wholeness that reneges on his true desire to sustain her presence. This moment is the exact moment when Nolan also turns away from his previous representation of trauma as, unlike his other protagonists who are either forced to sacrifice themselves or remain caught in a closed structural loop of trauma, Cobb achieves the catharsis that he so desperately seeks. Yet, the film undermines this from the spectator's vantage point by choosing to emphasize the spinning top as a guarantor of reality. Nevertheless, the fictional spaces of cinema and dreams are important to Nolan's films because, as divided subjects, we crave the restoration of wholeness that would make it possible to overcome or transcend the experience of loss. Where cinema exploits this relationship by perpetually deferring the spectator's desire, Nolan's cinema foregrounds it by demonstrating that it is only through the fantasy of completion that one can become aware of the enjoyment that the falsity of the fiction provides. In the context of classical cinema narration, it is our investment as spectators in the fictional story that sustains our desire to fill the lack and establish a unified self. However, Nolan's films undermine this logic by revealing the falsity of the fiction and the necessity of this falsity for the enjoyment of his films. He does so, not by overtly drawing our attention to the cinematic apparatus, but rather by embracing the spectator's willingness to be deceived – to question whether the top keeps spinning – to subsequently reveal the reasons for this deception. As a result, the truth emerges through the false or to use the film's own terminology 'the dream has become their reality'.

NOTES

1. An act which, paradoxically, conforms to the logic of reality despite maintaining the belief that she exists only in the dream-world.

2. In *Inception*, Nolan's thematic preoccupation with loss is alluded to from the outset in a scene in which Cobb momentarily visualizes his children in limbo. This fleeting image of James and Phillipa is a recurrent motif throughout the film that reflects the guilt he feels for abandoning them as a result of his involvement in Mal's death. As such, the images of his children are an indexical sign – an emanation of the past – which retrospectively points towards the repressed trauma of his wife's suicide thereby immersing the spectator in the specific temporal configuration of *après-coup* discussed in detail in Chapter 2. These brief shots of Cobb's children function according to the logic of *après-coup* because the imagery of his children is not explained until a much later point in the film. Therefore, the meaning of their appearances emerges through a process of retroactive resignification.

3. Firstly, as Cobb's totem originally belonged to Mal it lacks a specific attachment to him, which Arthur explains is necessary for the totem to operate successfully. Secondly, as Cobb explained to Ariadne how his (Mal's) totem works it is subject to further possible manipulation. Thirdly, as I have already pointed out, the totem's behaviour cannot tell Cobb whether or not he is dreaming but rather, whether or not he is in someone else's dream.

4. Anders Bergstrom points out that Cobb's experience of 'becoming' is restricted, in part, due to his preference to dwell in the past upon images of his dead wife (2013: 206–07).

5. *Inception's* metafictional references mean that it can also be situated within a certain theory of the postmodern for which the concepts of pastiche and intertextuality are of central importance (see Dyer 2006). In particular, Richard Dyer argues that the very essence of pastiche is its 'knowing imitation' of both culturally and historically recognizable texts (2006: 3). He notes that it 'imitates other art in such a way as to make consciousness of this fact central to its meaning and affect', thereby exposing a certain degree of complicity with its audience that is evident in Nolan's own filmmaking practises. Take, for example, the gravity defying set-pieces that occur during the middle of the Cobb's mission. Nolan readily admits that these scenes are indebted to Stanley Kubrick's *2001: A Space Odyssey* (1968) and equally, in the final third of Inception, Cobb's assault on a snow-covered fortress unmistakably pays homage to *On Her Majesty's Secret Service* (1969) (see Jolin 2010: 92). In this way, the spectator's encounter with *Inception* is a multifaceted interaction with a number of other pre-existing narratives that foregrounds a relationship with the past which extends beyond the present moment. This is while, at the same time, Nolan re-writes or re-translates the spectator's memories of these instants in light of new contexts. Or, as Carlos Gutiérrez-Jones puts it, 'the audience is able to successfully navigate *Inception* at the height of its narrative complexity by tapping its own memories of mediascapes that are being overwritten by Nolan' (2015: 113).

Beyond the Void: *Interstellar* and the Possibility of Post-Traumatic Growth

We've always defined ourselves by the ability to overcome the impossible.

– Cooper, *Interstellar*

There is a scene in *Interstellar* when Cooper (Matthew McConaughey) admits to his 10-year-old daughter Murph (Mackenzie Foy/Jessica Chastain/Ellen Burstyn) that he has no idea when he will return from his mission to find a new habitable planet which can sustain human life. She begs him to stay but he nevertheless resists and instead tries to comfort her as she cries. Eventually, though, she turns away from him in anger thereby forcing him to leave when their relationship is at its most strained. Later in the film, this emotional scene is returned to and repeated albeit from a different vantage point as Cooper watches the same events unfold whilst trapped in a space created within a black hole. This moment, which seems to represent the literal incarnation of an out-of-body experience akin to those felt during a traumatic event (see Spiegel and Cardeña 1991), is clearly significant for Cooper as it is only one of a handful to evoke a strong emotional reaction during its repetition. Even though Cooper is not able to change the past, he is subsequently able to re-translate its meaning in line with possibilities of 'working-through' (Freud [1914] 1958) trauma discussed in the previous chapter. What is significant about this scene is that the focus on the experience of trauma remains a fundamental aspect of Nolan's filmmaking, evident even here in a $165 million budget Hollywood blockbuster (Box Office Mojo 2016). Given this emphasis, it would be natural to consider *Interstellar* as a continuation of Nolan's thematic interests as trauma and loss remain central to the narrative. However, *Interstellar* also develops a strain of sentimentality and melodrama that emerges at the end of *Inception*, *The Dark Knight Rises* and, to a lesser extent, *The Prestige*, which all place a noticeable emphasis on romantic or familial unions indicating a variation on the type of approach taken towards trauma evident in his previous films. In those films listed, trauma and loss function as catalysts for the characters' positive changes and growth, whereas in Nolan's preceding films the repetitive nature of the traumatic experience often correlates to each film's structural organization and thematic concerns as well as presenting characters who frequently remain caught in a cycle of repetition. While *Interstellar* remains thematically in keeping with Nolan's interest in trauma with its focus on an absent father who chooses to abandon his children, in other ways the film has a contradictory relationship with his filmmaking to date as it rejects the atemporal formal structures that are so central to his depiction of trauma elsewhere. The purpose of this chapter is to explore the filmmaker's approach to trauma in *Interstellar* with an emphasis on what I perceive to be Nolan's growing embrace of melodrama, which itself shares a longstanding connection with psychoanalysis.

The link between melodrama and psychoanalysis was first established by Thomas Elsaesser in his influential article 'Tales of sound and fury: Observations on the family melodrama' ([1972] 1991: 68–91). In it, he suggested that melodrama, particularly those films produced in Hollywood during the 1940s, could be analysed using Freud's *The Psychopathology of Everyday Life* and his work on dreams (Freud [1972] 1991: 82). He argued that melodrama could be read as a fundamental critique of middle-class American society produced by the combination of stylistic elements related to *mise-en-scène* including colour, costume, music, camera, lighting, performance and the rhythmic qualities of everyday speech which expose subversive elements and internal contradictions within the social order. Following Elsaesser, Peter Brooks argued that the Freudian concepts of repression and the return of the repressed are embedded into the melodramatic form which externalizes the complex psychic conflicts that are entrenched within what he termed the 'moral occult' ([1976] 1995: 5). For Brooks, the moral occult was analogous to Freud's unconscious where our 'most basic desires and interdictions lie' ([1976] 1995: 5). Melodrama, then, according to Brooks, is the result of the encounter between our instinctual impulses and the necessarily repressive nature of the social order.

Moving the discussion away from the formative influence of those Hollywood films produced during the 1940s and 1950s, a number of feminist scholars have since expanded the definitions within which melodrama has been traditionally understood by providing a historical framework that outlines the development of melodrama while, at the same time, foregrounding the issues of female identity, representation and spectatorship in Hollywood cinema (see Mulvey 1978; Creed 1978; Brunsdon 1982). Writing in 1987, Christine Gledhill considered the inter-related cultural, historical, ideological and aesthetic dimensions of melodrama to argue that, prior to the renewed interest in those films produced during the 1940s and 1950s, critics had typically referred to melodrama in the pejorative sense (1987: 5). A fundamental tenet of such criticism was not only that melodrama lacked the cultural value and intellectual legitimacy of either tragedy or realism, but that its broadly defined appeal to women undermined its critical worth. For Gledhill, one of the most significant areas of research for feminist film scholars lay in contesting the view that the term melodrama only applied to women's films and female audiences (1987: 12–13). Largely influenced by Gledhill, in her seminal article 'Melodrama revisited', Linda Williams proposed a distinction between melodrama as a genre addressing a predominantly female spectatorship (see Elsaesser [1972] 1991), from melodrama as a more expansive mode – one that she considers to be the dominant form of American cinema (1998: 42). By positioning melodrama as the dominant narrative mode of storytelling in popular American culture, Williams not only liberates it from the confines of a certain historical period, she also expands the criteria for recognizing the constituent elements of what she considers to be the melodramatic mode. Williams identifies five defining features of melodrama. First, she proposes that melodrama 'begins, and wants to end, in a space of innocence'; second, melodrama 'focuses on victim-heroes and on recognizing their virtue. Recognition of virtue orchestrates the moral legibility that is key to melodrama's function'; third, melodrama 'borrows from realism but realism serves the melodramatic passion and action'; fourth, melodrama 'involves a dialectic of pathos and action – a give and take of "too late" and "in the nick of time"' and fifth, melodrama presents 'characters who embody primary psychic roles organized in Manichean conflicts between good and evil' (1998: 65–77).[1]

Implicit in Williams's reading of melodrama is the psychoanalytic perspective that underpins much of her work taken elsewhere (see Williams 1991, 2000, 2001). For instance, echoing Sigmund Freud ([1930] 1961c: 36), she suggests that in melodrama the longing to return a space of innocence can be coded in terms of a regressive desire to return to the body of the mother (Williams 1991: 10–11).[2] Freud's famous observation in *Civilization and Its Discontents* that the house can be considered 'a substitute for the womb – one's first dwelling, probably still longed for' ([1930] 1961c: 36), finds a significant parallel in melodramatic narratives which frequently draw attention to the notion of the home as a maternal space. As Williams notes, melodrama is 'often suffused with nostalgia for rural and maternal origins that are forever lost yet – hope against hope – refound, reestablished or, if permanently lost, sorrowfully lamented' (1998: 65). One can argue that the maternal origins that Williams refers to in her work does not manifest itself in *Interstellar* as a distinct motherly presence but rather in the form of planet Earth. In the film, it is the failure of Earth to sustain human life and Cooper's necessary search for a new habitable home planet that can be perhaps interpreted as the ultimate form of primal separation. Indeed, given that the Earth is commonly regarded as the fundamental source of all life it should come as no surprise that such a diverse range of cultures have made the connection between the maternal aspects associated with women's birthing capabilities and 'mother' nature (see Eaton 2006: 1110). Nonetheless, whether Williams's notion of maternal origins is conceptualized in relation to a biological woman or through the Earth's symbolic imbrication with the female, her argument clearly shares a lineage with past psychoanalytic discourses relating to the significance of maternal loss and its impact upon the formation of the subject (see also Schur 1953; Arlow 1963). This obsession can be more broadly linked to narrative cinema as a quest for the 'lost-object' and pervades the film throughout.

Interstellar is, according to Jacqueline Furby, fundamentally concerned with negotiating loss on a number of levels (2015: 253). In addition to the Earth's inability to provide for its inhabitants, she also suggests that several of the relationships that form the emotional and ideological centre of the film also orbit around loss linked to the failure of paternity. For instance, Cooper abandons his children and may not be able to keep his promise to return; Professor Brand (Michael Caine) lies to his daughter Amelia (Anne Hathaway) and sends her into space knowing that he will never see her again; and Cooper's son Tom (Casey Affleck) is unable to raise his first child who dies most likely as a result of the cancer that similarly effects his second born. Elsewhere, as Furby notes, even the poem 'Do Not Go Gentle into That Good Night' (Thomas [1939] 1971), which is quoted periodically throughout the film, is also concerned with negotiating loss. Perhaps nowhere is loss more evident than in Nolan's approach towards time in *Interstellar*, which he perceives to be the film's central antagonist (Nolan cited in Mitchell 2014). Fittingly, in her discussion of pathos and action, Williams refers to the importance of time and the inescapable nature of the past for understanding the melodramatic mode when she writes that most 'melodrama is an expression of feeling toward a time that passes too fast' (1998: 74). Ironically, in *Interstellar* it is the slowing of time that poses the greatest risk to the crew's hopes of saving the people left on Earth for whom, comparatively speaking, time does move too fast. As the crew travel towards potentially habitable planets within another galaxy, their experience of time slows as the gravitational force of a nearby black hole increases. The dilation and contraction of time in these scenes introduces what Furby refers to as a 'race-against-time element' (2015: 251), that is in keeping with Williams's comments regarding the essence of the melodramatic mode which 'seems to rest in those moments of temporal prolongation when "'in the nick of time" defies "too late"' (1998: 69). For Williams, suspense and tension arise in melodrama from the possibility that the hero might not return to save the day before a fixed deadline, a characteristic frequently realized through the formal act of cross-cutting between two or more characters and scenes often in different spatial dimensions. In *Interstellar*, Nolan does utilize parallel editing during the film's final act to compound this tension but, in many ways, it is the crew's encounter on Miller's planet earlier in the film that best demonstrates the temporal dialectic that Williams outlines.

The importance of time is invoked from the outset of the sequence on Miller's planet when Cooper reminds the crew that, due to the relativistic effects of time dilation, one hour spent there equates to seven years back on Earth. When they arrive on the surface, the accompanying non-diegetic score is infused with the sound of numerous clocks ticking at variable speeds further heightening the significance of each second spent on the planet. Given the significance of encountering obstacles in classical Hollywood narrative syntax, the mission predictably goes wrong, and the crew are forced to spend longer than anticipated on the planet. Upon returning to the Endurance spacecraft Cooper fully realizes the dramatic implications of the few hours spent on Miller's planet when the crew calculates that the delay lasted, in Earth time, 23 years and 4 months. Rather than opting to convey the passage of time through conventional editing techniques such as cross-cutting or montage, Nolan instead focuses on Cooper's emotional response to a backlog of recorded messages that have been sent by his family during his absence. Vivian Sobchack notes that:

> The effects on the crew as well as on those at home are made powerfully and poignantly explicit through a series of video communications transmitted to the crew from Earth. Over a dilated and hence brief period of time on the ship, to a crew that looks much as they did when they boarded, the videos from home show what seem to be rapidly aging loved ones [...] all of whom report on family illnesses, deaths both natural (Cooper's father-in-law) and cancerous (Cooper's young grandson), and increasing terrestrial misery.
>
> (Sobchack 2014)

The recognition of lost time and actual loss evoked in the video messages as well as by Cooper's emotional reaction to them can be directly linked to Williams's dialectic of pathos and action as, in melodrama, she argues, '[w]hat counts is the feeling of loss suffused throughout the form' (1998: 70). Williams says that, in these films, emotional excess is often derived from grief and pathos is experienced by those characters that are forced to comprehend the 'irreversibility of time' (1998: 69). As Cooper sits watching his son and daughter age over the series of recordings, the camera lingers on his face as he begins to weep uncontrollably. Each video captures a moment in time: his son's transition from adolescence into adulthood, the news of his father-in-law's passing as well as the birth and premature death of his grandson. It is the succession of these moments that encapsulates an overwhelming sense of loss. Williams says that, 'time is the ultimate object of loss' (1998: 69) and it is Cooper's emotional outburst that, while largely in keeping with the typical excess that many critics associate with melodrama (see Nowell-Smith 1977: 113–18; Elsaesser [1972] 1991; Brooks [1976] 1995: 11–12), represents his reluctant acceptance of the relentlessness of time's arrow.

As Williams convincingly argues, the temporal structure of melodrama is intimately bound to the forward march of time in which characters strive to reunite with loved ones prior to an imposed deadline (1998: 69). From this dialectic, a tension arises that is strong enough to elicit a somatic response of tears from the spectator, which is often mirrored by the characters on-screen. Williams argues that 'the precise trigger to crying occurs at the moment when agnition reduces the tension between desire and reality' (1998: 69). She provides the example of a father who is unable to make peace with his dying son before his passing, but it is not difficult to conceive how Cooper's absence from a number of crucial moments in the life cycles of others might function in a similar way. Williams concludes by remarking that, '[t]he tension ends [...] because desire is finally shown to be futile' (1998: 69–70). In other words, we not only cry when the characters cry, we cry when we realize that their desire for reconciliation cannot be realized or, to use Williams's phrasing, 'we cry when something is lost and it cannot be regained' (1998: 69). Temporally speaking, then, melodrama emerges from the tension between fidelity to the past and the movement towards an inevitable future or between continuity and change. Cooper's uneasy acceptance of the unidirectional movement of time becomes increasingly obvious as the film progresses especially when it is revealed that the failed expedition to Miller's planet has cost them 'decades'. At this point, Cooper's immediate response is to desperately seek any means of undoing the past. He says, 'Is there any possibility, some kind of a way we could maybe – I don't know, jump into a black hole, gain back the years?' His desire to somehow alter the course of past events corresponds to what Williams identifies as melodrama's 'larger impulse to reverse time' (1998: 74).

While Cooper's comments might be too literal to be suitable for the purposes of analysis here, it is possible to consider them in relation to Williams's broader proposal that the 'main thrust of melodramatic narrative [...] for all its flurry of apparent linear action, is to get back to the beginning' (1998: 74). Here, Williams is not only referring to the physical or symbolic dimension of the home – what she labels the 'space of innocence' or 'maternal place of origin' (1998: 65), she is also acknowledging a distinct temporal dimension. She returns to this subject in her book about racial melodrama, *Playing the Race Card* (2001), but in the second instance it is not simply a straightforward repetition of the same argument but rather a slight variation of the statement that alters its emphasis from a literal understanding of the 'beginning' as a geographic, symbolic or temporal dimension to one that can be interpreted as being a more generalized understanding of nostalgia. She writes, '[t]he "main thrust" of melodramatic narrative, for all its flurry of apparent linear action, is to get back to', then the texts diverge in phrasing with 'the beginning' replaced by 'what *feels* like the beginning' (2001: 35, original emphasis). The stress that Williams places on the word 'feels' tellingly exposes the impossibility of such a return as well as hinting at the intrinsic loss also associated with it. In doing so, this emphasis draws attention to melodrama's inherent nostalgic preoccupations, which share certain characteristics with trauma including a sense of rupture and discontinuity, the impossibility of a cure, irrecoverable loss and incomplete mourning. Indeed, for Sara R. Horowitz '[s]ince trauma resembles nostalgia in these senses, there is sometimes a slippage between the two' (2010: 49).

There's No Place like Home

In *Interstellar*, nostalgia (from the Greek word *nostos* meaning return home or homecoming and *algia* meaning pain or longing) takes a number of different forms with the most visible being that Nolan's depiction of rural America is steeped in a vision of the United States and American home life framed through the lens of Americana. According to Christine Sarah Steinbock the word Americana, 'evokes a myriad of antique, rustic, and nostalgic associations' (2014: 21). But it is possible to define a common understanding of the term based on its frequent association with American history and traditions (see Whitlow and Krysl 2014: 1). Americana's reverence for the past, a vision of a time when American life was simpler, is embedded throughout *Interstellar* in its depiction of several things related to the United States including the western homestead, pickup trucks and the national pastime of baseball. Elsewhere, the film's underlying thematic lamentation of a pioneering spirit associated with western expansionism is embodied in the characterization of Cooper as a former NASA pilot. At one point in the film, he remarks, 'It's like we've forgotten who we are – explorers, pioneers, not caretakers'. For Cooper, the exhaustion of Earth's resources is not something worth dwelling upon or even striving to remedy. Instead, what he chooses to lament is the loss of a distinctive American identity that is linked to traditions of US expansionism and Manifest Destiny. Cooper's reminisces are therefore in keeping with discourses surrounding westward expansion such as Frederick Jackson Turner's 1893 frontier thesis which linked the emergence of a 'dominant individualism' (1921: 37) in American culture to the pioneer pressures of physical hardship and isolation. He suggested that the 'disappearance of the frontier' (1921: 306) represented a threat to democratic institutions and American identity concluding that overseas expansion was both a necessary and inevitable solution.

Taking this sentiment as a point of departure, the narrative of *Interstellar* is never divorced from this romanticized vision of American identity, albeit one that is paradoxically caught between nostalgic invocations of the past and the benefits of modern technology. This conflict is perhaps nowhere more evident than during a scene that shows Cooper's eventual return home, albeit not to his actual home but rather a simulacral recreation of it built on the space station as a living history museum. The scene begins as Cooper enters the replica of the old farmhouse with a tour guide who innocently remarks, 'Home, sweet home'. While this statement is perhaps intended to be welcoming, it is immediately undercut by the following comment that everything has been 'replaced' and put back where it belongs. There is an irony here in that these remarks draw attention to the disjunctive relationship between Cooper's perception of his homecoming as the realization of a utopian ideal and the impossibility of this reality, which is that, while everything is the same – nothing is the same. As the scene progresses, Cooper tentatively looks around the house before gently running the tips of his fingers over the dining room table. This subtle gesture draws attention to the lack of dust he would have expected to encounter on Earth, highlighting the fundamental discrepancy between the real and the simulation thereby foregrounding that *his* home has changed and is no longer what it once was. In some respects, this moment bears the thematic traces of a longer scene from Nolan's earlier film *Memento* in which the protagonist hires a female escort to recreate the moments leading up to his wife's apparent murder.

During this scene from *Memento*, Leonard (Guy Pearce) asks the woman to place his wife's personal belongings around his motel room, pretending as if they were her own. The escort initially interprets this request as being part of an elaborate sexual fetish, however, despite its seemingly peculiar nature, the significance of this request should not be underestimated as it effectively enables Leonard to reproduce the familiarity and safety of the domestic space in the moments prior to the traumatic home invasion.[3] As instructed, the escort then waits until Leonard falls asleep before sliding out of the bed and slamming the bathroom door. Moments later he wakes up and reaches over to her side of the bed to feel the residual warmth of her body. What follows is a series of fleeting shots that linger on his wife's things – an old worn book, a small bedside clock and a childhood teddy bear – each of which would ordinarily function as signifier of the past but, due to his temporary disavowal of the current situation, are imbued with a sense of presentness. At this moment, the combination of visual and haptic stimuli alongside the effects of his pre-existing medical condition and his somnolent state enable Leonard to temporarily regress to a period prior to the unconscious trauma, albeit one that he now participates in as a falsified form of lived experience. As he moves to the bathroom, however, the reality of the past begins to encroach upon the present. Fragments of the unconscious trauma momentarily appear on-screen indicating a psychological break with this regressive state of memory and his temporary self-deception. Upon opening the door to the bathroom and seeing the escort, the illusion of his wife's presentness is shattered completely and Leonard is returned to the reality of his everyday existence. Referring to the objects that Leonard uses to recreate the domestic space in the liminal setting of his motel room, William G. Little writes that 'Leonard does repeatedly try to manipulate souvenir-like objects; however, the goal of this action is not to frame desire's play but rather to transcend it' (2005: 73). For Little, Leonard's attempt to recreate the past according to an illusionary fantasy of the home foregrounds his desire to transcend both the practical and ontological barriers that prevent him from reinstating the psychological state of innocence that preceded the traumatic loss. Regrettably, this endeavour is, as Leonard repeatedly discovers, an impossible task. For both Leonard and Cooper, the home or the 'lost-object' cannot be in the simulacral recreation of it. The lost-object is not present, nor can it be represented, rather the lost-object appears to be time itself. The kind of nostalgia we see in Nolan's films is thus a visualization of the painful yearning to return to an idealized (and therefore always absent) past that is broadly in keeping with the development of the concept as a critical term since it was first articulated in 1688 by a medical student named Johanes Hofer.

Initially conceived of as a medical condition relating to Swiss mercenaries suffering from an intense and often debilitating longing for home, the term nostalgia has since evolved from a yearning for a particular place to a longing for an idealized past, that no longer exists or potentially never existed in the first place (see also Wilson 2005: 22–23; Schweizer 2013: 26). In her discussion of feminist fiction, literary scholar Roberta Rubenstein says that:

> Nostalgia encompasses something more than a yearning for literal places or actual individuals. While homesickness refers to a spatial/geographical separation, nostalgia more accurately refers to a temporal one. Even if one is able to return to the literal edifice where s/he grew up, one can never truly return to the original home of childhood, since it exists mostly as a place in the imagination.
> (Rubenstein 2001: 4)

For Rubenstein, even if one were able to enact a geographic return it would not be to the home for which one yearns. The place of return has not only been distorted through the lens of memory and desire, but it has also changed over time – become different from itself. Furthermore, even if it had not, the returner is now so widely different from whom they were when they left that such a return is rendered impossible. In both *Memento* and *Interstellar*, while the protagonists can re-experience the home as a physical space this return is insufficient and as a consequence, they both remain unsatisfied. Amelia DeFalco argues that the evolution of the term nostalgia, that is, the shift in emphasis from a place to a time can be considered in relation to the psychoanalytic notion of desire as it makes 'the object of desire irrecoverable, producing an inevitably frustrated longing' (2004: 29). She echoes the sentiment of Rubenstein's comments when she says that, 'though one may return to the homeland, one can never turn back time' (2004: 29). Implicit in these observations is the recognition that, by identifying the topography of nostalgia in relation to a temporal dimension rather than its prior articulation as a spatial one, a sense of *irrecoverable* loss emerges as a constituent component of the concept. This has meaningful implications for how nostalgia can be conceptualized in relation to psychoanalysis, trauma and psychoanalytic theories of desire which, as we have already seen, suggest that the 'object of desire' is perpetually deferred (see Lacan [1957] 1977b: 175).[4]

In her chapter appropriately titled 'Objects of desire', Susan Stewart argues that the nostalgic's relationship to the past is necessarily predicated on loss (1993: 145). According to Stewart, the subject longs to return to a time of lost innocence that predates their own ability to provide a narrative of moments that are no longer present. To illustrate her point Stewart uses the example of acquiring a souvenir to argue that, while such an object remains capable of evoking the past and returning the subject to that moment in time, it simultaneously cannot help but signify the intrinsic loss of that moment. Even though the souvenir preserves the past, the subject cannot transcend the loss, rather, it functions as a mitigation of the loss – a lessening of its power.[5] The souvenir, therefore, exists in the indeterminate gap between the past and the present remaining symbolically incomplete so that it might recall a moment in the past, now lost, to which it refers to when correspondingly supplemented by a narrative conveyed by the subject in the present.

For Stewart, nostalgia is thus established in relation to the fundamental loss that defines it and the desire that sustains it which is why her statement that '[t]he nostalgic is enamoured of distance, not of the referent itself' (1993: 145)[6] is in many ways, akin to Todd McGowan's comments regarding the nature of the subject's relationship to desire. He says:

> Desire finds its satisfaction not through the success of attaining its aim but through the repetition of failing to do so. Those who have gotten what they want can readily attest to the disappointment of desire that follows from achieving the goal.
>
> (McGowan 2012b: 158)

According to McGowan, it is the failure of the subject's desire that inaugurates a closed loop whereby desire remains unfulfilled, perpetually repeating itself in such a way that points towards the fundamental lack inherent in being. As divided subjects, we crave the restoration of wholeness that would make it possible to overcome or transcend the experience of loss while, at the same time, resisting such fantasmatic completion. This is because it is through the splitting of the subject that an object emerges that orientates the subject's desire. Without this fundamental loss, we would have no cause for desire and so exist in a regressive state of pure *jouissance* or enjoyment. As a consequence, the object that we desire is always reducible to being the path to another object. A similar pattern emerges when considering the structural function of nostalgia. Horowitz notes that:

> There is also something deeply disingenuous about nostalgia, this aching to return to another place, another time. The yearner does not really wish to go back. Insofar as our personal and historical experiences have created the beings that we are in the present moment, to return is to undo ourselves, the selves that we have become as a result of experience, adaptation, assimilation. One aspect of nostalgia, as we understand the term today, then, is that the yearner does not really wish to return. Instead, the yearner wishes to continue to yearn to return—that is, it is the yearning that is desired, and not the actual return.
>
> (Horowitz 2010: 49)

Similarly, for Stewart, it is the unbridgeable gap between the past and the present that serves to sustain the nostalgic impulse. As Stewart points out, the gap exists because erasing the gap would necessarily 'cancel out the desire which is nostalgia's reason for existence' (1993: 145). It is time that sustains the gap between desire and the object.

The nostalgic's desire to reverse time to a period of innocence, a sentiment often shared by those who undergo a traumatic experience (see Arnold-de Simine 2013: 63), is frequently framed as a response to loss and it is melodrama's emphasis on the past where loss is most clearly expressed and felt. David Grimstead theorizes that melodrama 'conceives the "promise of human life" not as a revolutionary future, but rather as a return to a "golden past"' arguing that it depicts, 'less how things ought to be than how they should have been' (cited in Gledhill 1987: 21). For Grimstead along with Williams, melodrama is a 'backward-looking form' (2001: 36) while Gledhill has suggested that 'melodrama's search for something lost, inadmissible, repressed, ties it to an atavistic past' (1987: 32). From this perspective, the nostalgic impulse underpinning melodrama can be understood as being fundamentally regressive. On the one hand, it is clear that nostalgic recollections reinforce our perception of time as a linear movement from the past to the present (see Boym 2001; Dickinson and Erben 2006); however, our subjective experience of nostalgia simultaneously rejects this chronologically ordered temporal flow in favour of the disjointed and fragmented experience of memory. Cultural critic Rey

Chow poses the question, '[i]nstead of thinking that nostalgia is a feeling triggered by an object lost in the past (a mode of thinking that remains linear and teleological in orientation), could we attempt the reverse?' (1998: 135). She says, '[c]ould the movement of nostalgia be a loop, a throw, a network of chance, rather than a straight line?' (1998: 135). This simultaneity of backward and forward movements in time bears a structural resemblance to the bidirectionality of *après-coup* described by Lacan whereby a past traumatic experience is repeated in the present. Unlike the experience of trauma, though, which often generates a closed loop of repetition, nostalgia arguably makes dealing with the loss to some extent possible if the subject views the past as being a foundation for the future. In her influential book *Screening the Past*, Pam Cook identifies the therapeutic aspects of nostalgia when she considers that, instead of 'being seen as a reactionary, regressive condition imbued with sentimentality, [nostalgia] can be perceived as a way of coming to terms with the past, as enabling it to be exorcised in order that society, and individuals, can move on' (2005: 4).[7] Cook notes that the sense of loss evoked by a nostalgic encounter is particularly potent because it is predicated on an *acceptance* that the past is gone forever.

In *Interstellar*, Cooper's reconciliation with Murph is perhaps the clearest indication that the past is irretrievable but also that this loss *might* form the basis of developmental progression. When Cooper finally reunites with his daughter the gap between his desire and the lost-object seems to disappear and yet, what a detailed textual analysis of this scene reveals is the impossibility of obtaining the lost-object. Upon greeting her he realizes that the 10-year-old Murph he left on Earth is now aged over 100 years old. Nevertheless, he can fulfil his promise to return and this scene towards the film's conclusion sees them together at last. Despite their reconciliation, however, Murph almost immediately sends Cooper away perhaps recognizing that there is something incomplete about the resolution of their relationship as the reunion between them is, to use Williams's phrasing, inevitably 'too late' (1998: 69). While he has indeed kept his promise to return to her, an aged Murph tells him that no parent should have to watch their child die, emphasizing that her own children are there to comfort her in her last hours. This reminder, which is visually reinforced by the presence of numerous other people in the room encroaching upon what should be an intimate moment between them, foregrounds the fact that Murph has lived most of her life without him, indicating that this reconciliation is perhaps only a partial consolation. Even though Murph, through the course of her own life, now understands her father's reasoning for abandoning her, his redemption comes at a price. Therefore, what lingers over the image of them is the underlying acceptance that they cannot turn back time and salvage what has been lost. This is poignantly symbolized when Cooper retreats from the room maintaining his gaze upon Murph who tellingly does not return it.

Instead, she emphasizes the distance between them by embracing those around her who eventually block his line of sight entirely, thereby revealing the inherent gap between desire and the object framed here as an irrecoverable loss. When Murph sends Cooper away he instinctively understands that her reason for doing so is based on their inability to regain the time they have lost together. Consequently, he unquestionably accepts her decision rather than resisting the temptation to stay with her despite this being his sole aim for much of the film. In what follows, it is implied that Cooper subsequently embarks on a new mission to rendezvous with Amelia on Edmunds's planet where a fresh start awaits. This offers a theoretical blank slate upon which to build a new future unbound by the unconscious traumas of the past. The presence of the flag of the United States of America, however, seen erected on Edmunds's planet, arguably undermines this proposition as it points towards the overt perpetuation of the historical and cultural traditions of western colonialism, thereby contradicting the possibility of a real fresh start free from the memories of the past. On this basis, even though Cooper can accept the past and move beyond his sentimental attachment to his daughter he cannot break free of the loss that structures his being.

In her discussion of melodrama, cinema and trauma, E. Ann Kaplan argues that in melodramatic narratives the spectator encounters trauma through a combination of the film's themes and techniques (2001: 204). However, these films frequently end in such a way to communicate a clear sense of closure and often even point towards the possibility of a cure that reconciles the unconscious trauma into a coherent future-orientated narrative. Here lies the essence of what I argue distinguishes *Interstellar* from Nolan's other films. While it remains in keeping with his interest in trauma through the thematic enactments of nostalgia, repetition and return, his treatment of trauma in the film is arguably different as it betrays his previous emphasis on the stylistic and structural repetition attached to the experience of trauma. Instead, from one perspective, the final third of *Interstellar* offers a simple cure for trauma that is in keeping with the forward moving momentum of closure offered by many mainstream Hollywood narratives.

Unlike the other protagonists from Nolan's films who frequently remain caught within the closed structural loop of the trauma, perhaps destined to perpetually return to the site of loss, *Interstellar* is possibly the only one of Nolan's films to present the protagonist as having the capacity – unlike every divided and lacking subject – to seemingly overcome loss. Other characters in his current filmography have, in many respects, given up on a future-directed desire, whereas Cooper can perceive the experience of trauma not as something to be endured but rather something that can potentially be mastered. By the end of the film, Cooper is, at least superficially, no longer a divided subject and instead occupies an impossible position of fantasmatic completeness. Unlike *Following, Memento, The Dark*

Knight trilogy and *Inception*, which all, at least from the perspective of one possible interpretation, conclude with the protagonist caught in a perpetual cycle of repeating the trauma, *Interstellar* is perhaps the only one of Nolan's films to date[8] to present the protagonist as having a clearly defined and unquestionably realized transformational arc. Cooper's narrative journey contains both redemption and resolution thereby breaking the pattern of repetition and the cyclical movement of time associated with the experience of trauma. As Furby notes:

> Whereas the past often contains an irreconcilable traumatic loss for many of Nolan's protagonists, Cooper's past is not yet finished, not closed off from the present and he is able to communicate with his daughter in the past, and visit her in the future (or rather *her* future) at which point he receives forgiveness and is able to move on with his life [...]. Protagonists of other Nolan films are not so fortunate, and they remain stuck in a series of temporal waiting rooms.
>
> (Furby 2015: 253, original emphasis)

In some respects, these ideas are most explicitly demonstrated elsewhere in a sequence towards the end of the film which shows Cooper entering what is referred to as 'the tesseract'.

The tesseract is a place where the linear time experienced on Earth intersects with the fourth-dimensional fabric where time is not only infinite but a physical and navigable dimension. By floating up or down, left or right, Cooper can traverse both space and time across a seemingly infinite series of three-dimensional iterations of Murph's bedroom. In this environment, there are no temporal paradoxes because the past, present and future all exist simultaneously. Here, Cooper is able to return to the past in a way that not only facilitates his ability to relive previous events but foregrounds the possibility that he might be able to imbue them with new meaning. Specifically, if we consider that the primary moment Cooper re-experiences from the vantage point of the tesseract is his decision to abandon Murph then it is possible to understand how this memory functions as his fundamental regret. While he is not able to alter this moment, he is able to re-translate its meaning and it is this ability that largely distinguishes him from Nolan's other protagonists who remain unable to overcome the experience of loss.

Cooper's experience of the tesseract does align him with another character from Nolan's films to date who also utilizes a physical space to return to various moments in time. In *Inception*, Cobb (Leonardo DiCaprio) tells Ariadne (Ellen Page) that he obsessively revisits a number of these snapshots because they are moments that he regrets. Even though he expresses a desire to change the past, he later succumbs to the impossibility of doing so. However, during the film's climax, Nolan permits Cobb to return to his principal regret, thereby allowing the character to finally re-translate its meaning. In the concluding scene, Cobb can see the faces of his children again and, upon reconciling with them, the memory of his role in his wife's suicide is re-translated. This restorative ending implies that Cobb can attain some form of redemption and move on; however, as Mark Fisher notes, 'this ending has more than a suggestion of wish-fulfilment fantasy about it' (2011: 38). In any case, this sense of 'closure' does not extend to the spectator who remains unsure of whether Cobb returns to reality or is stuck in a perpetual dream-state.

Conversely, in *Interstellar*, there is no question as to whether Cooper's experience of the tesseract is real or not based on the textual evidence presented and neither is the film's ending open to interpretation in perhaps the same manner of *Memento*, *The Prestige*, *Inception* and *The Dark Knight Rises*.[9] Instead, *Interstellar* concludes with a forward movement in time relative to the beginning that extends outward to the spectator's experience of the film. Where the diegetic misdirection and deceptions of *Following*, *Memento*, *The Prestige* and *Inception* invite the spectator to repeatedly return to the text in search of further meanings and clues, *Interstellar* does not contain the same distinct level of playfulness with film form and even the core mysteries related to the identities of 'they' as well as the 'ghost' in Murph's room are solved well before the film's final frame. Instead, *Interstellar* simply relies on the revelation of a twist ending to engineer repeat viewings. Nevertheless, this technique, of course, still recalls the process of deferred or retroactive meaning that Paul Sutton establishes in his discussion of cinematic *afterwardsness* (see 2004). What all this amounts to then, is that the spectator's experience of the film is relatively straightforward when compared to Nolan's previous atemporally structured narratives thereby rendering his treatment of trauma somewhat diluted. Where *Following*, *Memento*, *The Prestige* and *Inception* demand that we pay particularly close attention to each film and move the necessary narrative pieces of each puzzle into place, often vicariously experiencing the cognitive shifts of the traumatic experience in the process, in *Interstellar* what Nolan presents is effectively a chronological account of Cooper's departure from, and return to, those he loves.

Broadly speaking, in terms of structure and form, *Interstellar* is remarkably linear. Sobchack notes that '[u]ncharacteristically, but appropriately, Nolan has chosen to contain and clarify these multidimensional scientific puzzles as well as the film's central but spatially and temporally fractured father-daughter relationship in a classically constructed narrative served by traditional continuity editing' (2014: n.pag.). Equally, where flashbacks have been employed at various points throughout the film they are clearly signposted by psychological or aural cues and thus create a pattern of intelligible causation underlying the temporal ordering of the events. Furthermore, the film arguably abandons the central and ongoing ambiguities evident in *Memento*, *The Prestige* and *Inception*. There are no puzzles to solve and ostensibly no loose ends to tie up. The spectator can, and indeed may return to *Interstellar* a number of times, but the potential to generate new meanings based on the textual information available is limited by the imposition of a conventional ending whereby the hero's journey is complete albeit with the caveat that another quest awaits him.[10] Instead, the capacity to produce a different or revised interpretation of the film beyond the enframed image exists within the spectator who returns to it having been changed by the present and other experiences between each viewing. The spectator's desire is not sustained by some inherent falsity within the text that renders the narrative ambiguous in any way but rather by our own experience of the inherent gaps that structure our symbolic reality. This is to say that, if a film were truly completely satisfying in a way that resolved desire, we would not want to watch it again. Of course, as the film is fixed but the viewing of it is not, seeing a film again renders its meanings differently thereby sustaining our desire regardless of our knowledge of the narrative.

The Possibility of Post-Traumatic Growth

The actual ending of *Interstellar* is, then, arguably a concession to sentimentality, melodrama and the ability of the individual to seemingly obtain the lost-object because, when Cooper is released from Murph's timeline (and his own), the film suggests that he can escape the temporal loop created by the traumatic experience. Unlike *Following*, *Memento*, *The Dark Knight* trilogy and *Inception*, which – at least from one perspective – utilize a combination of film form and thematic content to communicate the protagonist's ongoing experience of being trapped in time, in *Interstellar* Cooper's reunion with Murph indicates that he can break the cycle of traumatic repetition, thereby suggesting the possibility of what Richard G. Tedeschi and Lawrence G. Calhoun refer to as 'post-traumatic growth' (Tedeschi and Calhoun 1995). As the term 'growth' implies, this is a process that can contribute to positive changes because of the struggle with trauma or any highly stressful event. This discourse of post-traumatic growth is by no means new when one considers, for example, the ancient mythological story of the Egyptian phoenix rising from the ashes or the Christian parable of Jesus raising Lazarus from the dead. Nevertheless, its development as a clinical tool has flourished since the turn of the millennium alongside a shift away from an emphasis on simply documenting the pathological effects of trauma (see Calhoun and Tedeschi 2014: ix).

In principle, Tedeschi and Calhoun identify three general domains where growth can occur: (1) changes in the sense of self, (2) changes in interpersonal relationships and (3) changes in one's philosophical outlook on life (see 1996). In the first instance, changes in the sense of self reflect an individual's sense of becoming a better person. In the second instance, an improvement in personal relationships reflects an individual's perceived awareness of closer and more intimate ties to their immediate family and friends. Finally, in the third instance, changes in one's philosophical outlook on life reflect an increased appreciation for an individual's own sense of self alongside an improved awareness of new opportunities and a heightened awareness of what is important in life (Calhoun and Tedeschi 2014: 66). According to Calhoun and Tedeschi, for post-traumatic growth to occur, 'something has to replace the goals and beliefs from which a survivor of trauma and loss has necessarily disengaged' (2001: 165). In other words, the traumatic experience must be integrated into the development of the self or, considered from a slightly different perspective, whatever has been lost must be regained. This is somewhat problematic when considered in relation to the temporality of trauma discussed throughout this book, a notion summarized by Ivana Milojevic who emphasizes the potential risks associated with post-traumatic growth. She says, 'neither grief nor trauma recovery follows a predictable line. Both can have periods of progression and/or regression as a response to various internal and external stimuli [...] Post-traumatic growth is not linear; rather it is multidimensional' (Milojevic 2013: 264). For Milojevic, our experience of trauma does not function in accordance with a linear understanding of time but rather operates in response to the subjective experience of memory meaning that it is not resolved in quite the straightforward manner implied by term 'growth'.

Nevertheless, the principle way that post-traumatic growth is dramatized in the final moments of *The Prestige, Inception, The Dark Knight Rises* and *Interstellar* is in the disguise of love. Love is presented in these films as being a form of treatment for those who have undergone a traumatic experience. Indeed, the notion that love (romantic or familial) can be part of the therapeutic process is widely supported by several psychologists (see Woodward and Joseph 2003). Clare Woodward and Stephen Joseph identify the experience of love and nurturing, both by the self and others as one of what they term to be 'vehicles of change' (2003: 281) for post-traumatic growth. This sentiment is echoed by a number of characters at various points throughout *Interstellar* but perhaps nowhere more explicitly than in Amelia's monologue during which she outlines what she perceives to be the defining qualities of love. She says:

> Love isn't something we invented – it's observable, powerful. It has to mean something [...] Maybe it's some evidence, some artefact of a higher dimension that we can't consciously perceive [...] Love is the one thing we're capable of perceiving that transcends dimensions of time and space.

This character's conviction in the transcendent power of love represents Nolan's most explicit attempt to express the significance of love to date, and it is here that a challenge to the inescapable nature of the traumatic experience begins to emerge. The suggestion that love exists beyond time and space ultimately calls into question the inherent impossibility of obtaining the lost-object. Where desire exists to reproduce itself, love attempts to fill the void by eradicating desire (which points towards the experience of loss created by the splitting of the subject), thereby erasing the impact of trauma. Building on the theories of Lacan, Ehsan Azari writes that 'we may well uphold the idea that when there is love at play, desire disappears' (2008: 44). He goes on to remark that, '[w]hen one desires something, one tries to deprive oneself of that object [...] The opposite is true for love, as it always creates the *illusion* of fusion with the object' (2008: 44, emphasis added). Elsewhere in his discussion, he argues that 'love provides a short circuit for desire and in some ways rescues a subject from the overwhelming trail of desire. Unlike desire, love may reach its impossible goal, and this very feature raises love beyond the boundary of desire' (2008: 45). It would appear that to love (as distinct from the desire to be loved by an other) requires, according to Lacan, a renunciation of the lost-object. Towards the end of *Seminar XI* Lacan notes that '[l]ove which it seems to some that I have downgraded can be posited only in the beyond where at first it renounces its object' (1977d: 262). Such love is, however, as Lacan informs us 'impossible' ([1975] 1998: 87) as to be in love in this sense is to separate oneself from the void that one must lack to maintain subjectivity.

Nevertheless, in *The Prestige, Inception, The Dark Knight Rises* and *Interstellar*, narrative closure is organized around a redemptive conclusion to the protagonist's journey through an implied union that bears the hallmarks of love. In *The Prestige*, a Borden (Christian Bale) reunites with his daughter and in *Inception* – even though Cobb's familial reconciliation with his children is positioned as being subject to debate from the spectator's perspective – the ending seems to imply the character's cathartic redemption. This notion is supported by Nolan when he says 'I choose to believe that Cobb gets back to his kids' (Nolan cited in Fisher 2011: 38). Elsewhere, in *The Dark Knight Rises*, Selina Kyle's (Ann Hathaway) presence with Bruce Wayne (Christian Bale) during the film's climax represents the fulfilment of Alfred's (Michael Caine) paternal desire for Wayne 'to find a life, to find someone' and in *Interstellar*, even though a romantic subplot between Cooper and Amelia was removed from the final version of the screenplay, a connection between the two characters remains and Cooper's decision to join her during the film's climax represents an implied union of sorts as they will be the only two inhabitants on the planet tasked with the primary aim of setting up a human colony.

Significantly, however, in all of the previous examples given, the union is undermined or at the very least de-emphasized at the expense of the remaining mysteries that remain unsolved: Cobb's reunion with his children is diluted in favour of the spinning top and while there is textual evidence indicating Wayne's survival in *The Dark Knight Rises*, the possibility that this sequence is a form of wish-fulfilment cannot be ruled out. In *The Prestige*, it is clear that the protagonist has been reunited with his daughter although the film refuses to clarify whether the man who returns is her biological father and this is further subsumed by Cutter's (Michael Caine) enigmatic closing monologue. In each example then, there is a sense that, on the one hand, these films provide the spectator with the object of desire while, on the other that each film indicates this search is in many ways futile and leads us astray from where pure *jouissance* or enjoyment might be found. Consider, once again, Cooper's reconciliation with Murph in *Interstellar*. Even though the film's entire narrative has been geared towards this single moment, Nolan does not dwell on it for long and it is noticeably brief when contextualized within the film's overall near three hours running time. Perhaps then, the lack of emphasis placed upon this scene is befitting of the film's underlying message relating to its articulation of desire; even when one obtains the object of desire one remains unsatisfied or, at the very least, duped into a false state of consciousness whereby they believe that they have found the elusive lost-object. Those that place a value on the reconciles at the end of these films are, therefore, lulled into a fallacy that obscures the loss that is a necessary component of the traumatic experience and the ensuing possibility of post-traumatic growth. Loss underwrites the experience of trauma (e.g. the irretrievable time between Cooper and Murph, Mal's [Marion Cotillard] suicide, the death of Borden's twin and so on) and so the desire for substitute objects (Cooper's search for Amelia, Cobb's relationship with his children, Borden's reunion with Jess [Samantha Mahurin] etc.) remains a potent force that continually reminds us of the trauma that structures our existence. While these films do suggest the possibility of healing and growth, it is open-ended rather than closed indicating a perpetual search rather than something found. In the specific context of *Interstellar*, even though the narrative suggests that we can travel into the emptiness and vastness of space, Nolan indicates that the capacity to move beyond the void inherent in subjectivity is an illusion. Instead, we are always slaves to trauma and desire.

NOTES

1. Ben Singer has referred to melodrama as a 'cluster concept', a term 'whose meaning varies from case to case in relation to different configurations of a range of applicable features' (2001: 44). Like Williams, he identifies five key features of melodrama: pathos, heightened emotionality, moral polarization, nonclassical narrative mechanics and spectacular effects.

2. Of course, this desire should not be taken literally but rather viewed symbolically as an expression of a psychological yearning to return to the security, stability and innocence of childhood and early youth.

3. This request is particularly important when it comes to understanding the logic of his desire for it reveals his need to be partially ignorant of the arrangement, thereby contributing towards the illusion of his wife's presence.

4. David Sigler (2004) goes so far as to claim that the notion of nostalgia parallels Lacan's *objet a* in that neither can be located or recovered and so are both the object of intense longing.

5. In the previous example given taken from *Memento*, Leonard is able to momentarily transcend this loss but only through the act of fetishistic disavowal.

6. See also Alison Blunt who similarly notes that 'a nostalgic desire for home has come to represent a wider "desire for desire"' (2005: 14).

7. See also Michel Foucault (1988: 12) who suggests that nostalgia can be positive as long as it does not emerge from a contempt for the present.

8. While the endings of *Insomnia* and *The Prestige* are, to an extent, concluded with a relatively clear sense of resolution, in both scenarios a sacrifice is required in order to overcome the traumatic encounter. Along these lines, as Claire Sisco King points out, 'the act of sacrificial death is itself a traumatic one' (2011: 17). Consequently, these sacrifices can be considered to perpetuate a trauma, thereby ensuring that trauma is seen as existing as a closed loop.

9. A number of users of several online forums have discussed the possibility that Cooper's entrance into the tesseract represents his own personal experience of the after-life making the film's conclusion a rather elaborate fantasy (see O'Connell 2014).

10. This is not to say that there are not gaps in the narrative. However, these are largely catered for by the film's own narration. Those that continue to insist that there are other means by which the film and the ending can be understood seemingly do so due to an over investment in the directors' authorial signature rather than being based on a sustained and critical evaluation of the textual evidence available.

Keep Calm and Carry On: Combating Cultural Trauma in *Dunkirk*

Take me home.

– Tommy, *Dunkirk*

Towards the end of *Dunkirk* (2017), Tommy (Fionn Whitehead), Alex (Harry Styles) and a few other soldiers take shelter in a grounded fishing trawler hoping that the tide will eventually carry it away from the shores of Northern France. The current pulls the boat out to sea, but the hold begins to take on water forcing the soldiers to hastily abandon the sinking ship. Tommy and Alex manage to escape to the surface where they swim towards a nearby Naval Destroyer in the hope of rescue. As they approach the ship, however, an enemy aircraft flies overhead dropping several bombs that hit their intended target causing catastrophic damage to the vessel. The ship subsequently capsizes compelling Mr Dawson (Mark Rylance) to manoeuvre his small boat – the Moonstone – to within reach of the survivors, but the bomber responsible for the initial attack returns to strike again. This time, a Royal Air Force pilot – Farrier (Tom Hardy) – shoots down the enemy aircraft causing it to plummet into the sea. While the Moonstone makes a speedy getaway, the downed plane ignites the oil that has leaked from the sinking ship causing the deaths of the remaining Allied soldiers stranded in the water. This brief description of what appears to be a linear series of events betrays the complexity of the film's editing which reworks the dominant cinematic codes of representation associated with mainstream cinema to construct a language capable of depicting the traumatic experience of war.

The film is divided into three distinct perspectives across three different time-spans, regularly cutting between each narrative thread. The events during the segment entitled 'The Mole' last one week and introduce the viewer to Tommy, Alex and several other soldiers who are desperate to escape the beach of Dunkirk. Set on water, 'The Sea' roughly spans a 24-hour period and follows Mr Dawson as he and his son Peter (Tom Glynn-Carney) and their friend George (Barry Keoghan)

133

set sail towards Dunkirk as part of the operation to rescue some of 400,000 British and Allied soldiers trapped by German forces. In the segment titled 'The Air', two RAF pilots led by Farrier engage enemy planes in a series of dogfights lasting approximately 60 minutes. Rather than ordering them in sequence, the different lines of action intersect. To complicate matters further, events that occur in one narrative thread are shown and then reshown in another from a different perspective generating a sense of confusion, disorientation and repetition that is consistent with the traumatic experience of war.

In his influential essay 'War and representation', Fredric Jameson (2009) suggests that the depiction of war in art poses distinct challenges to, and questions about, the nature of representation. His main argument is that the 'existential experience of war belongs to a category of collective realities which *exceed* representation fully as much as they do conceptualization' (2009: 1547, emphasis added). Similarly, the American film director Sam Fuller who himself was an infantryman during the Second World War famously remarked that '[t]o make a real war movie would be to occasionally fire at the audience from behind the screen during a battle scene' (cited in Kennedy 2004). But, as Joshua Hirsch reminds us, the attempt to communicate traumatic events is not restricted to the memory of the lived experience and can find expression in both the denotive content of visual language and the formal construction of a text (2003: 19). In *Dunkirk*, the disrupted temporality of the film – a technique that Nolan has employed in *Following*, *Memento* and *The Prestige* among others – provides the spectator with what is perhaps the closest approximation to the experience of war by emulating the symptoms of trauma using the visual and formal properties of cinema.

So far, throughout this book, I have analysed Nolan's films using a psychoanalytic framework that accounts for the way that the spectator vicariously experiences trauma and loss at the level of theme, structure and *mise-en-scène*. What is striking about his previous films is his ability to foster a compulsion to repeat and replay his films. Likewise, *Dunkirk* can be interpreted along similar lines. To begin with, the film marks a return to the atemporal structures of Nolan's earliest films thereby encouraging the spectator to adopt an active position in relation to the text and to engage in repeat viewings. *Dunkirk* is also the director's most overt thematic engagement with trauma which is perhaps unsurprising given the war genre's capacity to portray soldiers who have been traumatized during combat. Where *Dunkirk* differs from Nolan's other work, however, is the film's close relationship to actual historical events. *Dunkirk* is the first time that Nolan has attempted to depict an 'authentic' version of history. Consequently, the film engages in a discourse about the past that contains an implicit political dimension. My own approach to studying *Dunkirk*, then, begins by acknowledging a necessary shift in my critical analysis of his work which has, up to this point, focused on individual rather than collective responses to trauma.

While the film represents a continuation of the themes of trauma and loss that I have identified elsewhere in Nolan's films, *Dunkirk*'s engagement with the cultural trauma of the Second World War requires a broader understanding of the distinction between individual and collective responses to trauma, and the formation of identity.[1] For this reason, I begin by briefly discussing the psychoanalytic origins of cultural trauma before going on to address the way that the cultural memory of the Second World War has been shaped by subsequent cinematic depictions of the war. I pay particular attention to a number of British war films produced during the 1950s, identifying a parallel between the tone of those films released in the aftermath of the Second World War and those films and television programmes released in the lead up to, and following the British referendum on membership of the European Union (EU). I conclude by suggesting that the depiction of events surrounding the period of the Second World War in these more recent texts can serve as a potent source of national identity in times of social, economic and political uncertainty. Where those films released during the 1950s offered a nostalgic retreat from contemporary problems, *Dunkirk* too provides a commentary on the present by attempting to revise the memory of a cultural trauma located in the past.

Towards a Psychoanalytic Theory of Cultural Trauma

It is rather fitting that my analysis of Nolan's films comes to an end by examining *Dunkirk* because a discussion of the war film aptly returns us to one of Sigmund Freud's seminal discussions of trauma stemming from his research on shell-shocked soldiers in *Beyond the Pleasure Principle* ([1920] 1955b). In the aftermath of the First World War, Freud was forced to revise his theories of trauma to account for the many psychologically damaged soldiers returning from battle. Prior to 1920, Freud had indicated that most neurotic symptoms could be understood in relation to psychosexual trauma. However, the overwhelming number of veterans who exhibited characteristic symptoms of trauma required that he reappraise these initial assertions in light of the many horrors of war. In *Beyond the Pleasure Principle*, Freud restructured his earlier model of trauma to account for the phenomenon of 'shell-shock' or 'war neurosis' by emphasizing the compulsion to repeat painful, even unbearable experiences. He proposed that the shock of intense unexpected traumatic experiences ruptured the 'protective barrier' designed to prevent excessive stimuli from entering consciousness resulting in symptoms such as repeated flashbacks and nightmares ([1920] 1922: 30). The war played a significant part in pushing Freud to re-evaluate the difference between an external and an internal assault on the ego by acknowledging that traumatic events could originate from collective experiences, such as war.

In his last work prior to his death, *Moses and Monotheism* ([1939] 1964b), Freud further conflated individual and cultural trauma by using the same dynamic that he had employed in relation to individual patients to examine Judaic culture. Freud proposed that the history of Judaism could be understood in relation to a traumatic event, namely the murder of Moses. According to Freud, the version of Moses referred to in the Bible was an Egyptian priest who was killed by a band of Israelites because of his attempt to impose a monotheistic religion upon them. Those responsible for his death repressed the memory of his murder, but traces of the crime remained and subsequently resurfaced in the form of a belated return to Mosaic law. Cathy Caruth, in her reading of *Moses and Monotheism*, demonstrates how the text itself – a revised account of the biblical Exodus narrative – not only articulates the apparent traumatic origins of Jewish traditions but also constitutes the inscription of a traumatic event: that of Freud's enforced exile from Vienna in 1938 under the threat of Nazi persecution (1996: 20). Caruth's deconstruction of Freud's final work thus reveals how his fictionalized account of Judaic culture is connected to contemporaneous historical events indicating a broader capacity for literary, filmic and other texts to 'speak about and *speak through* the profound story of traumatic experience' (1996: 4, emphasis added).

The shift from individual to cultural trauma that takes place in Freud's final work is expanded upon by the sociologist Neil J. Smelser who goes so far as to suggest that, however catastrophic, '[n]o discrete historical event or situation automatically or necessarily qualifies in itself as a cultural trauma' (2004: 35). Smelser indicates that it is the passage of time that effectively permits catastrophic events to transform into cultural traumas. Cultural trauma is thus never experienced directly but only after a period of latency. Cultural traumas, he argues, are 'for the most part *historically made*, not born' (2004: 37, emphasis added). To qualify as a cultural trauma, Smelser suggests that an event must be memorialized by those, directly and indirectly, affected, while subsequent generations must engage in 'compulsive examining, and reexamining, bringing up new aspects of the trauma, reinterpreting, reevaluating, and battling over symbolic significance' (2004: 54). One of the principal ways in which this has been encouraged is through the aid of cinematic representation. Jeremy Havardi (2014) suggests that the powerful nature of cinema has shaped public memories of the past. He says:

With its seamless presentation of visual images, sounds and compelling narrative, film has an unrivalled emotional impact on its audiences. It transmits its messages with a unique visual potency, and casts such a glow over its audience that it can cement stereotypes and images in the popular imagination.

(Havardi 2014: 3)

Likewise, in his work *American Cinema/American Culture* (2012), John Belton suggests that films mediate our relationship to the past by providing a lens through which they observe the trauma of war (2012: 218). He argues that the generic conventions of the war film shape our understanding of real wars and in doing so, remind us why we fight and what we stand to lose in the process. Elsewhere, Elisabeth Bronfen draws attention to how memories of war depicted on-screen interact with the present when she says, '[t]he past that haunts us is also a past that we can never fully master. Instead, to restage the past on screen is to make present the cultural memory that shaped contemporary society' (2010: 10). Cultural trauma is thus constituted as a site of retroactive negotiation that is informed by the convergence of history, individual memory and popular culture.

The Cultural Trauma of the Second World War

In 1939, Britain entered the Second World War as one of the leading imperial powers. After six years of conflict, however, the country emerged occupying a drastically different position within the global political and economic order (Davies and Sinfield 2000: 1). In addition to the 264,000 military casualties and 90,000 civilian deaths, large parts of the United Kingdom sustained heavy damage during the German air raids between 1940 and 1941, leaving much of the country's public infrastructure – railways, roads, schools and hospitals – in ruins. Likewise, food shortages made rationing necessary until the early 1950s and the British economy became heavily reliant on financial aid from the United States in the first years of post-war reconstruction. Despite these setbacks, Sonya Rose indicates that the period surrounding the Second World War is collectively remembered as a time when the British people 'put aside their everyday involvements and individual concerns, joined hands, and came to the nation's defence. Public memories of the war continue to recall this as a historical moment when the nation was truly united' (2003: 1–2). Many films released in the aftermath of the war such as *Angels One Five* (1952), *The Dam Busters* (1955), *The Battle of the River Plate* (1956), *Reach for the Sky* (1957) and *Danger within* (1958) contributed to this spirit of national unity by celebrating the wartime heroics and sacrifices of servicemen, as well as those fighting on the home front.

There is a shared consensus among several writers, directors and critics, however, that those British war films produced and released during the 1950s also represented a nostalgic escape designed to mask the decline of the British Empire and the weakening of Britain's status as a world power. Roy Armes, for instance, suggests that these war films offered 'strong evidence of a reaction against contemporary social change' dismissing them as 'archaic memories of a self-deluding era's retreat into a cosy never-never land' (1978: 179). Similarly, Neil Rattigan attributes the popularity of these films among British filmmakers and audiences to a pervading sense of nostalgia at a time of extreme social upheaval at home (1994: 146). As the wartime period of austerity continued and the international prestige of the British Empire began to wane, he says, these films were 'a way to instantly hark back to that mythic time when (it was believed) the British people stood alone but together, bravely faced adversity of the most fearsome type and bested it' (Rattigan 1994: 146). The British film director and commentator Lindsay Anderson comes to a similar conclusion in his essay 'Get out and push!' which condemned British war films for being ideologically complicit with a Conservative outlook on the past. These films, he says, portray Britain as 'a country without problems in which no essential changes have occurred for the last fifty years, and which still remains the centre of an Empire on which the sun will never have the bad manners to set' (Anderson 1957: 141). Viewing these films considering the sociopolitical contexts of their production and reception during the 1950s reveals a great deal about the prevailing attitudes of those people who made them and those people who paid to see them.

Writing upon the occasion of the royal premiere of Leslie Norman's *Dunkirk* (1958), the film critic William Whitebait lamented the British public's infatuation with the Second World War. He wrote, '[a] dozen years after World War II we find ourselves in the really quite desperate situation of not being sick of war but hideously in love with it' (1958: 432). While the period following the end of the Second World War may seem far removed from the social reality of contemporary Britain, there nonetheless remains a significant comparison to be made not least in terms of an apparent desire to return to the images of war on screen. Taken together, *Dad's Army* (2016), *Swallows and Amazons* (2016), *Pegasus Bridge* (2017), *Churchill* (2017), *Dunkirk*, *Darkest Hour* (2017), *The Bookshop* (2017), *Their Finest* (2017) and *The Guernsey Literary and Potato Peel Pie Society* (2018) represent a cluster of films that return to the cultural traumas of the Second World War and often appeal to a reactive Englishness – as opposed to Britishness – which is politically conservative and predominantly white. This trend has not been restricted to film and includes television programmes such as *Downton Abbey* (2010–16), *Call the Midwife* (2012–present), *Poldark* (2015–present), *The Crown* (2016–present), *Victoria* (2016–present) and *War and Peace* (2016). Among these, *Dunkirk* has been the most commercially successful and is therefore worthy of attention in terms of what it might reveal about the culture within which it was produced (Box Office Mojo 2018).

For many British commentators, the appeal of *Dunkirk* can be connected to the growing presence of nostalgia – particularly that which focuses on restoring an idealized version of the past – across various aspects of contemporary culture (see Rose 2017; Jack 2018). In his work *Yearning for Yesterday*, the sociologist Fred Davis proposed that nostalgic episodes can be frequently connected to 'present fears, discontents, anxieties, or uncertainties' (1979: 34) and while it is beyond the scope of this study to provide a detailed analysis of the sociopolitical land-scape in Britain, a brief acknowledgement of the major global events that have shaped the cultural context of the new millennium will be useful to understand how nostalgia has become a defining feature of the modern condition. After 9/11 and the launch of the War on Terror, the level of perceived threats across the globe has intensified, coinciding with a rise in the amount of information available in the globalized era. The media coverage of terrorist attacks in London, Paris, Nice, Madrid, Istanbul and Mumbai, among others, have further exacerbated global fears rendering the past, in hindsight, more homogenous. Likewise, the prolifer-ation of economic instability, particularly after the 2008 global financial crash, has prompted a surge in nostalgic sentiment for the post-war period of economic prosperity during which the British government invested heavily in the creation of the welfare state, as well as comprehensive healthcare and education systems (Hatherley 2017).

The combined effects of the War on Terror and the global financial crisis have contributed to a marked increase in resentment about the impacts of globalization across certain segments of western societies. According to Roland Robertson, the nostalgic impulse is a direct response to the perceived threats of globalization. He postulates that the gradual shift towards global homogeneity has reinforced the desire to maintain traditions in the form of a 'wilful nostalgia' (1992: 155). He refers to the period of rapidly accelerating globalization in the late nineteenth and early twentieth centuries 'that witnessed the flowering of the urge to invent traditions' (1992: 155). Similarly, John Hill puts forward that nostalgia 'is both promoted by globalization and directed against it in so far as the break-up of bounded social systems, the border-crossing and deterritorialization of culture char-acteristic of globalization also encourages a longing for the "security" of place and tradition' (1999: 75). As I have discussed elsewhere in Chapter 6, this longing can be connected to a desire to return home. Using language that is reminiscent of Lacan's own writing on the concept of lack, Susan Mackey-Kallis argues that the quest for home is a common feature of many mainstream narratives and transcends genres because of its universal appeal to 'wholeness' (2002: 2). However, Emmett Early suggests that the home motif is particularly relevant to films about war (2003: 8). Sean Carter and Klaus Dodds contend that the home is often idealized in these films because it represents a utopian space far removed from the conflict that is used to 'highlight everything that the war zone is not' (2014: 98). In *Dunkirk*, the home becomes more than a geographical location or a spatial construct, functioning instead as a signifier of hope. This is perhaps nowhere more clearly communicated than during the climactic rescue of the soldiers towards the end of the film.

The sequence begins when Commander Bolton (Kenneth Branagh) notices several shapes in the distance. A nearby soldier, Colonel Winnant (James D'Arcy), hands him a pair of binoculars and asks, 'What do you see?' The two men look to the horizon for a moment before Bolton utters the word 'Home'. With that, the non-diegetic score abruptly shifts from a constant metronomic staccato to an elegiac string adaptation of 'Nimrod', the famous Adagio by the British composer Sir Edward Elgar. At the same time, the scene cuts to a series of shots that reveal a fleet of civilian boats heading towards the shores of Northern France. The music begins to build to a crescendo and the sequence returns to Bolton whose eyes begin to well up with tears as he gazes upon the approaching armada. At this point in the film, the combination of sound, visuals and story elements produces a moment of melodrama. Nolan's use of classical music is particularly significant in this regard because the piece elicits an affective response from the spectator by working together with the film's *mise-en-scène* to underscore the narrative action. However, Nolan also provides an additional layer of emotional depth to the scene by choosing a piece of music that, for British viewers at least, has distinct patriotic associations with an idealized version of the past.

Over the last 100 years, 'Nimrod' has become etched onto the British public's cultural consciousness through a repeated association with several historically significant nationally specific events. In 1997, for example, the piece was played at the funeral of Diana, Princess of Wales and in 2012, the piece marked the beginning of the opening ceremony of the London Olympics.[2] One of the reasons for Elgar's enduring appeal in Britain is that it rarely escapes consideration within a discourse of national identity. When asked to explain the significance of 'Nimrod' to *Dunkirk*, for example, the film's composer – Hans Zimmer – replied: 'It's part of English culture, since it was written. It's quite the opposite to the national anthem – it's more the emotional anthem to a nation' (Ryzik 2017). One of Zimmer's collaborators, Benjamin Wallfisch, remarked in the same interview that: 'There's a sort of nobility about it, which I think British people aspire to' (Ryzik 2017). For his part, Nolan has referred to 'Nimrod' as 'a theme as beloved to the English as Dunkirk itself' (2017), but he has also admitted that Elgar's composition carries a special meaning having been played at his father's funeral (Ryzik 2017). Consequently, Nolan's decision to include an ode to Elgar's most famous work in *Dunkirk* is significant because it dramatically highlights the way that art can draw from a repository of both individual and cultural memories to create meaning.

Besides the strong patriotic undertones of 'Nimrod', musician Barry Smith notes that Elgar's work is also 'tinged with more than a hint of melancholy, of an almost bitter-sweet nostalgia, a looking back to something unattainable. With Elgar it was the values of a fast-fading, ebbing away of the Empire and all it stood for' (2001: 2). It is fitting, then, that *Dunkirk* – a film which ostensibly laments the loss of values so closely associated with the 'Dunkirk Spirit' – should adopt Elgar's most famous anthem at a time of profound political, social and economic uncertainty in Britain. Nevertheless, far from making a political statement with the film, Nolan, it would seem, has attempted to distance *Dunkirk* from such debates by initially stating that he approached the story 'from the point of view of the pure mechanics of survival rather than from the politics of the event' (Sexton 2017). In a separate interview with *The Telegraph*, however, Nolan strikes a more conciliatory tone when discussing the film's potential political meaning remarking:

> If you're asking me about what I prefer to call the resonance of the story, to me it's about European unity, the desperate attempt to keep the French in the war. Dunkirk has always been a Rorschach test for people, but I think the confusion we see today between patriotism and nationalism is extremely tricky. I don't believe that we want any political faction to own patriotism, or to own Dunkirk. These are points of national pride.
>
> (Collin 2017)

Despite this sentiment, towards the end of *Dunkirk*, a distinct nationalist agenda seems to come to the fore as images of the stranded soldiers rejoice at the arrival of the so-called 'little ships' to the tune of Elgar's theme. The subsequent shots of their triumphant return to an idealized version of Britain and Commander Bolton's decision to remain on the beach 'For the French', further contribute towards a nostalgic narrative of British exceptionalism and imperial values.

John Corner (2018) points out that the overall sentiment of the film's ending is broadly steeped within the emotionally affirming mythic tonalities of the way that the history of Dunkirk has been collectively remembered and embraced as part of British identity. He says:

> The determined positivity of national mood in the face of setback is heightened by its contrast with the shame and criticism which some of the soldiers are shown to be expecting, thereby stabilizing the film's core values and linking its various fictive depictions to a dominant version of the national-historical.
>
> (Corner 2018)

For Corner, *Dunkirk* contributes to the prevailing mythic national-historic narrative of the 'Dunkirk spirit' that was nurtured in Britain during the wartime years by both politicians and the media (Calder 1992). The myth of Dunkirk was, at the time, a carefully constructed piece of propaganda that portrayed Britain as a unified land of 'ordinary people' contributing to the war effort. Since then, the cultural memory of the events has been used by a range of politicians and cultural commentators at different times of national crises. Margret Thatcher and several other leading Conservative politicians, for example, evoked the 'Dunkirk Spirit' in 1982 to galvanize British support for the Falklands War (Calder 1992: xiv). According to Mark Connolly, '[t]he myth of Dunkirk and the "Dunkirk spirit" have become vital to our self-perceptions, for they underline and confirm our sense of apartness, of otherness, of self-reliance and insularity, of coolness under tremendous pressure, of surviving' (2014: 54). These ideas are embodied by the collective memory of the 'little ships' operated by civilian crews which assisted in the evacuation and subsequently became national symbols of British resilience (Calder 1992: 26). Yet, as Angus Calder reveals, '[f]ew members of the British Expeditionary Force owed their passage to "little ships"' (1992: 97). In *Dunkirk*, Nolan contributes to the dominant nation-historic myth of Dunkirk by building towards the climactic rescue of the soldiers and emphasizing the role of the little ships.

That the attempts to rewrite or reimagine what Winston Churchill labelled a 'colossal military disaster' have been ideological in nature is self-evident. But, the repeated return to this historical moment across both film and television evidences a more complex relationship with a cultural discourse that extends beyond the appropriation of the past for political means. In reality, references to this event can be understood within the broader psychoanalytical context of the return of the repressed. Like individual trauma, cultural trauma must also be repressed. As Freud notes, however, the mechanism of repression as a process is doomed to fail because the repressed material ultimately breaks through into consciousness and manifests as unwanted symptoms ([1914] 1958: 150). In this example, the repeated return to the events of Dunkirk across a variety of cultural artefacts is seemingly testament to an unresolved fixation with its history that is perhaps connected to an element of psychic trauma. The unpleasant repressed truth of the humiliating defeat continues to manifest, yet the symbolic function of the little ships plays a crucial role in rewriting the past.

Dunkirk: Remain or Leave

The renewed focus on the Second World War across both film and television seems to answer a cultural need brought on by present anxieties and insecurities. In Chapter 6, I discussed this desire as an *individual* pathology related to nostalgia. However, nostalgia not only operates as a personal experience but also as a *collective* phenomenon. Where the nostalgia commonly refers to a person's distinctly unique memories, collective nostalgia invokes a shared perception of the way that society used to be. There is a considerable amount of overlap between these two types of memory, but one key distinction lies in the way that collective nostalgia can reflect a broader social consciousness. Janelle L. Wilson points out, for example, that '[c]ollective nostalgia can serve the purpose of forging a national identity, expressing patriotism. It also might reflect selective remembering and selective forgetting that occur at the collective level' (2005: 31). Nostalgia is thus central to narratives of how we define ourselves, both through our perception of an imagined home and in relation to others. This understanding of the ways that nostalgia can be expressed by cultural texts and articulated by those in positions of power provides one possible explanation for the shift in British political discourse during the decade leading up to the 2016 referendum on membership of the European Union – more commonly known as Brexit.

Nostalgic invocations of tropes related to the Second World War by politicians and the media occurred frequently throughout the Brexit campaign (Eaglestone 2018). For example, when asked whether the British government was ready for potentially tense negotiations with EU leaders, the former Brexit Secretary David Davis announced, '[o]ur civil service can cope with World War Two, they can easily cope with this' (McDonald 2017). Similarly, the former United Kingdom Independence Party (UKIP) leader, Nigel Farage, also repeatedly referred to the Second World War in his comments relating to the Vote Leave campaign declaring, 'I believe [...] that in many ways this referendum on EU membership is our modern-day Battle of Britain' (2015). Sophie Gaston and Sacha Hilhorst argue that the nostalgic rhetoric employed by both politicians and the media during the EU referendum campaign was an important factor in contributing to the outcome (2018: 70). Likewise, the contribution of popular cultural texts to sociopolitical debates should not be dismissed, especially given the abundance of films connected to the Second World War, including *Dunkirk*, that have been released in the years leading up to, and following, the referendum which invite the viewer to adopt a nostalgic gaze onto an idealized version of the past. Referring to the war film, Belton notes that '[t]he genre has become a battleground on which different political factions have fought with one another over the hearts and minds of [...] moviegoers' (2012: 205), and while *Dunkirk* was conceived sometime before the referendum it has since been utilized as a vehicle through which political commentators have attempted to shore up support for the result (see McKinstry 2017). During an interview with *Screen*, Nolan vehemently denied the film's inferred connections to the politics of Brexit stating that:

Interpreting the events of 1940 through a modern lens is frankly disrespectful to the people who lived through the real-life events. This is something that happened in 1940, not something that's happening in 2017. Brexit happened while we were shooting and was as much a surprise to us as to everybody else. As a filmmaker, you can't control the world that your film goes out into. What you can do is be true to the real-life events and what they meant to the people who were involved in them. Dunkirk is a story about community. It's a story about people coming together in the face of evil. And I think different political groups taking that to mean different things means they are necessarily ignoring certain elements of the film.

(Wiseman 2017)

Nevertheless, despite his claims to the contrary, Nolan's own admission in a separate interview that *Dunkirk can* be interpreted through the lens of *other* contemporary events – specifically the Mediterranean Migrant crisis of 2015–16 (Berman 2017) – fails to take into consideration the established connections between anxieties relating to immigration and Britain's decision to leave the EU (see Goodwin and Milazzo 2017). Consequently, while Nolan may be reluctant to acknowledge the film's direct relationship to Brexit, *Dunkirk*'s celebration of values which are perceived to have been fostered during the Second World War in Britain (Harris 2004: 317), cannot help but feed the national image of British exceptionalism at a time of deep social, political and economic uncertainty.

While Nolan's personal relationship with the politics of Brexit seems to be somewhat contradictory based on his comments in various interviews, the film itself can be read in relation to a rising tide of nationalist sentiment in Britain. When viewed through the prism of contemporary events, *Dunkirk* – alongside several other concurrent film releases relating to the Second World War – provides a commentary on the present by reconsidering the impact and meaning of events that are deeply embedded within the British psyche. Like those war films produced in the immediate aftermath of the Second World War, the general sentiment of *Dunkirk* contributes to the revision of a historically significant event. In this instance, the film is part of a wider ongoing social project to rewrite the evacuation of Dunkirk as the defiant victory of the so-called 'little boats'. This collaboration with the existing national-historic myth relating to Dunkirk takes on a particular significance when considered within the broader sociopolitical climate of nostalgic nationalism in Britain during the lead up to and following the EU referendum. However, it should be noted that the final shot of the film complicates this reading to some extent.

At the end of *Dunkirk*, the soldiers are welcomed home as heroes but the last shot of the film – a close up of Tommy's face – problematizes the relationship between *Dunkirk*'s otherwise celebratory tone and the claims that it supports a nostalgic form of nationalism. During this scene, men, women and children rush to greet the returning soldiers as Tommy reads out a famous speech by Winston Churchill designed to rally the support of the British people. In the speech itself, Churchill called for national unity and resolve in the face of adversity, but these words seem to run counter to Tommy's instinct for survival evidenced throughout the film. The final shot of his facial expression, therefore, highlights a discrepancy between how the returning soldiers will likely be perceived by the public and the reality of their traumatic experiences. In an interview that precedes the screenplay for the film, Nolan discusses the character's motivation in this scene stating that: 'he's trying to process the words he's just read from this very eloquent politician and trying to reconcile that with his experience. Hopefully, the audience is trying to do the same thing, through his eyes' (2017: xv). In truth, however, the film's final shot is, like many of Nolan's films, ambiguous and open to interpretation. Even though the filmmaker has encouraged the spectator to experience the evacuation of *Dunkirk* as a secondary witness to the trauma of war via the formal and stylistic construction of the film, the meaning of Tommy's expression remains unclear, thus rendering a political interpretation of this moment largely redundant. In effect, the final shot does not address the politics of the event, but rather, it reminds us that behind the myth of *Dunkirk*, actual soldiers and people's lives were irrevocably changed by the trauma of war.

NOTES

1. This chapter does not seek to offer a conclusive statement regarding the film's historical accuracy, although some of what I discuss involves examining the appropriation of certain myths associated with the events of *Dunkirk* which, in turn, necessitates an engagement with the concept of nostalgia outlined in Chapter 6.

2. An estimated 31 million people watched the funeral of Diana, Princess of Wales, and 27.3 million people saw the opening ceremony of the London 2012 Olympics. At the time of writing, these events are two of the most watched television broadcasts in the United Kingdom (Duncan 2017).

Conclusion: Ending at the Beginning with *Doodlebug, Following* and *Memento*

It's all about endings, it's about knowing where you want to go.

– Nolan cited in YTS Digital Films 2011

At the end of *Doodlebug*, Nolan's three-minute short film about a man attempting to catch an insect in his apartment, it becomes apparent that the claustrophobic space in which the events have unfolded is, in fact, a room-within-a-room, a series of duplicate apartments each smaller than the last endlessly repeating in what amounts to a stylistic homage to the recursive Droste Effect (a picture within a picture within a picture that can, in theory, continue *ad infinitum*). At its core, the narrative depicts a tormented man stuck in a perpetual loop of self-inflicted pain. Images of his anguish and despair alongside the prevalence of clocks ticking on-screen and on the soundtrack foreground immediate parallels to both *Memento* and *Inception*, but it is the film's twist ending – that the 'insect' is a miniature version of the man pursuing it – which most clearly bears the artistic imprint of Nolan's unique directorial style while foreshadowing many of the themes that are apparent in his later films including the trappings of time, identity, obsession and paranoia.

Will Brooker points out that, even though there is a vast financial and creative difference between *Doodlebug* and Nolan's big-budget films such as *Interstellar*, what is notable about his career trajectory is not how far he has come but rather, 'how close he remains to his earlier visions, or how consistently he *returns* to them' (2015: xi, emphasis added). With this in mind and in addition to the conclusions already drawn at the end of each chapter, this final chapter revisits Nolan's early films – both *Following* and *Memento* – in much the same way that the spectator is encouraged to do so while watching them: by retroactively reconsidering their meaning at the end. This approach not only allows for a re-evaluation of these films considering Nolan's subsequent career development, but it also enables an analysis of the stylistic and thematic traces that have emerged as an outcome of

146

the discussions presented thus far relating to Nolan's representation of trauma. In what follows, I focus on each film's respective ending to argue that they are indicative of Nolan's filmmaking to date which I suggest repeatedly conveys trauma and loss at the level of theme, structure and *mise-en-scène* as well as the spectator's compulsion to repeat and replay his films.

In many respects, even though this book has so far examined a wide range of scenes from a number of Nolan's films, implicit in almost all those analysed is the importance of their endings. Instances such as whether Ellie (Hillary Swank) chooses to divulge Detective Dormer's (Al Pacino) indiscretions at the end of *Insomnia*, the proper meaning of Cutter's (Michael Caine) closing narration in *The Prestige* and the fate of Cobb's (Leonardo DiCaprio) spinning top in the final moments of *Inception* are just a few examples of the unanswered questions that encourage the spectator to repeatedly return to these films in search of further meanings. Unlike many mainstream films which are often governed by a logic of desire that orientates the protagonist (and by proxy, the spectator) towards an object that offers the momentary and illusory satisfaction of desire, by deploying these ambiguous and often indeterminate endings Nolan sabotages the spectator's desire for completeness by prompting an encounter with the traumatic Real. In Nolan's films, satisfaction can – although invariably does not – emerge from a linear pursuit of the object of desire (as is the case in many conventional Hollywood narratives). Instead, the spectator's enjoyment of his films is in the repetition associated with the failure of desire. In *Following*, Nolan's debut feature film, repetition emerges as a central theme that guides the spectator's response and involves them in the shared realization that, in the end, like the protagonist, they too have been duped by the way in which the chain of events has unfolded.

Following: Nolan Begins

During the opening post-credit sequence of *Following* a young man, or Bill (Jeremy Theobald) as he is sometimes referred to, attempts to rationalize his motives for 'shadowing' seemingly random people. He tells a police officer (John Nolan) that 'the following is my explanation. Well, more of an account of what happened'. While this line of dialogue is intended to be expository in nature, it performs the dual function of introducing the protagonist and emphasizing that Bill's 'account' is implicitly only one part of or one perspective on, the whole story. This line of dialogue, therefore, alludes to a hidden layer of meaning that exists just beneath the film's surface, which occasionally ruptures the narrative in the form of allegory and metaphor but whose meaning only becomes fully evident during the film's climax. The veiled reference contained within the opening line of dialogue also acts as a primer for the narrative given that, unbeknownst to Bill (and the spectator), his version of events is only partially complete as his perspective of them has been engineered and orchestrated by a mysterious stranger known by the name of Cobb (Alex Haw).

Andrew Kania confirms that even though Bill thought he was actively following, 'he was, in fact, being led' (2015: 176). He goes on to suggest that Bill's failure to register Cobb's manipulation is also shared by the spectator who experiences an analogue in their structural relationship to the film. For Kania, the spectator's belief in the possibility of a future-orientated explanation that will retroactively assign meaning is precisely how they capitulate to the deception that occurs at the level of the filmic discourse. This is perhaps why at the end of the film – when all that remains of Bill's account is a shoebox full of evidence that falsely implicates him in a murder committed by Cobb – the spectator experiences the same response to this revelation that Bill does. In the final moments of the film, the phantom-like puppeteer status of Cobb is cemented with a cinematic flourish that depicts him literally vanishing into a crowd on a busy West End street. Cobb's disappearance via this transition is a fitting way to conclude the film as it momentarily foregrounds the role of an implied author who, like Cobb, has orchestrated the spectator's perception of the events. Where Bill remains largely blind to the way that Cobb has staged the events for him to encounter, the spectator too fails to recognize the way that Nolan structures the film around an awareness of their look. At this moment, then, just as Bill begins to comprehend Cobb's role in shaping his own narrative trajectory, the same can also be said of the spectator who briefly registers the absent yet structuring presence of the director before both the character and his creator vanish in the instant that the film concludes.

Discussing *Following*, Kania comments that the film's central puzzle is 'simply to figure out, from the non-linear narrative, what actually happens in the fictional world of the film – though the process of figuring this out is by no means simple' (2015: 176). But, Todd McGowan argues that if this is the central aim of the spectator then they are fundamentally misguided (2012: 33). Instead, the spectator of the film, indeed of all Nolan's films, 'must see the truth of the desire articulated by the filmic fiction' (McGowan 2012: 33). McGowan goes on to indicate that this does not require deciphering the plot or uncovering the ambiguities that it might contain, but rather that the truth of the desire is instead 'the truth of the filmic discourse itself' (McGowan 2012: 33). He says, '[t]he structure of every filmic discourse exposes a desire, and this is the desire that animates the film. By focusing on this desire, the spectator can discover the unconscious truth of the social order itself' (McGowan 2012: 33). As is often the case in Nolan's films, however, the spectator is all too frequently lured by the prospect of a hidden meaning. Even if the spectator claims to have discovered it, however, or sees it coming a second time around, there remains another layer, which seems to exist just out of reach. As a consequence, whether attempting to determine whether Bruce Wayne (Christian Bale) survived the explosion during the conclusion of *The Dark Knight Rises* or if Cooper (Matthew McConaughey) is successful in his mission to rendezvous with Amelia (Anne Hathaway) at the end of *Interstellar*, it is the spectator's investment in the object of desire – the hidden meaning – that diverts them away from understanding that in truth, the focus of these films is the subject's relationship to the experience of trauma. As Brooker suggests, '[t]he central enigma is, rather than a narrative hook, often the whole point: the restless ambiguity that stays with us after the film becomes the central meaning' (2015: xi–xii).

In the context of Nolan's first feature film, McGowan writes that '[u]nravelling the narrative development of *Following* requires identifying the logic of desire that structures it, not determining the linear chronology that it hides' (2012: 30). He adds, '[t]he idea of a hidden linear chronology – a story waiting to be deciphered from the filmic discourse – represents a lure for the spectator' (2012: 30). For McGowan, restoring the film's fragmented narrative to a linear order of events undermines the logic of desire that is evident in the pattern of shot-to-shot editing that structures the film, he says '[r]ather than showing a linear causality tied to the temporality of the clock, [Nolan] edits the film in a way that stresses the logic of desire' (2012: 29). Even though the film opens (and closes) with Bill's confession, it is the non-linear arrangement of the scenes in-between which reveals the logic of desire. Specifically, as *Following* unfolds in short, episodic, seemingly random narrative segments or what Jacqueline Furby labels 'discontinuous uncontextualized durational snapshots' (2015: 262), it is implied that this arbitrary arrangement of scenes will, once concluded, communicate meaning. Just as Lacan suggests that a sentence's meaning is derived retroactively from the effect of applied punctuation ([1981] 1993: 262–63), the spectator's investment in *Following* is based on an expected ending that will function in much the same way by providing a momentary pause in which meaning can be obtained. However, the non-linear structure of the film reveals that meaning is not solely derived from the movement towards the end, but rather through the structure of the experience itself.

Broadly speaking, whereas the linear presentation of cause and effect evident in conventional mainstream approaches to narrative allows the spectator to be aligned with the pursuit of an object of desire (i.e. finding love, achieving success, returning home and so on), a non-linear narrative can force the spectator to re-evaluate their relationship to the object by foregrounding their relationship to time. Such revisions, for instance, can indicate the inherent impossibility of obtaining the object by undermining the spectator's investment in causality. In her chapter on *Following* and existentialism, Erin Kealey writes that each scene 'becomes more like a piece of a jigsaw puzzle connected to various other pieces: remove any one and the surrounding others lose their context' (2015: 221). In *Following*, the introduction of each new individual narrative segment obstructs the linear movement of time but because the film provides subtle chronological markers – Bill's appearance for example – it suggests that the possibility of revealing the linear order of events (and thus the implicit secret) exists only to undermine it with each passing shift to a new segment. Accordingly, it motivates the spectator's desire in a Lacanian manner whereby desire is sustained by not encountering the object of desire, which, in this instance, is the illusory secret that the linear ordering of the plot seems to mask. By structuring *Following* in such a manner, Nolan establishes a foundation for his subsequent films that adhere to a structural, thematic and visual pattern of repetition associated with the intersection between trauma and desire.

In *Following*, the spectator does not engage with Bill's experience of trauma in perhaps the same way that, for example, the spectator of *The Dark Knight* trilogy or *Interstellar* does. As we have seen in Chapters 3 and 6, in these films – which occur later in Nolan's career – an encounter with the traumatic Real ruptures the narrative early on and thereafter functions as a focal point around which the remnants of the story orbit. Instead, in *Following*, the possibility that an encounter with the traumatic Real might occur structures the entire narrative. However, it is not until the film's climax when Bill finally recognizes that he has been duped by Cobb that the rupture finally occurs. At this moment, the camera lingers on Bill's blank expression as he, along with the spectator, attempts to reconcile what has happened. Here, Bill's catatonic rigidity and his loss of words exhibit symptoms of trauma (see Moskowitz 2004). However, it is also at this point that Nolan's representation of the traumatic experience extends outwards from the film's visual syntax to bridge the gap between the character's circumstances and the spectator's attempt to retroactively determine the linear ordering of the events. The spectator of *Following* is thus placed in the same position that Bill occupies throughout the diegesis, which involves the misguided pursuit of an object that superficially masks the trauma that they seek to escape. Where Bill seeks the truth of his own being, the spectator seeks the truth that the complex narrative seemingly hides not realizing that it is self-evident. Nolan's next film continues this dynamic with a narrative structure that forces the spectator to confront their own position as what McGowan refers to as a 'subject of desire' (2012: 41).

Memento

During the climactic scenes of *Memento*, Leonard (Guy Pearce) kills the drug dealer Jimmy Grantz (Larry Holden) having been led to believe by Teddy (Joe Pantoliano) that he is *the* John G. who apparently raped and murdered his wife. However, fearing that he has killed the wrong man, Leonard subsequently confronts Teddy who eventually reveals that he helped Leonard avenge his wife's assault[1] a year earlier. He tells Leonard that he wanted to use his inability to form new memories to profit from Jimmy's death. Among others, this revelation causes Leonard to create a false link between his wife's death and Teddy's license plate number which, when combined with his 'condition', effectively triggers a series of events that lead to Teddy's death.[2] As with *Following*, the climax of the film forces the spectator to re-evaluate everything that they have seen prior to this moment although, in this instance, it becomes clear that there exists a central ambiguity about the ending that undermines any clear sense of resolution. The doubt that Teddy casts on Leonard's narrative of events, the Polaroid evidence of Leonard's initial revenge killing as well as his own subsequent willingness to deceive himself by manipulating his 'condition' means that the spectator is confronted with a number of challenges to their preconceptions regarding Leonard's past, his motivations and his morality.

The climactic revelation at the end of *Memento* has the effect, then, of transforming the entire narrative. It retroactively (re)frames each character's actions by providing a previously unknown context, that of Leonard's wilful self-deception. The conclusion of the film also establishes that Leonard's conscious actions are guided by his unconscious and conscious desire to perpetuate (rather than conclude) the quest to find his wife's alleged killer. By burning the Polaroid evidence of his previous killings and falsely targeting Teddy as the new suspect of his investigation Leonard is able to sustain the motivation behind his revenge plot.[3] He is, therefore, a 'subject of desire' (2012: 41) as he acts in accordance with that which would sustain his desire rather than eliminate it to the extent that he even avoids the truth in order to continually (re)experience the trauma that underpins his existence (2012: 50). Just as Leonard is caught in the loop of desire, the film also, according to McGowan, 'makes it impossible for the spectator to escape the loop of desire' (2012: 56). In principle, this is due to the spectator's inability to draw a definitive conclusion from the events that unfold. Anna Kornbluh argues that the film functions by 'mobilizing in the spectator the desire to decide whodunit and, simultaneously, rendering this desire not only impossible to fulfil, but *false*, and as such, *irrelevant*' (2004: 135, original emphasis). Here, *Memento* shares an affinity with a number of Nolan's other films, which similarly position the spectator as a subject of desire. For example, one watches *Insomnia* with the desire to solve the mystery of the murder, but the film reveals that this crime has nothing to do with what ultimately motivates Detective Dormer's (Al Pacino) actions. Instead, in *Insomnia* the truth of the film emerges from an understanding of Dormer's relationship to his past act of planting evidence. Similarly, as I have shown in Chapters 5 and 6, in *Inception* and *Interstellar* the spectator's desire to witness each protagonist's quest to be successfully reunited with their children betrays where the truth of each film resides. In the former, the question as to whether the top keeps spinning diverts the spectator's attention away from realizing the potential of fictions to dramatically reshape our perception of reality and in the latter, the spectator's emotional investments in Cooper's reunion with Murph (Mackenzie Foy/Jessica Chastain/Ellen Burstyn) means that his willingness to abandon her for a second time is largely forgiven despite his motivation to leave being, on both occasions, based on a selfish desire to be an explorer rather than a father. In all these examples, the point is that the narrative lure of these films is not to obtain the object of desire but rather to understand the desire that animates the search, something that is invariably rooted in the subject's relationship to trauma.

Shelia Kunkle suggests that what is exposed in these types of films that are not principally motivated by the search for an object of desire is the 'circularity involved in the constitution of the subject itself' (2016: 11). Here, Kunkle is referring to Lacan's proposition discussed in Chapter 3 that it is only through the repression of the child's desire for the mother that they can enter the Symbolic. Yet, simultaneously, this separation sets into motion a circular process that is based upon their repeated attempts to return to the previous state of being. Thus, those films which employ the use of repetition, multiples, alternative realities or perhaps offer indeterminate resolutions – as Nolan's filmmaking frequently does – are the kinds of films that foreground, 'the gap or loop of the subject's causality' (2016: 11). For Kunkle, in the endings of these films, a traumatic encounter with the Real can occur during the spectator's realization that something has been missed (2016: 5). The gap in their knowledge is something that only returning to the text in the form of repetition can fill and yet, even when watching a film for a second time there remains the possibility that the gap may remain. Such endings, therefore, exhibit the value of the psychoanalytic approach adopted throughout this book as they 'demonstrate something important about the subject itself' (2016: 11).

The End Matters

As I have discussed elsewhere in Chapters 1 and 3, according to Lacan, the subject exists in an indeterminate state of perpetual lack. This lack is derived from the child's separation from the mother, an experience which creates the gap – the surplus of meaning that cannot be signified – that Lacan refers to as the Real. The Real, however, not only operates as lack but also as an excess because lack is founded upon the repression of desire that occurs during the child's entry into the Symbolic. As a consequence of that repression, the subject is caught in a condition of seeking to recover the absent, but impossible state of wholeness. Even though our day-to-day experience of reality contributes towards the overall impression of being on a linear path that begins with birth and ends with death, in truth our lives are organized according to a series of repetitions that emerge from need and satisfaction, desire and repression. Ultimately these films, therefore, foreground this process as they 'disorient our sense of our singular selves on a chronological path toward a certain end and short-circuit the dimensions of being and meaning' (Kunkle 2016: 11).

The desire for meaning, to draw together separate threads as a way of attempting to constitute the wholeness of being, is inherent to people and is perhaps one of the fundamental organizing principles, as well as the main appeals, of conventional stories (see Brooks [1984] 1992: 37). If a film rejects or defers the straightforward resolution of desire, however, it can be aligned with the Lacanian proposition that our experience of reality is structurally incomplete and because of that possibility, our response to it is frequently guided by further intrigue. The endings to many of Nolan's films to date, for instance, frequently rupture our conventional expectations by either concluding ambiguously, confronting us with a twist or leaving a number of questions unanswered. In doing so, these films open gaps that force us to insert our own interpretation while at the same time resisting a final definitive conclusion. In line with Paul Sutton's (2004) concept of cinematic *afterwardsness*, the moment that these films conclude, the spectator is provided with a temporary vantage point from which to view the events so that they might begin the process of retroactive analysis required to produce meaning and closure.[4] However, those films that contain gaps in the narrative or end indeterminately require the spectator to bridge these gaps, to fill in the missing details and to offer interpretations that nonetheless foreground the impossibility of closing off the text as well as drawing attention to the very excess generated by these interpretations.

Although the vast majority of Hollywood genre films attempt to provide some form of closure by tying up a story's loose ends thereby ensuring the momentary satisfaction of desire, Kunkle suggests that films which break out of the 'genre formula' make use of what she, building on the writings of Slavoj Žižek, refers to as 'blank spots' (1992: 6). By blank spots, Kunkle is referring to Žižek's discussion of narrative closure where *'the space of "what can be said", the subject's universe of meaning, is "always curved" by traumatic blanks,* organized around what must remain unsaid if this universe is to retain its consistency' (1992: 242, original emphasis). In other words, within a narrative there exists a paradoxical element that draws attention to the filmmaker's role in the construction of the text whose presence 'curves' the narrative space. Here, Žižek provides the example of the penultimate scene from *Psycho* (1960) during which Norman Bates (Anthony Perkins) raises his head and stares directly into the camera with a knowing expression that displays an awareness of our complicity in his actions while simultaneously reversing the gaze of the camera back onto us. At this moment the spectator shifts, as it were, from the position of an omnipotent transcendental subject to one where they feel as though they are directly addressed (Žižek 1992: 234). This shift prompts an encounter with the Real since it forces the spectator to confront their own subjectivity by acknowledging that they are accounted for within the film itself while, at the same time, presenting them with 'a trauma that goes beyond fantasy's ability to point us toward an object that would make everything all right' (Kunkle 2016: 6). Likewise, I have shown that Nolan's cinema prompts a similar type of engagement since it possesses the ability to disrupt the spectator's perceived mastery over the images presented by invoking an encounter with the traumatic Real.

Understood in Lacanian terms, Nolan's films *speak* to the spectator by calling attention to the filmic discourse in ways that Hollywood films rarely do by immersing the spectator in the narrative while simultaneously challenging their position of spectatorship. This occurs most visibly through the overt manipulation of time and space in his earliest films such as *Following* and *Memento*, but is also evident elsewhere in the achronological timelines of *The Prestige*, *Batman Begins*, *Inception* and *Dunkirk* as well as in the overarching circular temporal structure of *The Dark Knight* trilogy. In these films, the non-linear arrangement of scenes exposes the mechanisms of production thereby emphasizing the power of the filmic discourse over the narrative while, at the same time, also displaying the emotional investment that binds the spectator to the unfolding events. As I have shown in both *Following* and *Memento*, for example, the atemporal structure of these films provides the spectator with a confusing and fragmented viewing experience which would ordinarily promote an active awareness of the mechanisms designed to mask the falsity of the fictional world presented on-screen. However, given that the structures so closely mirror the experiences of each film's protagonist, these narratives function as both an invocation of the traumatic Real *and* a defence against it.

Beyond the formal construction of each film's sequences, Nolan's frequent use of an unreliable narrator in a number of his non-franchise films can also be considered a tool that self-consciously points towards the role of an implied author who, on one level, is responsible for immersing the spectator in the unreliability of the account provided by the characters but is also, on a deeper level, responsible for revealing the selectivity of the events presented. In *Following*, even though the protagonist is a *reliable* narrator, it is his belief in the truth that means he doesn't foresee the trap into which he falls. As a result, the spectator cannot help but be deceived by his voice-over narration, a narration that aims to prove his innocence but ultimately condemns him to prison. In *Memento*, the spectator's investment in Leonard's quest for revenge emerges from the lie that he tells himself, a lie that retroactively produces an altogether different perspective of the narrative events. This trend continues in *Insomnia*, discussed in Chapter 2, where Detective Dormer's decision to frame a suspect is hinted at throughout but only fully revealed towards the film's conclusion. Unlike *Memento*, Dormer's lie is a constant burden that he carries with him, but the film uses misdirection as well as the narrative construction to implicate the spectator in the lie. Elsewhere, in *The Prestige*, the pattern of shot-to-shot editing deceives the spectator in such a way that lures them to place an undue emphasis on the magicians' secrets. Finally, in *Inception*, the spectator's commitment to Cobb's willingness to embark on one last job so that he might be able to return home to his children is undermined when it is revealed that what he seeks is to absolve his own role in his wife's suicide.

In each of these films the unreliable narrator or, in some instances, the unreliable narrative representation that emerges through the pattern of shot-to-shot editing forces the spectator out of a position of passivity to understand the film and to produce meaning. However, each character's revelation occurs late enough in each respective narrative so that, by then, the spectator has already been made complicit in the character's actions meaning that the unreliable narrator draws attention to the character's psychology as much as the spectator's awareness of an implied author. Each film, therefore, invokes the Real while defending against it through the ways in which the spectator is accounted for within the film. What is conspicuously absent, however, from these observations about Nolan's films is a discussion of *Interstellar* if only because the film does not contain an unreliable narrator nor does it attempt to deceive the spectator through the arrangement of scenes. Instead, in *Interstellar* the tesseract offers a metaphorical image of cinema, which, like the allegories of magic tricks and shared dreams of *The Prestige* and *Inception*, provides a subtler way for the filmmaker to comment on the filmic discourse without disrupting the audience's voluntary suspension of disbelief (see Olson 2015: 47).

As I have shown in Chapter 6, *Interstellar* is somewhat unique within Nolan's catalogue of films produced so far in that it marks an overt departure from the narrative organization of his previous films. In these other films, the experience of trauma is an absent yet structuring presence that frequently characterizes the temporal arrangement of the scenes via nonrealist narrational strategies, which occasionally rupture the diegesis in such a way that emphasizes its potency to stop the linear flow of time. By contrast, in *Interstellar*, the structure of trauma remains embedded within the narrative in terms of story and *mise-en-scène* but there is a markedly different attitude expressed towards trauma. This shift finds its antecedents in the concluding moments of *The Prestige* and *Inception* but is also evident elsewhere in the resolution of *The Dark Knight Rises*; nonetheless, it emerges most fully formed in *Interstellar*. Unlike *The Prestige*, *Inception* and *The Dark Knight Rises*,[5] which imply a possible path towards the resolution of trauma through the love of an other, Cooper's successful reconciliation with Murph clearly shows that he can break the closed temporal loop associated with the structure of trauma. Of significance is Nolan's decision to depict the cathartic moment that takes place between them upon his return. Whereas similar instances in both *Inception* and *The Dark Knight Rises* only hint at the reality of the familial or romantic union, Nolan's decision to allow the spectator to witness the moment that Murph and Cooper reunite in *Interstellar* is, on the surface, indicative of a growing embrace of sentimentality and melodrama in his approach to trauma. But, it should be added that the depiction of their reunion is tinged with sadness, the underlying implication being that what has been lost can never be recovered. According to this conception of trauma, even though an individual can adopt an accepting attitude towards by working-through the experience of trauma, we are ultimately unable to fully translate our pain and suffering into language. Instead, there is always something left over – a leftover Lacan calls desire. This is perhaps why, in the final scene of *Interstellar*, Cooper's willingness to leave his daughter for the second time in favour of seeking out a new frontier aligns him with the solitary hero of the classic western genre whose desire to extend the nation's border can never be satiated and so cannot live in the world they helped to create. It is this desire that once again points to the lack in being.

What this evidence further demonstrates is that in the confines of the cinema we can encounter the trauma of the Real. But, to do so it seems that the spectator cannot be a passive participant in the act of viewing. Instead, they must actively engage with the film on a psychological level. What this means is that a film must challenge the spectator in such a way that it generates moments where the Real ruptures the conventional passivity of the spectator/screen relationship. This evidence may help to explain why Nolan has emerged as one of the most critically and commercially successful directors of the twenty-first century. One of the guiding principles of Nolan's films is that, unlike his mainstream contemporaries, he can allude to the very dynamism of the spectatorial experience – to speak of the active and creative aspects of watching a film – while simultaneously immersing the spectator in the narrative. What this requires is the recognition that Nolan's films present us with a number of ways through which we might experience them. The most common perspective, shared by both critics and audiences alike, is that his films are mysteries waiting to be solved. But, another way of understanding his films is to recognize that to succumb to the lure of the secret – to try and obtain the object of desire – is to misapprehend the true meaning of the film, which is invariably a commentary on the subject's relationship to trauma.

My aim for this book was to explore how Nolan engages with and attempts to represent trauma. Ultimately, I was less interested in determining the impact of individual traumatic events than I was in examining the structure of the traumatic experience, which invariably begins on-screen but also extends outwards to the spectator's engagement with Nolan's films. The resulting implication was that the uniting feature of his films is the subject's relationship to trauma, which becomes visible through repetition at the level of theme, form and *mise-en-scène* as well as the spectator's compulsion to repeat and replay his films. The act of repetition – whether occurring in relation to the shape of Nolan's atemporal narrative structures or in the literal repetition of thematic motifs and entire scenes – foregrounds the way that film can mimic the structure of trauma as well as demonstrate the experience of its after-effects. Added to this, the spectator's willingness to replay his films allows them to vicariously experience the structure of trauma through an engagement with the cognitive shifts of traumatic memory. In addition, I have also demonstrated that when we come to analyse Nolan's films from the 2010s onwards, for example, in films such as *Inception*, *The Dark Knight Rises* and *Interstellar*, there is a noticeable shift in his treatment of trauma that is reflected in both the style and sentimental content of these films. This trend continues to a certain extent with *Dunkirk* (2017), a film focused on the successful evacuation of over 300,000 allied troops from Nazi-occupied France. It remains to be seen whether future Christopher Nolan films continue to explore his thematic emphasis on trauma. Needless to say, this kind of conjectural reasoning in constructing a plausible link to the themes that have dominated Nolan's career thus far, and which have been explored throughout this book, has the inadvertent effect of emphasizing one of the inherent limitations of the auteur theory.

A fundamental principle, as well as a central critique of the auteur theory, is, in many ways, its intrinsic revisionism. For example, much of the initial focus of French film critics such as Alexandre Astruc, André Bazin and François Truffaut concerned a complete *revaluation* of both French and Hollywood film canons. Similarly, in his influential 1962 essay, Andrew Sarris declared a pantheon of directors based on a *reassessment* of both films and filmmakers from Hollywood's past. To be considered an auteur, for Sarris, one must 'exhibit *recurrent* characteristics of style' (1962: 7, emphasis added), a notion that necessitates the existence of a corpus of films. Any critical assessment of the work produced by an auteur must therefore invariably engage in a holistic approach that, at the very least, considers more than one film. Consider, for instance, David Bordwell's statement that 'auteur criticism tries, in effect, to make aspects of the single film into narrational systems of a larger text, that of the *oeuvre*' (1985: 83, original emphasis). Such an approach is necessarily revisionist in nature and bears a structural similarity to the structural nature of trauma. In both instances, there is a tendency to impose a causal connection between the present and the past not merely retrospectively but retroactively. Where a traumatic event has the power to retroactively adjust our understanding of the past – altering it in the light of the present – the auteur critic constructs a revised history of an artist's body of work by identifying the authorial signature in those aspects of an individual film that are clearly related to the overall stylistic or thematic imprint of the director. This method, therefore, renders it possible to examine a film from a director that, intentionally or otherwise, endows their previous work with new meaning. Nolan, himself, acknowledges that it is the passage of time which allows meaning to be ascribed retroactively. He says:

> One of the things that troubles me and fascinates me about my world is that when you look back at film history, the connections between the films that are made in any given era are so clear and so obvious, yet they're not to us while we're actually making them. However much you might try to look at it from 50,000 feet, you really can't. So, for example, in the same way that if you look at how fears of communism manifested in 1950s science fiction, I think 20 years from now, people will look back at the films made in the wake of 9/11 and think the connections are stunningly obvious. But it's tough to live outside your own time.
>
> (Collin 2017)

In effect, then, Nolan's films not only involve trauma at the level of form and content, but the discourse of spectator and scholarly engagement that surrounds his films is also structured according to the temporal logic of trauma. By positioning him as an auteur Nolan's cinema is revealed to be a cinema of trauma.

NOTES

1. In terms of understanding the plot, it is significant that Teddy never refers to Leonard's wife's murder but rather her assault. This distinction lends his narrative of events some credibility due the level of consistency he maintains throughout.
2. Due to the complicated narrative structure, Teddy's death occurs at the beginning of the film but at the end of the narrative.
3. Leonard's willingness to destroy or fabricate false evidence is displayed at several other points throughout the film, but our investment in his quest for revenge blinds us to their size and importance. For instance, there are twelve pages of case notes missing from the police file related to the night of his wife's assault and the tattoos he has written on his body are also false leads.

4. There is a paradox here as meaning will necessarily always be incomplete for the simple reason that any formal ending (i.e. the cut to black or the beginning of the credits) is merely the springboard for further questions, speculation and analysis, because desire is manifest in an endless chain of signifiers, or the endless play of interpretation. Even in those films, which seemingly conclude unambiguously, the possibility to speculate about the characters' internal struggles exists after-the-fact as does the ability to retrospectively insert oneself into the plot to consider how one might have acted differently in a similar situation. In these scenarios, desire is sustained and the pursuit of meaning making continues.

5. In the climactic moments of *The Dark Knight Rises*, the ambiguous depiction of Bruce Wayne sat at a café in Florence is a form of closure for the spectator but not for the character. By living out Alfred's fantasy, Bruce's subjectivity remains bound to the gaze of an other and so implicitly remains a split subject. Even though the film seems to indicate that leaving Gotham provides him with a means to escape the trauma of his past, it is clear from this moment that he remains bound to it.

References

American Psychological Association (2000), *Diagnostic and Statistical Manual of Mental Disorders: DSM-IV-TR*, 4th ed., Washington, DC: APA.

Anderson, Lindsay (1957), 'Get out and push!', in T. Maschler (ed.), *Declaration*, London: MacGibbon & Kee, pp. 158–78.

Andrew, Geoff (2002), '*Insomnia*', *Timeout*, http://www.timeout.com/film/reviews/76055/insomnia.html. Accessed 18 August 2016.

Arlow, Jacob A. (1963), 'Conflict, regression, and symptom formation', *International Journal of Psychoanalysis*, 44, pp. 12–22.

Armes, Roy (1978), *A Critical History of British Cinema*, New York: Oxford University Press.

Armstrong, Richard (2012), *Mourning Films: A Critical Study of Loss and Grieving in Cinema*, Jefferson, NC: McFarland & Company Inc. Publishers.

Arnold-De Simine, Silke (2013), *Mediating Memory in the Museum: Trauma, Empathy, Nostalgia*, Basingstoke: Palgrave Macmillan.

Astruc, Alexandre (1948), 'The birth of a new avant-garde: La Caméra stylo', *L'ecran Français*, 141. Rpt. in P. Graham (ed.) (1968), *The New Wave*, Garden City, NJ: Doubleday, pp. 17–22.

Azari, Ehsan (2008), *Lacan and the Destiny of Literature: Desire, Jouissance and the Sinthome in Shakespeare*, New York: Continuum.

Baudry, Jean-Louis (1974), 'Ideological effects of the basic cinematographic apparatus', *Film Quarterly*, 28:2, pp. 39–47.

Beebe, John (1996), 'Jungian illumination of film', *Psychoanalytic Review*, 84:4, pp. 579–87.

Belton, John (2012), *American Cinema/American Culture*, 4th ed., New York: McGraw-Hill.

Benjamin, Walter ([1935] 1969), 'The work of art in the age of mechanical reproduction', in H. Arendt (ed.), *Illuminations*, New York: Schocken, pp. 217–52.

Bergson, Henri ([1896] 2004), *Matter and Memory*, New York: Dover.

—— ([1911] 2005), *Creative Evolution*, New York: Cosimo Classics.

Bergstrom, Anders (2015), 'The traces of "a half remembered dream": Christopher Nolan's *Inception* (2010), Wong Kar-wai's *2046* (2004), and the Memory Film', in R. J. A. Kilbourn and E. Ty (eds), *The Memory Effect: The Remediation of Memory in Literature and Film*, Ontario: Wilfrid Laurier University Press, pp. 195–210.

Bevan, Joseph (2012), 'Christopher Nolan: Escape artist', *Sight and Sound*, http://www.bfi.org.uk/news-opinion/sight-sound-magazine/features/christopher-nolan-escape-artist. Accessed 16 August 2016.

Bhatnagar, Gagan (2009), 'A psychoanalysis of *The Prestige*', *International Review of Psychiatry*, 21:3, pp. 276–77.

Birksted-Breen, Dana (2003), 'Time and the après-coup', *International Journal of Psychoanalysis*, 84, pp. 1501–15.

Blouin, Michael J. (2016), *Magical Thinking, Fantastic Film, and the Illusions of Neoliberalism*, New York: Palgrave Macmillan.

Blunt, Alison (2005), *Domicile and Diaspora: Anglo-Indian Women and the Spatial Politics of Home*, Oxford: Blackwell.

Bonanno, George A. and Keuler, David J. (1998), 'Psychotherapy without repressed memory: A parsimonious alternative based on contemporary memory research', in S. J. Lynn and K. M. McConkey (eds), *Truth in Memory*, New York: Guilford, pp. 437–63.

Bordwell, David (1985), *Narration in the Fiction Film*, Madison: University of Wisconsin Press.

Bordwell, David and Thompson, Kristin (2013), *Christopher Nolan: A Labyrinth of Linkages*, Madison, WI: Irvington Way Institute Press.

Bordwell, David and Carroll, Noel (eds) (1996), *Post Theory: Reconstructing Film Studies*, Madison: The University of Wisconsin Press.

Botez, Catalina (2015), 'Skin-deep memos as prosthetic memory in Christopher Nolan's *Memento* (2000)', in C. Rosenthal and D. Vanderbeke (eds), *Probing the Skin: Cultural Representations of Our Contact Zone*, Newcastle: Cambridge Scholars Publishing, pp. 312–34.

Box Office Mojo (2016), 'Christopher Nolan', http://www.boxofficemojo.com/people/chart/?view=Director&id=christophernolan.htm. Accessed 20 February 2015.

Boym, Susan (2001), *The Future of Nostalgia*, New York: Basic Books.

Breuer, Josef and Freud, Sigmund ([1895] 1957), 'Studies on hysteria' (trans. J. Strachey), in *The Standard Edition of the Complete Psychological works of Sigmund Freud*, vol. 2, New York: Basic Books.

Bronfen, Elisabeth (2012), *Specters of War: Hollywood's Engagement with Military Conflict*, New York: Rutgers.

Brooker, Will (2012), *Hunting the Dark Knight: Twenty-First Century Batman*, New York: I. B. Tauris & Company.

Brooks, Peter ([1976] 1995), *The Melodramatic Imagination: Balzac, Henry James, Melodrama and the Mode of Excess*, New Haven and London: Yale University Press.

—— ([1984] 1992), *Reading for the Plot: Design and Intention in Narrative*, Oxford: Claredon Press.

Brown, William (2014), 'Complexity and simplicity in *Inception* and *Five Dedicated to Ozu*', in W. Buckland (ed.), *Hollywood Puzzle Films*, New York and London: Routledge, pp. 125–40.

Brunsdon, Charlotte (1982), 'A subject for the seventies', *Screen*, 23:3–4, pp. 20–29.

Buckland, Warren (ed.) (2009), *Puzzle Films: Complex Storytelling in Contemporary Cinema*, Chichester: Wiley-Blackwell.

—— (ed.) (2014), *Hollywood Puzzle Films*, New York: Routledge.

Burnetts, Charles (2015), '"Downwards is the only way forwards": "Dream space", parallel time and selfhood in *Inception*', in M. Jones and J. Ormrod (eds), *Time Travel in Popular Media*, Jefferson, NC: McFarland & Company Inc Publishers, pp. 234–46.

Busch, Fred (2005), 'Conflict theory/trauma theory', *Psychoanalytic Quarterly*, 74, pp. 27–45.

Calder, Angus (1992), *The Myth of The Blitz*, London: Pimlico.

Calhoun, Lawrence G. and Tedeschi, Richard G. (1998), 'Posttraumatic growth: Future directions', in R. G. Tedeshci, C. L. Park and L. G. Calhoun (eds), *Posttraumatic Growth: Positive Changes in the Aftermath of Crisis*, Mahwah, NJ: Lawrence Erlbaum Associates, Publishers, pp. 215–38.

—— (2001), 'Posttraumatic growth: The positive lessons of loss', in R. A. Neimeyer (ed.), *Meaning Reconstruction and the Experience of Loss*, Washington, DC: American Psychological Association, pp. 157–72.

—— (eds) (2014), *Handbook of Posttraumatic Growth: Research and Practice*, London: Routledge.

Call the Midwife (2012–present, UK: Neal Street Productions).

Cameron, Allan (2008), *Modular Narratives in Contemporary Cinema*, Basingstoke: Palgrave Macmillan.

Carter, David (2019), *Inception*, New York: Columbia University Press.

Carter, Sean and Dodds, Klaus (2014), *International Politics and Film: Space, Vision, Power*, London: Wallflower Press.

Caruth, Cathy (1995), *Trauma: Explorations in Memory*, Baltimore, MD: Johns Hopkins University Press.

—— (1996), *Unclaimed Experience: Trauma, Narrative and History*, Baltimore, MD: Johns Hopkins University Press.

—— (2014), *Listening to Trauma: Conversations with Leaders in the Theory and Treatment of Catastrophic Experience*, Baltimore, MD: Johns Hopkins University Press.

Chow, Rey (1998), *Ethics After Idealism: Theory, Culture, Ethnicity, Reading*, Bloomington: Indiana University Press.

Clark, Melissa (2002), 'The space-time image: The case of Bergson, Deleuze, and *Memento*', *The Journal of Speculative Philosophy*, 16:3, pp. 167–81.

Coixet, Isabel (2017), *The Bookshop*, UK: Diagonal TV.

Collin, Robbie (2014), 'Christopher Nolan interview: "I'm completely invested in every project I do"', *The Telegraph*, 31 December, http://www.telegraph.co.uk/culture/film/11317410/Christopher-Nolan-interview-Im-completely-invested-in-every-project-I-do.html. Accessed 16 August 2016.

—— (2017), 'Christopher Nolan interview: "To me, Dunkirk is about European unity"', *The Telegraph*, https://www.telegraph.co.uk/films/0/christopher-nolan-interview-dunkirk-european-unity/. Accessed 12 February 2018.

Cook, Pam (2005), *Screening the Past: Memory and Nostalgia in Cinema*, London: Routledge.

Corner, John (2018), 'Nolan's *Dunkirk*: A note on spectacle, history and myth', *Open Screens*, https://openscreensjournal.com/articles/10.16995/os.3/. Accessed 21 September 2018.

Coveney, Peter and Highfield, Roger (1990), *The Arrow of Time*, New York: Ballantine Books.

Creed, Barbara (1978), 'The position of women in Hollywood melodramas', *Australian Journal of Screen Theory*, 4, pp. 27–31.

———— (2000), 'Film and psychoanalysis', in J. Hill and P. Church Gibson (eds), *Film Studies: Critical Approaches*, Oxford: Oxford University Press, pp. 75–88.

Darius, Julian (2011), *Improving the Foundations: Batman Begins from Comics to Screen*, Illinois: Sequart Research and Literacy Foundation.

Davies, Alastair and Sinfield, Alan (eds) (2000), *British Culture of the Post-War: An Introduction to Literature and Society 1945–1999*, London: Routledge.

Davis, Fred (1979), *Yearning for Yesterday: A Sociology of Nostalgia*, New York: Free Press.

De Valk, Mark and Arnold, Sarah (2013), *The Film Handbook*, London: Routledge.

Defalco, Amelia (2004), 'A double-edged longing: Nostalgia, melodrama, and Todd Haynes's *Far from Heaven*', *Iowa Journal of Cultural Studies*, 5, pp. 26–39.

Deleuze, Gilles (1986), *Cinema I: The Movement-Image*, London: Athlone.

———— (1989), *Cinema 2: The Time-Image*, London: Athlone.

Deleuze, Gilles and Guattari, Felix (1972), *Anti-Oedipus: Capitalism and Schizophrenia* (trans. R. Hurley, M. Seem and H. R. Lane), Minneapolis: University of Minnesota Press.

Demme, Jonathan (1991), *The Silence of the Lambs*, USA: Orion Pictures.

Dickinson, Hilary and Erben, Michael (2006), 'Nostalgia and autobiography: The past and the present', *Auto/Biography*, 14:3, pp. 223–44.

Downton Abbey (2010–16, United Kingdom: Carnival Film & Television).

Duncan, Amy (2017), 'Princess Diana's funeral is named most-watched live TV event with 31 million viewers', *Metro*, https://metro.co.uk/2017/09/06/princess-dianas-funeral-is-named-most-watched-live-tv-event-with-31-million-viewers-6906781/?ito=cbshare. Accessed 28 October 2017.

Dyer, Richard (2006), *Pastiche: Knowing Imitation*, London and New York: Routledge.

Eaglestone, Robert (ed.) (2018), *Brexit and Literature*, London: Routledge.

Early, Emmett (2003), *The War Veteran in Film*, Jefferson, NC: McFarland.

Eaton, Heather (2006), 'Ecofeminism', in R. S. Keller, R. R. Ruether and M. Cantlon (eds), *Encyclopedia of Women and Religion in North America*, Bloomington: Indiana University Press, pp. 1110–17.

Edwards, Gareth (2010), *Monsters*, USA: Magnet Releasing.

Elm, Michael (2014), 'Screening trauma: Reflections on cultural trauma and cinematic horror in Polanski's film oeuvre', in M. Elm, K. Kobalek and J.B. Köhne (eds), *The Horrors of Trauma in Cinema: Violence Void Visualization*, Newcastle Upon-Tyne: Cambridge Scholars, pp. 46–67.

Elsaesser, Thomas ([1972] 1991), 'Tales of sound and fury: The family melodrama', in M. Landy (ed.), *Imitations of Life*, Detroit: Wayne State University Press, pp. 68–91.

———— (2009), 'The mind-game film', in W. Buckland (ed.), *Puzzle Films: Complex Storytelling in Contemporary Cinema*, Chichester: Wiley-Blackwell, pp. 12–41.

Gondry, Michel (2004), *Eternal Sunshine of the Spotless Mind*, USA: Focus Features.

Eberl, Jason T. and Dunn, George A. (eds) (2017), *The Philosophy of Christopher Nolan*, Lanham, MA: Lexington Books.

Evans, Dylan (1996), *An Introductory Dictionary of Lacanian Psychoanalysis*, London: Routledge.

Farage, Nigel (2015), 'Farage on Friday: EU referendum is our modern day Battle of Britain', *Express*, https://www.express.co.uk/news/politics/590396/ Nigel-Farage-European-Union-EU-referendum-Battle-of-Britain. Accessed 11 July 2016.

Feinberg, Scott (2015), 'Christopher Nolan on "*Interstellar*" critics, making original films and shunning Cellphones and Email (Q&A)', *The Hollywood Reporter*, http://www.hollywoodreporter.com/race/christopher-nolan-interstellar-critics-making-760897. Accessed 16 August 2016.

Felman, Shoshana and Laub, Dori (1992), *Testimony: Crises of Witnessing in Literature, Psychoanalysis, and History*, New York: Routledge.

Fisher, Mark (2006), 'Gothic Oedipus: Subjectivity and capitalism in Christopher Nolan's *Batman Begins*', *ImageTexT: Interdisciplinary Comics Studies*, 2:2.

—— (2011), 'The lost unconscious: Delusions and dreams in *Inception*', *Film Quarterly*, 64:2, pp. 37–45.

Foster, Hal (1996), *The Return of the Real: The Avant-Garde at the End of the Century*, Cambridge: MIT Press.

Foucault, Michel (1977), 'What is an author?', in D. Bouchard (ed.), *Language, Knowledge, Counter-Memory: Selected Essays and Interviews*, Ithaca, NY: Cornell University Press, pp. 113–38.

—— (1988), 'Interview with R. Martin: Truth, power, self', in L. H. Martin, H. Gutman and P. H. Hutton (eds), *Technologies of the Self: A Seminar with Michel Foucault*, London: Tavistock Publications, pp. 9–15.

Fradley, Martin (2013), 'What do you believe in? Film scholarship and the cultural politics of the *Dark Knight* franchise', *Film Quarterly*, 66:3, pp. 15–27.

Freud, Sigmund ([1920] 1922), *Beyond the Pleasure Principle* (trans. C. J. M. Hubback), London and Vienna: International Psycho-Analytical.

—— ([1895] 1950), 'Project for a scientific psychology', in J. Strachey (trans. and ed.), *The Standard Edition of the Complete Psychological Works of Sigmund Freud*, vol. 1, London: Hogarth, pp. 281–397.

—— ([1918] 1955a), 'From the history of an infantile neurosis', in J. Strachey (trans. and ed.), *The Standard Edition of the Complete Psychological Works of Sigmund Freud*, vol. 17, London: Hogarth, pp. 3–122.

—— ([1920] 1955b), 'Beyond the pleasure principle', in J. Strachey (trans. and ed.), *The Standard Edition of the Complete Psychological Works of Sigmund Freud*, vol. 18, London: Hogarth, pp. 7–64.

—— ([1914] 1957a), 'Repression', in J. Strachey (trans. and ed.), *The Standard Edition of the Complete Psychological Works of Sigmund Freud*, vol. 14, London: Hogarth, pp. 146–58.

—— ([1917] 1957b), 'Mourning and melancholia', in J. Strachey (trans. and ed.), *The Standard Edition of the Complete Psychological Works of Sigmund Freud*, vol. 14, London: Hogarth, pp. 243–58.

—— ([1914] 1958), 'Remembering, repeating, and working-through', in J. Strachey (trans. and ed.), *The Standard Edition of the Complete Psychological Works of Sigmund Freud*, vol. 12, London: Hogarth, pp. 209–41.

—— ([1901] 1960a), 'The psychopathology of everyday life', in J. Strachey (trans. and ed.), *The Standard Edition of the Complete Psychological Works of Sigmund Freud*, vol. 6, London: Hogarth, pp. 1–291.

—— ([1905] 1960b), 'Jokes and their relation to the unconscious', in J. Strachey (trans. and ed.), *The Standard Edition of the Complete Psychological Works of Sigmund Freud*, vol. 8, London: Hogarth, pp. 1–238.

—— ([1923] 1961a), 'The ego and the id', in J. Strachey (trans. and ed.), *The Standard Edition of the Complete Psychological Works of Sigmund Freud*, vol. 19, London: Hogarth, pp. 12–59.

—— ([1899] 1961b), 'Screen memories', in J. Strachey (trans. and ed.), *The Standard Edition of the Complete Psychological Works of Sigmund Freud*, vol. 3, London: Hogarth, pp. 303–22.

—— ([1930] 1961c), 'Civilization and its discontents', in J. Strachey (trans. and ed.), *The Standard Edition of the Complete Psychological Works of Sigmund Freud*, vol. 21, London: Hogarth, pp. 59–145.

—— ([1896] 1962a), 'The aetiology of hysteria', in J. Strachey (trans. and ed.), *The Standard Edition of the Complete Psychological Works of Sigmund Freud*, vol. 3, London: Hogarth, pp. 191–221.

—— ([1896] 1962b), 'Further remarks on the neuro-psychosis of defence', in J. Strachey (trans. and ed.), *The Standard Edition of the Complete Psychological Works of Sigmund Freud*, vol. 3, London: Hogarth, pp. 162–88.

—— ([1933] 1964a), 'New introductory lectures on psychoanalysis', in J. Strachey (trans. and ed.), *The Standard Edition of the Complete Psychological Works of Sigmund Freud*, vol. 22, London: Hogarth, pp. 5–182.

—— ([1939] 1964b), 'Moses and monotheism: Three essays', in J. Strachey (trans. and ed.), *The Standard Edition of the Complete Psychological Works of Sigmund Freud*, vol. 23, London: Hogarth, pp. 3–140.

—— ([1899] 1965a), 'Screen memories', in J. Strachey (trans. and ed.), *The Standard Edition of the Complete Psychological Works of Sigmund Freud*, vol. 3, London: Hogarth, pp. 301–22.

—— ([1900] 1965b), 'The interpretation of dreams', in J. Strachey (trans. and ed.), *The Standard Edition of the Complete Psychological Works of Sigmund Freud*, vols. 4 and 5, New York: Avon Books.

Furby, Jacqueline (2006), 'Rhizomatic time and temporal poetics in *American Beauty*', *Film Studies*, 9:1, pp. 22–28.

—— (2015), 'About time too: From *Interstellar* to *Following*, Christopher Nolan's continuing preoccupation with time-travel', in J. Furby and S. Joy (eds), *The Cinema of Christopher Nolan: Imagining the Impossible*, London: Wallflower Press, pp. 246–66.

Furby, Jacqueline and Joy, Stuart (eds) (2015), *The Cinema of Christopher Nolan: Imagining the Impossible*, New York: Wallflower Press.

Gabbard, Glen. O (ed.) (2001), *Psychoanalysis and Film*, London: Karnac.

—— (2007), 'Foreword', in A. Sabbadini (ed.), *Projected Shadows: Psychoanalytic Reflections on the Representation of Loss in European Cinema*, London: Routledge, pp. xv–xix.

Galloway, Steven (2014), 'Angelina Jolie, Christopher Nolan and Director A-List on their toughest decisions, "dreadful" first cuts and Mike Nichols', *The Hollywood Reporter*, http://bcove.me/0jn04qbz. Accessed 27 January 2015.

Garcia, J. L. A. (2006), 'White nights of the soul: Christopher Nolan's insomnia and the renewal of moral reflection in film', *Logos: A Journal of Catholic Thought and Culture*, 9:4, pp. 82–117.

Gargett, Adrian (2002), 'Nolan's *Memento*, memory, and recognition', *CLCWeb: Comparative Literature and Culture*, 4:3.

Gassert, Ágnes (2012), 'Prestidigitation: Some reflections on cinema in the digital age', in Á. Pethő (ed.), *Film in the Post-Media Age*, Newcastle Upon-Tyne: Cambridge Scholars Publishing, pp. 207–26.

Gaut, Berys (2011), 'Telling stories: Narration, emotion, and insight in *Memento*', in N. Carroll and J. Gibson (eds), *Narrative, Emotion, and Insight*, University Park, PA: Pennsylvania State University Press, pp. 23–44.

Gertz, Nurith and Khleifi, George (2008), *Palestinian Cinema: Landscape, Trauma and Memory*, Edinburgh: Edinburgh University Press.

Gledhill, Christine (1987), 'The melodramatic field: An investigation', in C. Gledhill (ed.), *Home Is Where the Heart Is: Studies in Melodrama and Woman's Film*, London: BFI, pp. 1–39.

—— (1988), 'Pleasurable negotiations', in D. E. Pribram (ed.), *Female Spectators: Looking at Film and Television*, London: Verso, pp. 64–89.

—— (2000), 'Rethinking genre', in C. Gledhill and L. Williams (eds), *Reinventing Film Studies*, Oxford: Oxford University Press, pp. 221–43.

Goodwin, Matthew and Milazzo, Caitlin (2017), 'Taking back control? Investigating the role of immigration in the 2016 vote for Brexit', *The British Journal of Politics and International Relations*, 19:3, pp. 450–64.

Gutiérrez-Jones, Carlos (2015), 'Escaping one's self: Narcissism and cycles of violence in *Inception* and *Looper*', in C. Gutiérrez-Jones (ed.), *Suicide and Contemporary Science Fiction*, Cambridge: Cambridge University Press, pp. 102–28.

Hamad, Hannah (2011), 'Extreme parenting: Recuperating fatherhood in Steven Spielberg's *War of the Worlds* (2005)', in H. Radner and R. Stringer (eds), *Feminism at the Movies: Understanding Gender in Contemporary Popular Cinema*, London: Routledge, pp. 241–54.

Hanley, Richard (2009), '*Memento* and personal identity: Do we have it backwards?', in A. Kania (ed.), *Memento*, New York and London: Routledge, pp. 107–26.

Harris, Jose (2004), 'War and social history: Britain and the home front during the Second World War', in G. Martel (ed.), *The World War Two Reader*, New York and London: Routledge, pp. 317–35.

Hatherley, Owen (2017), *The Ministry of Nostalgia: Consuming Austerity (Keep Calm and Carry On)*, London: Verso.

Heckman, Daniel (2008), 'Unravelling identity: Watching the posthuman bildungsroman', *CTheroy.net*, http://www.ctheroy.net/articles.aspx?id=594. Accessed 20 March 2010.

Heilmann, Ann (2009), 'Doing it with mirrors: Neo-Victorian metatextual magic in *Affinity*, *The Prestige* and *The Illusionist*', *Neo-Victorian Studies*, 2:2, pp. 18–42.

Herman, Judith (1992), *Trauma and Recovery: The Aftermath of Violence – From Domestic Abuse to Political Terror*, New York: Harper Collins.

Hill, John (1999), *British Cinema in the 1980s: Issues and Themes*, Oxford: Oxford University Press.

Hill-Parks, Erin (2010), 'Discourses of cinematic culture and the Hollywood director: The development of Christopher Nolan's auteur persona', Ph.D. thesis, Newcastle: Newcastle University.

—— (2011), 'Identity construction and ambiguity in Christopher Nolan's films', *Widescreen*, http://widescreenjournal.org/index.php/journal/article/view/20. Accessed 30 April 2014.

—— (2015), 'Developing an auteur through reviews: The critical surround of Christopher Nolan', in J. Furby and S. Joy (eds), *The Cinema of Christopher Nolan: Imagining the Impossible*, London: Wallflower Press, pp. 17–30.

Hirsch, Joshua (2003), *Afterimage: Film, Trauma, and the Holocaust*, Philadelphia, PA: Temple University Press.

Hitchcock, Alfred (1950), *Stage Fright*, USA: Warner Bros.

—— (1960), *Psycho*, USA: Paramount Pictures.

Holmes, David S. (1990), 'The evidence for repression: An examination of sixty years of research', in J. L. Singer (ed.), *Repression and Dissociation: Implications for Personality Theory, Psychopathology, Health*, Chicago, IL: University of Chicago Press, pp. 85–102.

Horowitz, Sara R. (2010), 'Nostalgia and the Holocaust', in R. C. Spargo and R. M. Ehrenreich (eds), *After Representation? The Holocaust, Literature and Culture*, Rutgers: The State University, pp. 41–58.

Hunt, Peter R. (1969), *On Her Majesty's Secret Service*, UK: Eon Productions.

Ide, Wendy (2006), 'The Prestige', *The Times*, http://entertainment.timesonline.co.uk/tol/arts_and_entertainment/film/article629981.ece. Accessed 21 February 2009.

Iñárritu, Alejandro G. (2003), *21 Grams*, USA: Focus Features.

Ip, John (2010), 'The Dark Knight's war on terrorism', *Ohio State Journal of Criminal Law*, 9:1, pp. 209–29.

Ishii-Gonzales, Sam (2004), 'Mysteries of love: Lynch's *Blue Velvet*/Freud's Wolf-Man', in E. Sheen and A. Davison (eds), *The Cinema of David Lynch: American Dreams, Nightmare Visions*, London: Wallflower Press, pp. 48–60.

Jack, Ian (2018), '*Dunkirk* and *Darkest Hour* fuel Brexit fantasies – even if they weren't meant to', *The Guardian*, https://www.theguardian.com/commentisfree/2018/jan/27/brexit-britain-myths-wartime-darkest-hour-dunkirk-nationalist-fantasies. Accessed 21 September 2018.

Jameson, Fredric (2009), 'War and representation', *PMLA*, 124:5, pp. 1532–47.

Jancovich, Mark (1995), 'Screen theory', in J. Hollows and M. Jancovich (eds), *Approaches to Popular Film*, Manchester: Manchester University Press, pp. 123–50.

Janet, Pierre ([1919] 1976), *Psychological Healing: A Historical and Clinical Study*, New York: Arno Press.

Jones, Jack (2012), 'Christopher Nolan – Traditional taste', *Little White Lies*, http://www.littlewhitelies.co.uk/features/articles/christopher-nolan-traditional-taste-21121. Accessed 16 August 2016.

Joseph, Rachel (2011), 'Disappearing in plain sight: The magic trick and the missed event', *Octopus: A Visual Studies Journal*, 5, pp. 1–14.

Kaes, Anton (2011), *Shell Shock Cinema: Weimar Culture and the Wounds of War*, 3rd ed., Princeton: Princeton University Press.

Kang, Kathryn Muriel (2006), 'Agnostic democracy: The decentred "I" of the 1990s', Ph.D. thesis, Sydney: University of Sydney.

Kania, Andrew (2009), *Memento*, London: Taylor and Francis.

_____ (2015), '*Inception*'s singular lack of unity among Christopher Nolan's puzzle films', in J. Furby and S. Joy (eds), *The Cinema of Christopher Nolan: Imagining the Impossible*, London: Wallflower Press, pp. 175–88.

Kaplan, E. Ann (2001), 'Melodrama, cinema and trauma', *Screen*, 42:2, pp. 201–05.

——— (2005), *Trauma Culture: The Politics of Terror and Loss in Media and Literature*, New Brunswick and London: Rutgers University Press.

Kar-Wai, Wong (2004), *2046*, UK: Tartan Films.

Kealey, Erin (2015), 'No end in sight: The existential temporality of *Following*', in J. Furby and S. Joy (eds), *The Cinema of Christopher Nolan: Imagining the Impossible*, London: Wallflower Press, pp. 219–32.

Kermode, Mark (2014), '*Interstellar* review – if it's spectacle you want, this delivers', *The Guardian*, http://www.theguardian.com/film/2014/nov/09/interstellar-review-sci-fi-spectacle-delivers. Accessed 16 August 2016.

Kennedy, Harlan (2004), 'The big red one', American Cinema Papers, https://www.american-cinemapapers.com/files/TheBigRedOne.htm. Accessed 16 August 2016.

King, Claire Sisco (2011), *Washed in Blood: Male Sacrifice, Trauma, and the Cinema*, New Brunswick, NJ: Rutgers University Press.

King, Geoff (2014), 'Unravelling the puzzle of *Inception*', in W. Buckland (ed.), *Hollywood Puzzle Films*, New York and London: Routledge, pp. 57–71.

Kiss, Miklós (2012), 'Narrative metalepsis as diegetic concept in Christopher Nolan's *Inception* (2010)', *Film and Media Studies*, 5, pp. 25–54.

Kirby, Lynne (1988), 'Male hysteria and early cinema', *Camera Obscura*, 17, pp. 112–31.

Kornbluh, Anna (2004), 'Romancing the capital: Choice, love, and contradiction in *The Family Man* and *Memento*', in T. McGowan and S. Kunkle (eds), *Lacan and Contemporary Film*, New York: The Other Press, pp. 111–44.

Kracauer, Siegfried (2004), *From Caligari to Hitler: A Psychological History of the German Film*, Princeton, NJ: Princeton University Press.

Kubrick, Stanley (1968), *2001: A Space Odyssey*, USA: Stanley Kubrick.

Kunkle, Shelia (ed.) (2016), *Cinematic Cuts: Theorizing Film Endings*, Albany: State University of New York Press.

Lacan, Jacques ([1953] 1977a), 'The function and field of speech and language in psychoanalysis', in *Ecrits: A Selection*, London: Tavistock, pp. 30–113.

—— ([1957] 1977b), 'The agency of the letter in the unconscious or reason since Freud', in *Ecrits: A Selection*, London: Tavistock, pp. 146–78.

—— (1977c), *Ecrits: A Selection*, London: Tavistock.

—— (1977d), *The Seminar of Jacques Lacan Book XI: The Four Fundamental Concepts of Psychoanalysis* (ed. J. A. Miller, trans. A. Sheridan), New York: Norton.

—— ([1949] 1977e), 'The mirror stage as formative of the function of the I', in *Ecrits: A Selection*, London: Tavistock, pp. 1–7.

—— ([1953] 1982), 'Le symbolique, l'imaginaire et le réel', *Bulletin de l'Association freudienne*, 1, pp. 4–13.

—— ([1978] 1988a), *Book II: The Ego in Freud's Theory and in the Technique of Psychoanalysis* (ed. J. A. Miller, trans. S. Tomaselli), Cambridge: Cambridge University Press.

—— (1988b), *The Seminar of Jacques Lacan, Book I: Freud's Papers on Technique 1953–1954* (ed. J. A. Miller), Cambridge: Cambridge University Press.

—— ([1986] 1992), *The Seminar of Jacques Lacan, Book VII: The Ethics of Psychoanalysis 1959–1960* (ed. J. A. Miller, trans. D. Porter), New York and London: W. W. Norton & Co.

—— ([1981] 1993), *The Seminar of Jacques Lacan, Book III: The Psychoses, 1955–1956* (ed. J. A. Miller, trans. R. Grigg), London: Routledge.

—— ([1975] 1998), *The Seminar of Jacques Lacan, Book XX: Encore, On Feminine Sexuality, The Limits of Love and Knowledge 1972–1973* (ed. J. A. Miller, trans. B. Fink), New York: Norton.

LaCapra, Dominick (1998), *History and Memory after Auschwitz*, Ithaca: Cornell University Press.

—— (1999), 'Trauma, absence, loss', *Critical Enquiry*, 25:4, pp. 696–727.

—— (2001), *Writing History, Writing Trauma*, Baltimore: Johns Hopkins University Press.

Lackoff, George and Johnson, Mark (1980), *Metaphors We Live By*, Chicago: University of Chicago Press.

Laclau, Ernesto and Mouffe, Chantal (1985), *Hegemony and Socialist Strategy: Towards a Radical Democratic Politics*, London: Verso.

Langley, Travis (2012), *Batman and Psychology: A Dark and Stormy Knight*, Hoboken, NJ: John Wiley & Sons Inc.

Laplanche, Jean (1976), *Life and Death in Psychoanalysis*, London and Baltimore: Johns Hopkins University Press.

—— ([1987] 1989a), *New Foundations for Psychoanalysis* (trans. D. Macey), Oxford: Basil Blackwell.

—— (1989b), 'Temporality and translation: For a return to the question of the philosophy of time' (trans. T. Thomas), *Stanford Literature Review*, pp. 241–59.

—— (1994), 'Why Spielberg has distorted the truth', *The Guardian Weekly*, 3 April.

—— (1999a), 'Notes on afterwardsness', in *Essays on Otherness* (trans. J. Fletcher), London: Routledge, pp. 260–65.

—— (1999b), 'A short treatise on the unconscious', in *Essays on Otherness* (trans. J. Fletcher), London: Routledge, pp. 84–116.

Laplanche, Jean and Pontalis, Jean-Betrand (1973), *The Language of Psychoanalysis*, London: Hogarth.

Lawrence, Will (2010), 'Christopher Nolan interview for *Inception*', *The Telegraph*, http://www.telegraph.co.uk/culture/film/filmmakersonfilm/7894376/Christopher-Nolan-interview-for-Inception.html. Accessed 16 August 2016.

Lebeau, Vicky (2001), *Psychoanalysis and Cinema*, London: Wallflower.

Leiser, Erwin (1960), *Mein Kampf*, UK: Gala Film Distributors.

Lewis, Randolph (2009), '*The Dark Knight* of American Empire', *Jump Cut: A Review of Contemporary Media*, 51.

Lewis-Kraus, Gideon (2014), 'The exacting, expansive mind of Christopher Nolan', *New York Times*, http://www.nytimes.com/2014/11/02/magazine/the-exacting-expansive-mind-of-christopher-nolan.html. Accessed 16 August 2016.

Little, William. G (2005), 'Surviving *Memento*', *Narrative*, 13:1, pp. 67–83.

Loeb, Jeph (1996–97), *Batman: The Long Halloween #1-13*, New York: DC Comics.

Lowthorpe, Philippa (2016), *Swallows and Amazons*, UK: BBC Films.

Lyons, Diran (2006), 'Vengeance, the powers of the false, and the time-image in Christopher Nolan's *Memento*', *Angelaki: Journal of the Theoretical Humanities*, 2:1, pp. 127–35.

Mackey-Kallis, Susan (2002), *The Hero and the Perennial Journey Home in American Film*, Philadelphia: University of Pennsylvania Press.

Mactaggart, Allister (2010), *The Film Paintings of David Lynch: Challenging Film Theory*, Bristol: Intellect Books.

McGowan, Todd (2003), 'Looking for the gaze: Lacanian film theory and its vicissitudes', *Cinema Journal*, 42:3, pp. 27–47.

—— (2004), *The End of Dissatisfaction?: Jacques Lacan and the Emerging Society of Enjoyment*, Albany: State University of New York Press.

—— (2007a), 'The violence of creation in *The Prestige*', *International Journal of Zizek Studies*, 1:3, http://www.zizekstudies.org/index.php/IJZS/article/view/49/46. Accessed 24 August 2016.

—— (2007b), *The Real Gaze: Film Theory after Lacan*, Albany: State University of New York Press.

—— (2007c), *The Impossible David Lynch*, New York: Columbia University Press.

———(2009), 'The exceptional darkness of *The Dark Knight*', *Jump Cut: A Review of Contemporary Media*, 51.

——— (2011), *Out of Time: Desire in Atemporal Cinema*, Minneapolis: University of Minnesota Press.

——— (2012a), *The Fictional Christopher Nolan*, Austin: University of Texas Press.

——— (2012b), 'Should the Dark Knight have risen?', *Jump Cut: A Review of Contemporary Media*, 54.

———(2015a), 'Stumbling over the superhero: Christopher Nolan's victories and compromises', in J. Furby and S. Joy (eds), *The Cinema of Christopher Nolan: Imagining the Impossible*, London: Wallflower Press, pp. 164–74.

——— (2015b), *Psychoanalytic Film Theory and The Rules of the Game*, London and New York: Bloomsbury.

McGowan, Todd and Kunkle, Shelia (eds) (2004), *Lacan and Contemporary Film*, New York: Other Press.

——— (2004), 'Introduction: Lacanian psychoanalysis in film theory', in T. McGowan and S. Kunkle (eds), *Lacan and Contemporary Film*, New York: Other Press, pp. xi–xxix.

McKenna, M. (2009), 'Moral monster or responsible person: *Memento*'s Leonard as a case study in defective agency', in A. Kania (ed.), *Memento*, New York and London: Routledge, pp. 23–44.

Mendes, Sam (2000), *American Beauty*, UK: United International Pictures (UIP).

Metz, Christian (1982), *Psychoanalysis and Cinema: The Imaginary Signifier* (trans. C. Britton, A. Williams, B. Brewster and A. Guzzetti), Bloomington, IN: Indiana University Press.

Meyer, Catherine, Borch-Jacobson, Mikkel, Cottraux, Jean and Pleaux, Didier (2005), *The Black Book of Psychoanalysis: How to Live, Think and Get on Better Without Freud*, Paris: Les Arenes.

Michaels, Walter Benn (2007), 'The death of a beautiful woman: Christopher Nolan's idea of form', *Electronic Book Review*, http://www.electronicbookreview.com/thread/electropoetics/detective. Accessed 11 March 2010.

Miller, Frank (1986), *Batman: The Dark Knight Returns*, London: Titan Books.

——— (1987), *Batman: Year One*, New York: DC Comics.

Milojevic, Ivana (2013), *Breathing: Violence In, Peace Out*, St Lucia, Queensland: University of Queensland Press.

Mitchell, Elvis (2014), 'Christopher Nolan: *Interstellar*', *KCRW*, http://www.kcrw.com/news-culture/shows/the-treatment/christopher-nolan-interstellar. Accessed 16 August 2016.

Molloy, Claire (2010), *Memento*, Edinburgh: Edinburgh University Press.

Morrissey, Belinda (2011), 'Impossible memory: Traumatic narratives in *Memento* and *Mulholland Drive*', in A. Sinha and T. McSweeney (eds), *Millennial Cinema: Memory in Global Film*, New York: Wallflower Press, pp. 97–116.

Moskowitz, Andrew K. (2004), '"Scared stiff": Catatonia as an evolutionary based fear response', *Psychological Review*, 111:4, pp. 984–1002.

Mottram, James (2002), *The Making of Memento*, London: Faber and Faber.

Mooney, Darren (2018), *Christopher Nolan: A Critical Study of the Films*, Jefferson, NC: McFarland & Company Inc Publishers.

Muller, Christine (2011), 'Power, choice, and September 11 in *The Dark* Knight', in R. J. Gray II and B. Kaklamanidou (eds), *The 21st Century Superhero: Essays on Gender, Genre and Globalization in Film*, Jefferson, NC: McFarland & Company Inc Publishers, pp. 46–60.

Mulvey, Laura (1975), 'Visual pleasure and narrative cinema', *Screen*, 16:3, pp. 6–18.

—— (1978), 'Notes on Sirk and melodrama', *Movie*, 25, pp. 53–57.

Naughton, John (2014), 'Christopher Nolan: The enigma behind *Interstellar*', *The Telegraph*, http://www.telegraph.co.uk/culture/film/film-news/11198035/Christopher-Nolan-the-enigma-behind-Interstellar.html. Accessed 16 August 2016.

Newell, Mike (2018), *The Guernsey Literary and Potato Peel Pie Society*, UK: Amazon Prime Video.

Ney, Jason. A (2013), 'Dark roots: Christopher Nolan and Noir', *Film Noir Foundation*, http://www.filmnoirfoundation.com/noircitymag/Dark-Roots.pdf. Accessed 7 February 2015.

Ní Fhlainn, Sorcha (2015), '"You keep telling yourself what you know, but what do you believe?": Cultural spin, puzzle-films, and mind games in the cinema of Christopher Nolan', in J. Furby and S. Joy (eds), *The Cinema of Christopher Nolan: Imagining the Impossible*, London: Wallflower Press, pp. 147–63.

Nielsen, Lance (2017), *Pegasus Bridge*, UK: Eagles Dare Productions.

Noé, Gaspar (2002), *Irreversible*, USA: Muse Productions.

Nolan, Christopher (1996), *Larceny*, UK: UCL Film Society.

—— (1997), *Doodlebug*, UK: Cinema 16.

—— (1998), *Following*, UK: Next Wave Films.

—— (2000), *Memento*, USA: Newmarket Capital Group.

—— (2002), *Insomnia*, USA: Alcon Entertainment.

—— (2005), *Batman Begins*, USA: Warner Bros.

—— (2006), *The Prestige*, USA: Warner Bros.

—— (2008), *The Dark Knight*, USA: Warner Bros.

—— (2009), *Columbia Pictures Film Noir Classics I*, USA: Sony Pictures.

—— (2010), *Inception: Shooting Script*, San Rafael, CA: Insight Editions.

—— (2010), *Inception*, USA: Warner Bros.

—— (2012), *The Dark Knight Rises*, USA: Warner Bros.

—— (2013), *The Dark Knight Trilogy: The Complete Screenplays*, Opus Screenplay Series, New York: Opus.

—— (2014), *Interstellar*, USA: Warner Bros.

—— (2017), *Dunkirk*, USA: Warner Bros.

—— (2017), *Dunkirk Soundtrack*, sleeve notes, New York: Sony Music Classical.

Nolan, Christopher and Belic, Roko (1989), *Tarantella*, UK: UCL Film Society.

Nolan, Christopher and Goyer, David S. (2005), *Batman Begins*, London: Faber and Faber.

Nolan, Jonathan (2001), 'Memento Mori', *Esquire*, 135, pp. 186–91.

Norman, Leslie (1958), *Dunkirk*, UK: Ealing Studios.

Nowell-Smith, Geoffrey (1977), 'Minelli and melodrama', *Screen*, 18:2, pp. 113–18.

O'Connell, Sean (2014), 'Why *Interstellar*'s ending doesn't mean what you think it means', *CinemaBlend*, http://www.cinemablend.com/news/Why-Interstellar-Ending-Doesn-t-Mean-What-You-Think-It-Means-68115.html. Accessed 7 February 2015.

Olson, Jonathan (2015), 'Nolan's immersive allegories of filmmaking in *Inception* and *The Prestige*', in J. Furby and S. Joy (eds), *The Cinema of Christopher Nolan: Imagining the Impossible*, London: Wallflower Press, pp. 44–61.

O'Neil, Dennis and Giordano, Dick (1989), 'The man who falls', *Secret Origins*, New York: DC Comics.

Panek, Elliot (2014), '"Show, don't tell": Considering the utility of diagrams as a tool for understanding complex narratives', in W. Buckland (ed.), *Hollywood Puzzle Films*, New York and London: Routledge, pp. 72–88.

Parker, Jo Alyson (2004), 'Remembering the future memento: The reverse of time's arrow and the defects of memory', *Kronoscope*, 4:2, pp. 239–57.

Parker, Oliver (2016), *Dad's Army*, UK: DJ Films.

Paul, Ian A. (2010), 'Desiring-machines in American cinema: What inception tells us about our experience of reality and film', *Senses of Cinema*, http://sensesofcinema.com/2010/feature-articles/desiring-machines-in-american-cinema-what-inception-tells-us-about-our-experience-of-reality-and-film/. Accessed 5 June 2014.

Perdigao Lisa K. (2015), '"The dream has become their reality": Infinite regression in Christopher Nolan's *Memento* and *Inception*', in J. Furby and S. Joy (eds), *The Cinema of Christopher Nolan: Imagining the Impossible*, London: Wallflower Press, pp. 120–31.

Pheasant-Kelly, Frances (2011), 'The ecstasy of chaos: Mediations of 9/11, terrorism and traumatic memory in *The Dark Knight*', *Journal of War and Culture Studies*, 4:2, pp. 235–49.

—— (2015), 'Representing trauma: Grief, amnesia and traumatic memory in Nolan's new millennial films', in J. Furby and S. Joy (eds), *The Cinema of Christopher Nolan: Imagining the Impossible*, London: Wallflower Press, pp. 99–119.

Poldark (2015–present, UK: Mammoth Screen).

Rattigan, Neil (1994), 'The last gasp of the middle class: British war films of the 1950s', in W. W. Dixon (ed.), *Re-Viewing British Cinema, 1900–1992: Essays and Interviews*, Albany: State University of New York Press, pp. 143–53.

Read, Peter G. (1991), *Gemmology*, Oxford: Butterworth-Heinemann.

Rehling, Nicola (2009), *Extra-Ordinary Men: White Heterosexual Masculinity in Contemporary Popular Cinema*, Lanham, MA: Lexington Books.

Resnais, Alain (1956), *Night and Fog*, USA: The Criterion Collection.

—— (1959), *Hiroshima Mon Amour*, USA: Zenith International Films.

Ressner, Jeffrey (2012), 'The traditionalist – Christopher Nolan', *DGA*, http://www.dga.org/Craft/DGAQ/All-Articles/1202-Spring-2012/DGA-Interview-Christopher-Nolan.aspx. Accessed 8 July 2014.

Robertson, Roland (1992), *Globalization: Social Theory and Global Culture*, London: Sage.

Rofé, Yacov (2008), 'Does repression exist? Memory, pathogenic, unconscious and clinical evidence', *Review of General Psychology*, 12:1, pp. 63–85.

Rose, Sonya O. (2003), *Which People's War? National Identity and Citizenship in Wartime Britain 1939–1945*, Oxford: Oxford University Press.

Rose, Steven (2017), 'The Dunkirk spirit: How cinema is shaping Britain's identity in the Brexit era', *The Guardian*, https://www.theguardian.com/film/2017/jul/20/dunkirk-spirit-british-film-brexit-national-identity-christopher-nolan. Accessed 8 March 2018.

Rubenstein, Roberta (2001), 'Feminism, eros, and the coming of age', *Frontiers: A Journal of Women's Studies*, 22:2, pp. 1–19.

Russo, Paolo (2014), '"Pain is in the mind": Dream narratives in *Inception* and *Shutter Island*', in W. Buckland (ed.), *Hollywood Puzzle Films*, New York and London: Routledge, pp. 89–108.

Ryzik, Melena (2017), 'Ticking watch. Boat engine. Slowness. The secrets of the "*Dunkirk*" score', *New York Times*, https://www.nytimes.com/2017/07/26/movies/the-secrets-of-the-dunkirk-score-christopher-nolan.html. Accessed 27 March 2017.

Sabbadini, Andrea (ed.) (2007), *Projected Shadows: Psychoanalytic Reflections on the Representation of Loss in European Cinema*, London: Routledge.

——— (ed.) (2003), *The Couch and the Silver Screen: Psychoanalytic Reflections on European Cinema*, Hove and New York: Brunner-Routledge.

Sarah Steinbock, Christine (2014), *Facing the Future with a Foot in the Past: Americana, Nostalgia, and the Humanization of Musical Experience*, Ontario: Carleton University.

Sarris, Andrew (1962), 'Notes on the auteur theory in 1962', *Film Culture*, 27, pp. 1–8.

——— (1968), *The American Cinema: Directors and Directions 1929–1968*, New York: E. P. Dutton & Company.

Scherfig, Lone (2017), *Their Finest*, UK: BBC Films.

Schur, Michael (1953), 'The ego in anxiety', in R. M. Lowenstein (ed.), *Drives, Affects, and Behavior*, New York: International Universities Press, pp. 67–103.

Schweizer, Bernard (2013), 'Modernism and the referendum on nostalgia in Rebecca West's *Return of the Soldier*', in T. Clewell (ed.), *Modernism and Nostalgia: Bodies, Locations, Aesthetics*, New York: Palgrave Macmillan, pp. 25–35.

Scott, A. O. (2010), 'This time the dream's on me', *New York Times*, http://www.nytimes.com/2010/07/16/movies/16inception.html?_r=0. Accessed 5 October 2012.

Scott, Ridley (1982), *Blade Runner*, USA: Warner Bros.

Sexton, David (2017), '*Dunkirk*: Everything you need to know about the cinematic event of 2017', *The Standard*, https://www.standard.co.uk/go/london/film/dunkirk-everything-you-need-to-know-about-the-cinematic-event-of-2017-a3587021.html. Accessed 12 September 2017.

Shone, Tom (2014), 'Christopher Nolan: The man who rebooted the blockbuster', *The Guardian*, http://www.theguardian.com/film/2014/nov/04/-sp-christopher-nolan-interstellar-rebooted-blockbuster. Accessed 18 August 2016.

Sigler, David (2004), '"Funky days are back again": Reading seventies nostalgia in late-nineties rock music', *Iowa Journal of Cultural Studies*, 5, pp. 40–58, http://ir.uiowa.edu/ijcs/vol5/iss1/5. Accessed 13 November 2015.

Silverman, Kaja (1992), *Male Subjectivity at the Margins*, London: Routledge.

Singer, Ben (2001), *Melodrama and Modernity: Early Sensational Cinema and Its Contexts*, New York: Columbia University Press.

Skakov, Nariman (2012), *The Cinema of Tarkovsky: Labyrinths of Space and Time*, London and New York: I. B. Tauris.

Skjoldbjærg, Erik (1997), *Insomnia*, Norway: Norsk Film.

Smelser, Neil J. (2004), 'Psychological trauma and cultural trauma', in J. C. Alexander, R. Eyerman, B. Giesen, N. J. Smelser and P. Sztompka (eds), *Cultural Trauma and Collective Identity*, Berkeley and Los Angeles: University of California Press, pp. 31–59.

Smith, Barry (2001), 'Elgar and Warlock (Philip Heseltine)', *The Elgar Society Journal*, 12:1, pp. 2–20.

Smith, Basil (2007), 'John Locke, personal identity, and *Memento*', in M. Conrad (ed.), *The Philosophy of Neo-Noir*, Lexington, KY: The University Press of Kentucky, pp. 35–46.

Smith, Daniel W. (2012), *Essays on Deleuze*, Edinburgh: Edinburgh University Press.

Snyder, Zach (2013), *Man of Steel*, USA: Warner Bros.

Sobchack, Vivian (2014), 'Time passages', *Film Comment*, http://www.filmcomment.com/article/time-passages/. Accessed 12 March 2015.

Southworth, Jason (2011), 'Let me put my thoughts in you', in D. K. Johnson (ed.), *Inception and Philosophy: Because It's Never Just a Dream*, Malden, MA: Blackwell, pp. 31–45.

Spiegel, David and Cardeña, Etzel (1991), 'Disintegrated experience: The dissociative disorders revisited', *Journal of Abnormal Psychology*, 100:3, pp. 366–78.

——— (2005), *War of the Worlds*, USA: Paramount Pictures.

Stern, Lesley (1995), *The Scorsese Connection*, London: BFI.

Stewart, Garrett (2010), 'Pre-war trauma: Haneke's "The White Ribbon"', *Film Quarterly*, 63:4, pp. 40–47.

Stewart, Susan (1993), *On Longing: Narratives of the Miniature, the Gigantic, the Souvenir, the Collection*, Durham, NC: Duke University Press.

Sugarman, Alan (2003), 'A new model for conceptualizing insightfulness in the psychoanalysis of young children', *Psychoanalytic Quarterly*, 72, pp. 325–55.

Sutton, Paul (2004), 'Afterwardsness in film', *Journal for Cultural Research*, 8:3, pp. 385–405.

——— (2010a), 'Prequel: The "afterwardsness" of the sequel', in C. Jess-Cooke and C. Verevis (eds), *Second Takes: Critical Approaches to the Film Sequel*, Albany: State University of New York Press, pp. 139–52.

———(2010b). 'Cinematic spectatorship as procrastinatory practice', *Parallax*, 5:1, pp. 80–82.

Tedeschi, Richard G. and Calhoun, Lawrence G. (1995), *Trauma and Transformation: Growing in the Aftermath of Suffering*, Thousand Oaks, CA: Sage Publications.

——— (1996), 'The posttraumatic growth inventory: Measuring the positive legacy of trauma', *Journal of Traumatic Stress*, 9, pp. 455–71.

——— (2004), 'Posttraumatic growth: Conceptual foundations and empirical evidence', *Psychological Inquiry*, 15, pp. 1–18.

Tembo, Kwasu David (2015), 'On the work of the double in Christopher Nolan's *The Prestige*', in J. Furby and S. Joy (eds), *The Cinema of Christopher Nolan: Imagining the Impossible*, London: Wallflower Press, pp. 201–18.

Teplitzky, Jonathan (2017), *Churchill*, UK: Salon Pictures.

The Crown (2016–present, UK: Left Bank Television).

The Death Camps (1945), France: Les Actualités Françaises.

Thomas, Dylan ([1939] 1971), 'Do Not Go Gentle into That Good Night', in D. Thomas (ed.), *The Poems of Dylan Thomas*, New York: New Directions Publishing.

Thomas, Peter (2003), 'Victimage and violence: *Memento* and trauma theory', *Screen*, 44:2, pp. 200–07.

Toh, Justine (2010), 'The tools and toys of (the) war (on terror): Consumer desire, military fetish and regime change in *Batman Begins*', in J. Birkenstein, A. Froula and K. Randell (eds), *Reframing 9/11: Film, Popular Culture and the War on Terror*, New York: Continuum, pp. 127–40.

Trifonova, Temenuga (2002), 'Time and point of view in contemporary cinema', *CineAction*, 58, pp. 11–31.

Truffaut, Francois (1954), 'Une certaine tendance du cinéma français', *Cahiers du cinéma*, 31.

Turim, Maureen (1989), *Flashbacks in Film: Memory and History*, New York: Routledge.

Turner, Frederick. J (1921), *The Frontier in American History*, New York: Henry Holt and Company.

Van Der Kolk, Bessel and Van Der Hart, Otto (1995), 'The intrusive past: The flexibility of memory and the engraving of trauma', in C. Caruth (ed.), *Trauma: Explorations in Memory*, Baltimore: Johns Hopkins University Press, pp. 158–82.

Victoria (2016–present, UK: Mammoth Screen).

Vighi, Fabio (2006), *Traumatic Encounters in Italian Film: Locating the Cinematic Unconscious*, Bristol: Intellect Books.

Vukovic, Krešimir and Petkovic, Rajko (2013), 'Legendary caesar and the architect ariadne: Narrative, myth and psychology in Christopher Nolan's *Batman Begins*, *The Dark Knight* and *Inception*', *PSYART: An Online Journal for the Psychological Study of the Arts*, http://www.psyartjournal.com/article/show/vukovic-legendary_caesar_and_the_architect_ariad. Accessed 24 January 2014.

Walker, Janet (2005), *Trauma Cinema: Documenting Incest and the Holocaust*, Berkeley, CA: University of California Press.

——— (2001), 'Trauma cinema: False memories and true experience', *Screen*, 42:2, pp. 211–16.

War and Peace (2016, UK: BBC Cymru).

Weber, Thomas (2014), '*Caché* (2005), or the ongoing repression of traumatic memories', in M. Elm, K. Kabalek and J. B. Kohne (eds), *The Horrors of Trauma in Cinema: Violence Void Visualization*, USA: Cambridge Scholars Publishing, pp. 32–45.

Wexman, Virginia W. (1987), 'The trauma of infancy in Roman Polanski's *Rosemary's Baby*', in G. Waller (ed.), *American Horrors: Essays on the Modern American Horror Film*, Urbana and Chicago: University of Illinois Press, pp. 30–43.

Whitebait, William (1958), 'Bombardment', *New Statesman*, 55:1412.

Whitehead, Anne (2004), *Trauma Fiction*, Edinburgh: Edinburgh University Press.

Whitlow, Carolyn Beard and Krysl, Marilyn (eds) (2014), *Obsession: Sestinas in the Twenty-First Century*, Hannover: Dartmouth College Press.

Williams, Linda (1991), 'Film bodies: Gender, genre, and excess', *Film Quarterly*, 44:4, pp. 2–13.

—— (1998), 'Melodrama revisited', in N. Browne (ed.), *Refiguring American Film Genres: History and Theory*, Berkeley: University of California Press, pp. 42–88.

—— (2000), 'Film bodies: Gender, genre, and excess', in R. Stam and T. Miller (eds), *Film and Theory: An Anthology*, Oxford: Blackwell, pp. 207–21.

—— (2001), *Playing the Race Card: Melodramas of Black and White from Uncle Tom to O.J. Simpson*, Princeton, NJ: Princeton University Press.

Williams, O (n.d.), 'Hans Zimmer on scoring Batman', *Empire*, http://www.empireonline.com/interviews/interview.asp?IID=1532. Accessed 16 March 2015.

Wilson, Emma (2003), *Cinema's Missing Children*, London: Wallflower Press.

Wilson, Janelle L. (2005), *Nostalgia: Sanctuary of Meaning*, Lewisburg: Bucknell University Press.

Wilson, Scott (2008), *The Order of Joy: Beyond the Cultural Politics of Enjoyment*, Albany: State University of New York Press.

Wiseman, Andrea (2017), 'Christopher Nolan: Why "*Dunkirk*" is anything but a "Brexit movie"', *Screendaily*, https://www.screendaily.com/news/christopher-nolan-why-dunkirk-is-anything-but-a-brexit-movie/5124612.article. Accessed 18 December 2017.

Woodward, Clare and Joseph, Stephen (2003), 'Positive change processes and post-traumatic growth in people who have experienced childhood abuse: Understanding vehicles of change', *Psychology and Psychotherapy: Theory, Research, & Practice*, 76, pp. 267–83.

Wright, Joe (2017), *Darkest Hour*, UK: Working Title Films.

Yosef, Raz (2011), *The Politics of Loss and Trauma in Contemporary Israeli Cinema*, New York: Routledge.

YYS Digital Films, (2011), 'SBIFF 2011 – Modern Master Award to Christopher Nolan with special guest Leonardo DiCaprio', https://www.youtube.com/watch?v=6MF3iPmSgGE. Accessed 11 May 2013.

Žižek, Slavoj (1989), 'The undergrowth of enjoyment: How popular culture can serve as an introduction to Lacan', *New Formations*, 9, pp. 7–30.

—— (1991), *Looking Awry: An Introduction to Jacques Lacan through Popular Culture*, Cambridge, MA: MIT Press.

—— (1992), *Everything You Always Wanted to Know about Lacan (But Were Afraid to Ask Hitchcock)*, London: Verso.

—— (1999), *The Ticklish Subject: The Absent Centre of Political Ontology*, London: Verso.

—— (2008), *The Sublime Object of Ideology*, London: Verso.

—— (2011), *Living in the End Times*, London: Verso.

—— (2013), *Enjoy Your Symptom!: Jacques Lacan in Hollywood and Out*, New York: Routledge.

—— (2016), 'The Failure of *The Dark Knight Rises*', in S. Kunkle (ed.), *Cinematic Cuts: Theorizing Film Endings*, Albany: State University of New York Press, pp. 251–68.

Index

A

abandonment 2, 6, 41, 101, 105, 108,
110–11, 114, 116, 124, 126–27, 133

absence 4, 19, 21, 31, 49, 59, 74–76, 79–82,
89–90, 97, 101, 107, 114, 117–18,
121, 148

acceptance 54, 62, 118, 124–25

acting-out 14, 95–99, 104–05

affect 20, 27–28, 41, 105, 109, 112, 136,
140

afterwardsness 13, 38, 40, 46, 48–50, 56,
60–62, 68–69, 106, 127

ambiguity 5–6, 22, 34, 52, 80, 83, 100, 128,
145, 147–49

American
cinema 3–4, 115, 137, 154–55
culture 115, 137
history 119, 157
identity 119–20

Angier, Robert 29, 31, 72–73, 76–77,
79–90, 93–94

apparatus 90, 92, 110–11

après-coup 13, 38, 45–46, 48–49, 55–56,
60, 111, 124

Ariadne 18, 102, 104, 112, 126, 157

atemporal 15, 32, 59, 114, 127, 134, 152

audience 1, 3, 5–6, 8–9, 12, 19–20, 26, 29,
34, 48, 54, 65, 71, 76, 84, 87, 90–91,
98, 105, 108, 112, 115, 134, 137–38,
145

aural 29, 49, 56, 58–59, 69, 76, 99, 127

auteur 3–4, 6–10, 65, 90, 132, 148, 155
auteur theory 3–4, 10, 155

auto-translation 49–50, 60–61

B

Bale, Christian 1, 9, 53, 68, 71, 130, 149

Batman 6, 54, 58, 60–62, 64–70

Batman Begins 1, 6, 21, 53–65, 67, 69, 109

belated 40–41, 136

bidirectional 38, 46, 48–49, 56, 82, 124

blood-Spreading Motif 39, 42, 44–45, 48, 50

Borden, Alfred 71–73, 76, 79–81, 84–87,
91–94, 130–31

boundaries 3, 19–20, 22–23, 75, 102, 109,
130

Brexit 143–44, 155, 158

British 107, 134–35, 137–45, 154–55

Brooker, Will 9–10, 54, 103, 146, 149

Burton, Tim 54, 60–61

C

Caine, Michael 9, 13, 29, 53, 73, 102, 116,
130–31, 147

Calhoun, Lawrence G. 128–29, 156

Caruth, Cathy 2, 11, 19, 40, 51, 55, 59, 136

catharsis 4, 14, 95–96, 109, 111, 130

causality 39, 42, 58, 90, 127, 149

childhood 1–2, 24, 40–41, 53–55, 58, 60,
108, 120–21, 132

chronology 1, 16, 22, 32, 59, 123, 127, 149

circularity 13, 32, 35, 47, 53–54, 59, 61–62, 68, 72, 76, 84, 90, 114, 118, 126, 128, 130

classical cinema 4, 15, 21–22, 32, 34, 90, 111, 117

closure 22, 32–34, 50, 65, 68, 80, 91, 98, 101, 125, 127, 130

Cobb 1, 6, 14, 18, 95–99, 101–05, 107–08, 110–12, 126–27, 130, 148

cognitive processes 1, 12, 14, 48, 81, 91, 127

collective 15, 27, 97–98, 134–37, 141–43

complex narrative 13, 58, 73, 154

compulsion 13, 28, 74, 86, 98, 134–36, 147

conflict 27, 33, 98, 114–15, 120, 137, 140

conscious 22, 25–26, 36, 41–42, 44, 55, 59, 62, 80, 82, 103, 108, 112, 131, 136, 140, 142–43

Cooper 2, 113, 115–21, 124–28, 130–32, 149

Cotillard, Marion 9, 95, 131

crime 12–13, 39, 47–48, 50, 52, 58, 64–65, 97, 136

cultural
context 62, 139
memory 135, 137, 141–42
trauma 15, 133, 135–38, 142, 156

Cutter, John 13, 29, 33, 71, 73, 82, 84, 87–91, 94, 102, 131, 147

D

Dark Knight, The 1, 4, 6–9, 11, 13, 32, 53–54, 59, 62–70, 109, 113, 127–31, 149

Dark Knight Rises, The 1, 6–7, 54, 59, 62–63, 65–68, 70, 113, 127, 129–31, 149

Death 21, 53–56, 58–60, 64, 67, 69–70, 73, 79, 83, 99, 101, 104, 116–17, 133, 137

deception 13–14, 37, 39–40, 44–48, 50, 91, 103, 107, 109–11, 127, 148

deferred 27, 30, 32–34, 40–41, 45, 48–49, 64, 100, 111, 122, 127

desire 5, 8, 13–14, 22, 25–37, 47, 50–52, 55, 58, 64–65, 69, 71–76, 79–84, 90–92, 99–105, 107, 110–11, 114–15, 118, 121–26, 128, 130–32, 138–39, 142, 147–49

DiCaprio, Leonardo 2, 18, 95, 126, 147, 158

diegetic 35, 42, 44, 47, 51, 59, 62, 64–65, 73, 89–90, 92, 97, 99–100, 103, 105–06, 108, 110, 127

digital 7, 24, 59, 146

disavowal 23, 29, 47, 51, 75, 91, 96, 105, 107, 120, 132

displacement 30, 34–35, 66, 71, 74, 80–82

Doodlebug 1, 3, 7, 11, 15, 146, 153

Dormer, Detective 1, 28, 37–39, 42–45, 47–52, 68, 70, 147

dreams 10, 12, 18, 21, 25–26, 36, 41, 55–56, 95–100, 102, 104–05, 109–12, 114

duality 3, 72–73, 93

Dunkirk 1–3, 5, 7, 15, 133–35, 138–45, 153–55, 158

duplicate 17, 28, 66, 83–86, 146

E

endings 1, 6, 15, 22, 39, 52, 54, 64–68, 92, 96, 101–03, 105, 127–28, 130, 132, 141, 146–47, 149

F

failure 4, 17, 22, 27–28, 30–32, 34–35, 45, 47, 62, 65–66, 69, 91–92, 97, 102, 104, 107–08, 115–16, 118, 122, 142, 147–48

familial 113, 129–30

fantasmatic 32, 35, 69, 100, 105, 110, 123, 125

fantasy 24, 66–67, 69, 75–76, 96, 105–06, 111, 121, 127, 132

Farrier 133–34

fate 22, 33, 38, 52, 70, 93, 102–04, 147

female

  body 75

  characters 75

  identity 114

  power 75

  spectatorship 115

  subjects 75

fetishistic disavowal 105, 107, 132

Fischer, Robert 97–99, 102, 107–09

flashback 1, 17, 19–23, 36, 39, 47–49, 55, 59, 61, 69, 73, 98–99, 101, 127, 136, 157

flash-forward 73, 87

Following 1, 3–7, 11, 15, 44, 47, 125, 127–28, 134, 146–49

fort-da 32, 74, 86, 94

fragmentation 2, 10, 12, 20, 22, 56, 123, 149

franchise 14, 61, 64, 68

Freud, Sigmund 18–19, 24–25, 32, 36, 39–41, 45–46, 51, 54–56, 60, 73–75, 82, 86, 96–101, 113–15, 135–36, 142, 150, 152

Furby, Jacqueline 12–13, 62, 83–84, 116, 126, 149, 152–54, 157

future 12, 33, 41, 46, 55–56, 67, 77, 82, 98, 118, 123–26, 148, 154–55

G

gaze, the 27–29, 37, 80, 124, 140, 143

Genre 4, 6–7, 18, 20, 26, 97, 115, 134, 137, 139, 143

Gotham 56, 59, 64–69

Goyer, David S. 54, 60, 64–65

grief 4, 27, 79, 99, 101, 104, 117, 129

growth 14, 83, 108, 113, 128–29, 131

guilt 2, 4, 27, 38, 51, 60, 70, 95, 99, 111

H

Hardy, Tom 9, 108, 133

Harris, Harriet Sansom 17

Hathaway, Anne 9, 67, 116, 130, 149

Hollywood 3–5, 8, 15, 21–22, 67, 90, 93, 113–14, 117, 125, 147

hysteria 25, 40, 45

I

idealized 80, 96, 107, 120–21, 139–41, 143

identification 12, 28, 36, 74, 110

identity 9–11, 13–17, 34, 36, 38, 47, 49, 54, 58, 60–61, 64–69, 72–73, 77, 83, 86, 96, 106–11, 114, 119–20, 127, 135, 140–41, 143, 146

ideology 29, 67, 107, 114, 116, 138, 142

illusion 12, 19, 28–29, 33, 50, 71–72, 76, 80–81, 84, 87, 91–93, 102, 110, 121, 130–32, 147

Imaginary, the 27, 30, 36

immersion 12, 28, 84, 111

Inception 1–2, 4–7, 9, 11–12, 14, 18, 22, 33–34, 95–98, 100–01, 103–05, 107–13, 126–30, 146–47

infant 32, 60, 74, 82, 110

innocence 115, 118, 121–23, 132

Insomnia 1, 4, 6, 11, 13, 29, 37–39, 42–48, 50–51, 68, 72, 76, 132, 147

Interstellar 2, 4, 7, 12, 14–15, 97, 113–16, 119–21, 124–31, 146, 149

J

Jackman, Hugh 29, 72

Jankis, Sammy 16–17

jouissance 27, 50, 123, 131

justice 47, 50, 64–66

K

Kania, Andrew 11–12, 148, 152

King, Claire Sisco 12, 19–20, 68, 132

Kubrick, Stanley 4–5, 7, 112, 150

L

Lacan, Jacques 13–14, 27–30, 36, 38, 40, 45–46, 50, 54, 56, 60, 69, 71–76, 79, 81–83, 85, 90, 100, 105, 110, 122, 124, 130, 132, 139, 149

lack 14, 29–34, 53, 55, 66, 71–72, 74–75, 80, 84, 90, 92, 102, 110–11, 120, 122, 125, 130–31, 139

Laplanche, Jean 13, 24, 38, 40–41, 46, 49, 55, 60

Ledger, Heath 54, 65

limbo 97–99, 111

loop 35, 69, 101, 111, 122, 124–25, 128, 132, 146

loss 1, 14–15, 19–20, 23, 30–33, 37, 50, 53–54, 64–65, 67–68, 70–72, 74, 76–77, 80–81, 85, 92, 96–97, 99–100, 107, 111, 113, 116–17, 119, 121–26, 129–32, 134–35, 141, 147

lost-object 30–31, 50–51, 72, 76, 79, 82, 92, 99, 101, 116, 121, 124, 128, 130–31

love 4, 7, 14, 19, 27, 71, 80–82, 93, 99, 107, 117–18, 127, 129–30, 138, 149

lying flashback 48

M

mainstream cinema 12, 23, 51, 101, 125, 133, 139, 147

Mal 95–96, 98–100, 103, 110–12, 131

mask 28, 30, 38, 60, 67–68, 138

mastery 5, 21–22, 32–35, 74, 84, 91

maternal 32, 115–16, 118

McConaughey, Matthew 2, 113, 149

McGowan, Todd 10–11, 23–24, 26, 29, 31–32, 34–35, 39–40, 44–45, 47–48, 50, 62, 67–68, 77, 92–93, 100, 103–04, 107–09, 122, 148–49

McCullough, Julia 72–73, 76–82, 85, 93

melancholia 98–101, 107–08, 141

melodrama 14, 18, 113–19, 123, 125, 128, 131, 140

Memento 1, 4–6, 9, 11–12, 15–16, 21–22, 28, 33–34, 38, 44, 47, 76, 95, 97, 101, 120–21, 125, 127–28, 132, 134, 146

memory 1, 9–13, 15, 17–24, 32, 36, 38, 40–42, 44–45, 49, 54–56, 58–62, 64, 66, 74, 77, 81–83, 88, 93, 95–101, 104, 106, 108, 110–12, 121, 123, 125–27, 129, 134–38, 141–43

metonym 20, 30, 71–74, 80, 82, 93

Metz, Christian 23, 26–27, 110

mise-en-scène 13, 114, 134, 140, 147

missed encounter 28, 76, 79, 91

mourning 19, 27, 79–80, 98–101, 104, 107, 119

Murphy, Cillian 9, 97

myth 5, 54, 58, 61, 65, 109, 128, 138, 141–42, 144–45

N

Nachträglichkeit 13, 38–41, 44–46, 55–56, 60

narcissism 98, 100–101

narration 4, 21–23, 29, 73, 83–84, 111, 132, 147

narrative
cinema 6, 34, 90, 116, 153
closure 33–34, 91, 130
desire 33, 90
puzzles 1, 71
nonlinear 1, 12, 20, 148–49
repetition 72
structure 2, 5, 13, 15, 48, 50, 58, 61

nationalism 141, 144–45

neurosis 104, 135

nightmares 19, 36, 55, 59, 136

Nolan, Christopher 1–15, 18, 20, 24, 28–29, 32–35, 38–40, 42, 44–45, 47–50, 54–56, 60–61, 64–69, 71–73, 75–77, 84–87, 89–91, 93–97, 99, 102–05, 109–14, 116–17, 119–21, 125–27, 130–31, 134–35, 140–49, 151–55, 157–58

nostalgia 15, 107, 115, 118–25, 132, 135, 138–39, 141, 143–45, 155–56, 158

O

object-cause of desire 74, 100

objet a 27, 30–32, 35, 74–75, 79, 93, 100, 132

obsession 4–5, 18, 72, 80, 101, 116, 126, 146, 158

ontology 23, 61, 104, 106, 121, 159

P

Pacino, Al 1, 28, 37, 68, 147

pain 23, 35, 53, 70, 76, 82, 97, 107, 119, 121, 135, 146, 155

paranoia 101, 146

paternal 14, 97, 106–08, 116, 130

pathology 2, 92, 99, 101, 128, 142

pathos 115–17, 131

patriarchy 74–75, 107

patriotism 140–41, 143

pleasure 32, 73, 105, 135, 153

political 15, 107, 134–35, 137, 141–45, 159

Pontalis, Jean-Bertrand 40–41, 55

post-traumatic 14, 21–23, 69, 113, 128–29, 131, 157–58

post-war 137, 139

pre-conscious 25, 36

Prestige, The 1, 4–6, 9, 11–14, 29, 31, 33–34, 44, 71–73, 76, 78–79, 81–82, 84–93, 100, 102, 113, 127–32, 134, 147

primal 41, 45, 62, 82, 93, 115

psyche 23, 27, 40, 45, 99, 101, 110, 144

psychoanalysis 2, 10–11, 13, 15–16, 18–19, 23–27, 31, 35, 39–40, 46, 49, 60, 68, 71–72, 74–75, 82, 95, 98, 106, 109, 114–16, 122, 134–35, 142, 150–52, 156

psychological 9, 12–13, 38, 60, 67–68, 77, 97–98, 121, 127, 132, 135, 150, 152, 156–57

psychosexual 75, 135

R

reality 6, 12, 17, 19, 21, 23, 29, 33, 35, 66, 95–12, 118, 120–21, 127–28, 138, 142, 145, 154

recall 1, 22, 36, 41, 44, 55, 83, 96, 98, 106, 122, 137

redemption 4, 14, 68, 96, 107, 109, 124, 126–27, 130

referendum 135, 143–44, 155

regression 46, 107, 115, 121, 123–24

regret 18, 126

repetition 2, 10, 14–15, 17, 20, 22–24, 28, 31–32, 34–35, 39, 48, 50, 55, 59, 62, 68, 72–74, 76–77, 79, 83–87, 93, 96, 98–100, 110, 113–14, 118, 122, 124–26, 128, 134, 147

repression 12, 16–18, 24–25, 30, 35, 38, 40–41, 44–46, 55–56, 60–61, 67, 69–70, 76, 82, 98, 104, 111, 114, 123, 136

resignification 46, 111

re-translation 47, 49, 60–61, 64, 96, 104, 106, 108, 112–13, 126–27

retroactive 17, 34, 40–41, 45–46, 48, 50–51, 55–56, 58, 74, 77, 80, 82, 90, 92, 96, 111, 127, 137, 146, 148–49

revision 36, 41, 55, 106, 108, 128, 136, 144, 149

rules 6–7, 31, 152

S

sacrifice 66–70, 83, 92, 107, 111, 132, 137

Sarris, Andrew 3, 155

screen, the 8, 12, 18–19, 22, 28, 40, 49, 65, 84, 90, 92, 104–05, 137–38

self-reflexive 21, 64, 109

self-sacrifice 31, 66, 68-69

sentimentality 113, 124, 128

separation 29–30, 32, 74, 115, 121

Shelby, Leonard 1, 6, 16, 76, 101

shock 23, 27, 45, 59, 67, 135

Sobchack, Vivian 117, 127

social order 25–27, 114, 148

society 14, 75, 105, 107, 110, 114, 124, 137, 143

socio-political 3, 138–39, 143–44

spectator 2, 12–14, 16–18, 21–23, 26–29, 32–36, 39–40, 42, 44, 47–52, 54, 56, 58–59, 61–62, 64–65, 68, 76–77, 79–80, 84, 86–87, 89–97, 99, 102–06, 108–11, 118, 125, 127–28, 131, 134, 140, 145–49

spectatorship 38, 50, 60, 109, 114–15, 156

split 29–30, 110, 123, 130

Stewart, Susan 18, 122–23

subjectivity 22, 29–31, 42, 44, 49, 54, 60, 67, 81–82, 89, 100, 105, 130–31, 156

substitute 30, 74, 81–82, 115, 131

suicide 95–96, 98–101, 104, 111, 127, 131

Sutton, Paul 38, 49–50, 60–62, 106, 127, 156

Swank, Hilary 52, 70, 147

Symbolic, the 27, 29–31, 36, 59, 69, 75, 79

symptom 19, 27, 30, 40, 45–46, 134–36, 142, 159

T

technology 7, 12, 18, 24, 73, 97, 120

Tedeschi, Richard G. 128–29, 156

temporal 1, 12–14, 20–24, 28, 32–33, 40,

46, 48, 51, 53–54, 56, 58, 61–62, 65, 67–69, 72–73, 77, 82–84, 90, 93, 97, 111, 116–18, 121–23, 126–29, 134, 149

terrorism 6, 11, 139, 154

theme 1, 3–7, 9–10, 12–15, 20, 23, 38, 72–73, 84–86, 93, 109, 111, 113–14, 119–20, 125, 128, 134–35, 140–41, 146–47

Theobald, Jeremy 6, 147

timeline 1, 5, 12, 47, 77, 79, 98, 128

time-travel 2, 12

topographical 18, 36

totem 5, 101–03, 107, 112

tragedy 54, 65, 67, 76, 79, 115

trauma 1–2, 4–5, 10–16, 18–24, 26–28, 31–33, 35, 38, 40–41, 44–49, 51, 53–56, 58–62, 64–74, 76–77, 79, 82, 91–01, 103–04, 106, 110–11, 113–14, 119–20, 122, 124–38, 142, 145, 147, 149

traumatic

  encounter 23, 27, 40, 132

  event 1–2, 18, 21, 28, 31–32, 37, 40–42, 46, 54–55, 60, 113, 134, 136

  kernel 69, 77, 111

  loss 30, 32, 64, 68, 70, 72, 85, 121, 126

  memory 1, 12, 20–22, 36, 38, 55, 100, 154, 158

  signifier 47–48, 55, 72, 76, 103, 107

truth 12, 17, 19, 29, 37–39, 47–48, 51–52, 65, 67, 77, 79–80, 85, 91–92, 96, 98, 103, 105, 110–11, 142, 145, 148–49, 151

Turim, Maureen 22–23, 48, 157

U

unconscious

  desire 25–27, 47, 80–81, 100, 104–05

  trauma 14, 16, 24, 41, 44–45, 47, 58–59, 69, 76, 96, 101, 120, 125

utopian 120, 140

V

vicarious 2, 12, 14, 21, 35, 48, 54, 56, 76, 127, 134
victim 44, 47, 68, 75, 96, 115
violence 23, 28, 55–56, 76, 104, 107
void 14, 50–51, 91, 113, 130–31

W

Walker, Janet 20–21, 23
Warner Bros. 9
Wayne, Bruce 1, 21, 53–70, 130–31, 149
Whitehead, Fionn 133, 158
wholeness 30, 32–34, 71, 82, 90, 92, 110–11, 123, 139

Williams, Linda 115–19, 123–24, 131
wish-fulfilment 25, 66, 127, 131
witness 18–19, 21, 34, 45, 52, 58–59, 65, 76, 80, 87, 90, 100, 139, 145
Wolf-Man 24, 41, 45
work-through 14, 74, 95–99, 101, 103–04, 107–10, 113

Z

Zimmer, Hans 9, 59, 140, 158
Žižek, Slavoj 28, 35, 50, 71, 158